Global Institutions, Marginalization, and Development

MW00986958

For more than a century and a half, the most powerful national governments have created institutions of multilateral governance that promise to make a more inclusive world, a world serving women, working people, the colonized, the "backward," the destitute, and the despised. This book is a study of that promise and the real impact of this "actually existing" world government.

Global Institutions, Marginalization, and Development discusses what systems of global institutions have done, and what they have not done, to keep their promise to the truly disadvantaged. It examines whether the system will serve the world's least-advantaged, or marginalize them further.

The future will largely be determined by the understanding of the global political economy developed by the world's most powerful people – corporate leaders and government officials in the strongest states. Their worldviews, in turn, will be influenced both by the political action and the ideas of social movements, and by the views of those who study the global political economy. Whether it is the "economists and political philosophers" of the rich or the social movements of the disadvantaged that are most likely to influence the world's lawmakers and the processes by which they will complete the next generation of multilateral institutions are the central topics of this book.

Key content includes:

- World Organizations and Human Needs
- Liberal Internationalism
- Social Movements and Liberal World Orders
- Political Consequences of the New Inequality
- Leadership and Global Governance for the Information Age
- Marginalization and the Privileged

This book is important reading for anyone with an interest in international political economy, global governance, development and the politics of North–South relations.

Craig N. Murphy is Historian of the United Nations Development Programme while on leave from Wellesley College, where he is M. Margaret Ball Professor of International Relations. He was chair of the Academic Council on the UN System from 2002 to 2004, president of the International Studies Association in 2000 to 2001, and a founding editor of *Global Governance*, which received the 1996 award of the Association of American Publishers for the best new scholarly journal in business, the social sciences, and the humanities. One of the leading critical scholars in the field, he has published widely on international institutions and North–South relations.

RIPE Series in Global Political Economy

Series Editors: Louise Amoore (*University of Newcastle, UK*), Randall Germain (*Carleton University, Canada*) and Rorden Wilkinson (*University of Manchester, UK* and *Wellesley College, US*).

Formerly edited by Otto Holman, Marianne Marchand (both *University of Amsterdam*), Henk Overbeek (*Free University, Amsterdam*) and Marianne Franklin (*University of Amsterdam*).
The RIPE series editorial board are:

Math2ias Albert (*Bielefeld University, Germany*), Mark Beeson (*University of Queensland, Australia*), A. Claire Cutler (*University of Victoria, Canada*), Marianne Franklin (*University of Amsterdam, the Netherlands*), Stephen Gill (*York University, Canada*), Jeffrey Hart (*Indianna University, US*), Eric Helleiner (*Trent University, Canada*), Otto Holman (*University of Amsterdam, the Netherlands*), Marianne H. Marchand (*University of Amsterdam, the Netherlands*), Craig N. Murphy (*Wellesley College, US*), Robert O'Brien (*McMaster University, Canada*), Henk Overbeek (*Vrije Universiteit, the Netherlands*), Anthony Payne (*University of Sheffield, UK*) and V. Spike Peterson (*University of Arizona, US*).

This series, published in association with the *Review of International Political Economy*, provides a forum for current debates in international political economy. The series aims to cover all the central topics in IPE and to present innovative analyses of emerging topics. The titles in the series seek to transcend a state-centred discourse and focus on three broad themes:

- the nature of the forces driving globalization forward
- resistance to globalization
- the transformation of the world order.

The series comprises two strands:

The *RIPE Series in Global Political Economy* aims to address the needs of students and teachers, and the titles will be published in hardback and paperback. Titles include:

Transnational Classes and International Relations
Kees van der Pijl

Gender and Global Restructuring: Sightings, Sites and Resistances
Edited by Marianne H Marchand and Anne Sisson Runyan

Global Political Economy
Contemporary theories
Edited by Ronen Palan

Ideologies of Globalization
Contending visions of a new world order
Mark Rupert

The Clash within Civilisations
Coming to terms with cultural conflicts
Dieter Senghaas

Global Unions?
Theory and strategies of organized labour in the global political economy
Edited by Jeffrey Harrod and Robert O'Brien

Political Economy of a Plural World
Critical reflections on power, morals and civilizations
Robert Cox with Michael Schechter

A Critical Rewriting of Global Political Economy
Integrating reproductive, productive and virtual economies
V. Spike Peterson

Contesting Globalization
Space and place in the world economy
André C. Drainville

Global Institutions and Development
Framing the world?
Edited by Morten Bøås and Desmond McNeill

The Political Economy of European Integration
Theory and analysis
Edited by Erik Jones and Amy Verdun

Global Institutions, Marginalization, and Development
Craig N. Murphy

Routledge/RIPE Studies in Global Political Economy is a forum for innovative new research intended for a high-level specialist readership, and the titles will be available in hardback only. Titles include:

1. Globalization and Governance*
Edited by Aseem Prakash and Jeffrey A. Hart

2. Nation-States and Money
The past, present and future of national currencies
Edited by Emily Gilbert and Eric Helleiner

3. The Global Political Economy of Intellectual Property Rights
The new enclosures?
Christopher May

4. Integrating Central Europe
EU expansion and Poland, Hungary and the Czech Republic
Otto Holman

5. Capitalist Restructuring, Globalisation and the Third Way
Lessons from the Swedish Model
J. Magnus Ryner

6. Transnational Capitalism and the Struggle over European Integration
Bastiaan van Apeldoorn

7. World Financial Orders
An historical international political economy
Paul Langley

8. The Changing Politics of Finance in Korea and Thailand
From deregulation to debacle
Xiaoke Zhang

Global Institutions, Marginalization, and Development

Craig N. Murphy

Routledge
Taylor & Francis Group

LONDON AND NEW YORK

First published 2005 by Routledge
2 Park Square, Milton Park, Abingdon, Oxon OX14 4RN

Simultaneously published in the USA and Canada
by Routledge
270 Madison Ave, New York, NY 10016

Routledge is an imprint of the Taylor & Francis Group

© 2005 Craig N. Murphy

Typeset in Baskerville by
Florence Production Ltd, Stoodleigh, Devon
Printed and bound in Great Britain by
The Cromwell Press, Trowbridge, Wiltshire

All rights reserved. No part of this book may be reprinted or
reproduced or utilized in any form or by any electronic,
mechanical, or other means, now known or hereafter invented,
including photocopying and recording, or in any information
storage or retrieval system, without permission in writing from
the publishers.

British Library Cataloguing in Publication Data
A catalogue record for this book is available from the
British Library

Library of Congress Cataloging in Publication Data
A catalog record for this book has been requested

ISBN 0–415–70055–8 (hbk)
ISBN 0–415–70056–6 (pbk)

Contents

Series preface

Global Institutions, Marginalization, and Development draws together the selected work of Craig Murphy, one of the most influential scholars working in international studies and international political economy today. Though only having just celebrated his half century, Murphy's contribution to our understanding of the world around us has been a source of inspiration for the many that have come into contact with his teaching, research, and professional activities. In the classroom, Murphy's passion for, and insight into, questions of justice, power, marginalization, and governance have helped create an international relations programme at his home institution – Wellesley College – that values and celebrates the normative, the ethical, and the critical, as much as it values analytical rigor, interdisciplinarity, and field-based research. In the academy, and in particular during his tenures as President of the International Studies Association (ISA) and the Academic Council on the United Nations System (ACUNS) respectively, Murphy has helped secure a space for alternative and non-traditional ways of thinking about international studies; and in his intellectual scribblings he has helped establish and been associated with the development of a critical international political economy, a Gramscian-inspired "Italian School," and an alternative form of historical institutionalism.

But Murphy's work is not distinguished by its intellectual clarity and innovation alone; it is also uniquely personal. Few others balance their normative and analytical positions as powerfully and persuasively as Murphy, whose writings have been informed by a deep concern with the ethical claims which are made by and on behalf of those whose voices have often been overlooked or marginalized. Much like the work of Robert W. Cox, whose most recent book has also been published in this series, Murphy refuses to construct and convey knowledge about the world in a manner that divorces the knowing subject from the issues at hand. But more than this, he is also one of the few "critical" scholars who actively engages with mainstream work in international relations and international political economy. Craig Murphy is that rare scholar who is as much at home in theoretical debates as he is while undertaking detailed empirical studies.

This volume can be read as a collection of conversations exploring the various dimensions of Murphy's intellectual industry. It begins with an account of how almost by chance he fell upon a research topic to enable him to travel during his undergraduate years. Inevitably, that topic – the 1972 International Cocoa Agreement – was shaped as much by his convictions as it was by happenstance, which is what he would have us believe. This early research established the broad parameters of much of his own agenda for the next 30 years. He became interested in how ideas influence the material world; the role of international institutions (those bodies he deems the "world government that we actually have") in the dissemination of those ideas and in making a material difference; the reasons why certain "market-taming" mechanisms promising social justice generate dramatically different outcomes for those involved (in the case of the Cocoa agreement, a metaphorical license to print money for chocolate companies and a weapon in the Cold War arsenal for the West, as well as a contributing factor in the immiseration of Ghana's most vulnerable); and where alternatives to prevailing international political arrangements may arise and what we can do to assist them. In short, it became an investigation into the interrelationship between global institutions, marginalization, and development.

This book began as an idea for a collection that would bring together in one place a thematically connected set of writings, some of which have been published in slightly obscure (for North American audiences, at least) or less accessible places, and "topped" and "tailed" with a new introduction and conclusion. What has emerged is an altogether different beast. All of the chapters have been revised, updated, and painstakingly reworked into a highly developed, coherent whole. For those who know Craig Murphy, that he should take the task so seriously and endeavor to produce something of value beyond that of the original contributions will come as no surprise; for those who do not know him, his resistance to the pressure to publish, recycle, and rehash will come as a refreshing change.

The conversations that follow range extensively across questions of equality, justice, and need in the global political economy. Inevitably, each will be read in isolation, as well as part of the narrative that unfolds from the beginning to the end. However these conversations are read, all encourage the reader to ask important questions of the relationship between global institutions, marginalization, and development, and the manner in which we seek to attenuate the growing inequalities within and across the social world.

Louise Amoore, University of Newcastle, UK
Randall Germain, Carleton University, Canada
Rorden Wilkinson, University of Manchester, UK

Acknowledgments

I am grateful to Rorden Wilkinson and Seiji Endo for conceiving of this book, and to Wilkinson and Craig Fowlie for making it possible. Kurt Burch, Christopher Candland, Peter Haas, Randall Germain, and Stephen Gill helped me reshape and sharpen my arguments. Ellane Park helped me prepare the manuscript and kept my focus on my primary audience. My deepest thanks go to all of them, but most especially to my wife, JoAnne Yates, who has been with this since the beginning.

I also acknowledge:

Lynne Rienner Publishers for parts of Chapter 2 taken from "Global Institutions and the Pursuit of Human Needs," in Roger A. Coate and Jerel A. Rosati (eds) *The Power of Human Needs in World Society*. Boulder: Colo.: Lynne Rienner Publishers, 1988.

Polity Press for parts of Chapter 3 taken from *International Organization and Industrial Change: Global Governance since 1850*. Cambridge: Polity Press, 1994.

Routledge, an imprint of the Taylor & Francis Group, for parts of Chapter 4 taken from "The Historical Processes of Establishing Institutions of Global Governance and the Nature of the Global Polity," in Morten Ougaard and Richard Higgott (eds) *Towards a Global Polity*. London: Routledge, 2002.

Palgrave/Macmillan for parts of Chapter 5 taken from "The Functional Approach, Organization Theory, and Conflict Resolution," in Lucian M. Ashworth and David Long (eds) *New Perspectives on International Functionalism*. Houndsmills, Basingstoke: Macmillan Press, 1999.

Butterworth-Heinemann Ltd for parts of Chapter 6 taken from Craig N. Murphy and Enrico Augelli, "International Institutions, Decolonization, and Development," *International Political Science Review* 14(1, January 1993): 71–86 and parts of chapter 7 taken from "What the Third World Wants: An Interpretation of the Development and Meaning of the New International Economic Order Ideology." *International Studies Quarterly* 27(1, 1983): 55–76.

The Center for Social Research and Education for parts of Chapter 8 taken from "Freezing the North–South Bloc(k) after the East–West Thaw," *Socialist Review* 20(3, 1990): 25–46.

Blackwell Publishers for parts of Chapter 9 taken from "Global Governance: Poorly Done and Poorly Understood," *International Affairs* 76(1, 2000): 789–803 and for parts of Chapter 10 taken from "Political Consequences of the New Inequality," *International Studies Quarterly* 45(3, 2001): 347–356.

The Institute for International Trade and Cooperation of the Graduate School of International Studies, Ewha Women's University for parts of Chapter 11 taken from "Leadership and Global Governance in the Early Twenty-first Century," *Journal of International Studies* 1(1, 1997): 25–49.

The Forum of Democratic Leaders in the Asia-Pacific for parts of Chapter 11 taken from "Prospects for Cosmopolitan Democracy," *FDLAP Quarterly* 3(3, 1997): 12.

1 Institutions, marginalization, development

For more than a century and a half, the most-powerful national governments have created institutions of multilateral governance that promise to make a more inclusive world, a world serving women, working people, the colonized, the "backward," the destitute, and the despised. That promise and the real impact of this actually existing world government have been a focus of my work over many years. I have been interested in what systems of global institutions have done, and what they have not done, to keep their promise to the truly disadvantaged. My reading of the history of multilateral governance suggests that we are at a cusp, a transition, between the system that marked the decades after the Second World War and a more extensive system of international governance that will characterize the world for the next generation. That system may keep the long-standing promise to serve the world's least advantaged, or it may serve to marginalize them further.

The outcome will largely be determined by the evolving understanding of the global political economy developed by the world's most powerful—by corporate leaders and government officials in the most powerful states. Their worldviews, in turn, will be influenced both by the political action and the ideas of social movements representing at least some of the world's marginalized, and by the views of at least some of us who make a profession of studying the global political economy.

The "economists and political philosophers" to whom today's "practical men" are the most likely to be enslaved,[1] the social movements of the disadvantaged that are most likely to influence the world's lawmakers, the processes by which they will complete the next generation of multilateral institutions, and their likely consequences, are the topics of this book. It brings together the distinctive historical arguments I have made about the emergence of what is now called "global governance." The final chapters summarize the argument, expand on one theme—the possibilities for scholars and for the world's leaders to learn from the marginalized, and discuss the potentials inherent in the current moment when the long-established trajectory of liberal multilateralism is challenged by the aggressive expansion of a unilateralist American empire.

This first chapter identifies the issues that have concerned me throughout my studies of international institutions and contrasts the kinds of arguments I find persuasive with those that convince other scholars.

The issues

My scholarly preoccupations over the last 30 years owe much to the tediousness of the Christian ecumenical movement in the 1970s. In 1973, a group of scholars in Princeton, New Jersey, gave me and a half-dozen other American undergraduates the opportunity to spend a year conducting social research first in Europe (in Ireland, the Netherlands, or the United Kingdom) and then in the Third World (in Ghana, Jamaica, or Suriname). Each of us had only to settle on a reasonable research question and develop a plausible research design with the help of the faculty at our own colleges and a dozen eager scholars recruited from the six countries and the US. My first thought was to expand from a paper on the North American ecumenical movement written for my favorite first-year class, an interdisciplinary seminar on conflict resolution led by a very young Lynn Mather, who went on to head the Law and Society Association. Unfortunately, everything I read about the idiosyncratic, tiresomely earnest, and inconsequential twentieth-century attempts to unite denominations in Europe, the Caribbean, and Africa convinced me that there was no topic I wanted to research there.

I scrambled about, reading everything I could on the six possible countries and letting my general interests in negotiation and questions of social justice be my guide. They led me to the 1972 International Cocoa Agreement among the major producers of the commodity (including Ghana) and the major chocolate manufacturing countries (including the UK). In one form or another, the negotiations leading up to the agreement had been going on since the late 1940s, and virtually the same text ratified in 1972 had been on the table since the early 1960s. What explained the timing of the actual agreement? If the pieces had all been in place for a decade, why had it taken so long? I had the topic that would take me to England and Ghana, and, through it, a set of research questions that would take me from my teens into my forties.

Institutions

The International Cocoa Agreement was a typical post-Second World War Keynesian innovation. It created an organization that would help stabilize the price of the primary commodity by managing a buffer stock, buying cocoa when the world price was low and selling it when the price was high. Economists believed that price stability, by itself, would serve the interests of the tens of millions of impoverished cocoa farmers and farm workers who ultimately faced a monopsonistic group of buyers, dominated by a handful of global chocolate manufactures—Nestlé, Cadbury, Rown-tree, Hershey, M&M/Mars. The firms had the wherewithal to use cocoa futures' markets to protect themselves, and even to profit, from wild price fluctuations. The farmers did not. Moreover, privately, if not officially, everyone associated with the cocoa negotiations expected that the new organization would push cocoa prices higher relative to manufactured goods. It would work against helping the declining terms of trade of most raw materials that the UN Conference on Trade and Development's Raul Prebisch had identified as a consequence of the much greater market power of manufacturers (such as the chocolate oligopoly) as compared to that of the myriad of competing Third World producers (for example, cocoa farm-ers). At the margin, the bias of the buffer stock's managers would be toward maintaining higher prices. Thus, the commodity agreement would help redress the imbalance of power that the unregulated market created.

I later discovered that the Cocoa Agreement was just one of scores of examples of "purpose-oriented" (that is, "function-oriented") or "function-alist" international agreements envisioned since the 1850s by social tinker-ers like John Maynard Keynes. These were formal institutions designed to redress transnational imbalances of power by husbanding and amplifying the power resources of one social group vis-à-vis other, more powerful groups (see Chapters 3 and 11). In almost every case, the aim has been to achieve social harmony at the expense of an unfettered operation of the market that created the socially dysfunctional inequality in the first place.

My fundamental interest in market-taming international institutions stands in contrast to that of many American international organization scholars born in the middle of the twentieth century. They have been inter-ested in market-creating institutions, institutions that might help realize the theoretical benefits of comparative advantage. My differing interests made me more attuned than some other scholars to the host of never-realized pro-posals for international collaboration aiding the least advantaged that have been over the last two centuries. Powerful actors, motivated by narrow, short-term self-interest, are usually available to block such innovations, and the proposals then disappear from scholarly memory. I have also been more conscious of the experiments of this sort that have failed, as the Cocoa Agreement has, often because the powerful come to resent the bit of social leveling that the institution provides.

Marginalization

Yet, such experiments need not always fail. The powerful respond to more than narrow self-interest. Their timeframes can be longer. Clever institu-tional experiments can be put into place when the powerful are not fully aware of what is going on and then the institutions can, themselves, reshape the powerful's interests. The answer to the question about what took the Cocoa Agreement so long convinced me of these lessons. Reflection on that answer made me see the ethical issue at the center of questions about institutionalized international politics.

The delay in signing a cocoa agreement was not a matter of conflicting interests and greed. It was a matter of ideology and apathy. Throughout the 1960s, the major chocolate manufacturers gained little from the fluctuations in cocoa prices; only M&M/Mars pursued a strategy of seeking profit in the cocoa futures market. The British giants, Cadbury and Rowntree, were both still dominated by their namesakes, families of Quaker reformers who had a paternalistic interest in the welfare of the poorest producers in the former British colonies of Ghana and Nigeria. Moreover, as one of the Cadburys confided to me, the counter-cyclical business of producing mildly addictive sweets was a bit like printing money; in the 1960s, Cadbury's greatest worry was to find other large businesses in similar fields to purchase with their huge accumulation of relatively liquid capital.[2]

British policy toward the cocoa negotiations had been set after a brief consideration at a Cabinet meeting of the Conservative government of Alec Douglas-Hume: the negotiators were to back any agreement supported by the major British firms and by the Commonwealth producers, Ghana and Nigeria. The only other stipulation was that the agreement must also be acceptable to Britain's main Cold War ally, the United States.

That turned out to be the sticking point. No matter what arguments the other negotiators made, no matter what special concessions they offered, year after year, the Americans turned a deaf ear. The impasse was broken only in 1972 when an ambitious British negotiator saw the chance for advancement to the newly open job as sugar negotiator (a much bigger commodity, second in world trade to oil). As he told me, he cajoled his Permanent Secretary to ask his Minister to go back to the Cabinet and strike the clause about coordinating policy with the US. Reportedly, an exasperated Prime Minister Edward Heath took only a few seconds to comment that he could not imagine that they had once thought that the price of chocolate had anything to do with the battle against Communism. The decision was made and, given the UN formula that determined the sufficient number of producing and consuming countries to secure a commodity agreement, Britain's new policy allowed the long-delayed agreement to go forward.

When I left Britain with this story of what had happened, I merely thought it humorous. After being in Ghana a few months, I realized that it was tragic.

In the summer of 1973, Ghana was in the grips of the economic crisis that would last for at least two decades. An incompetent military government, recently brought to power by an "IMF (International Monetary Fund) coup"—Ghana's second coup, this one in response to the austerity measures imposed by creditors to deal with intractable deficits (Libby 1976)—had just instituted its vaguely absurd "Operation Feed Yourself" campaign.

Shopkeepers and secretaries diligently tried to raise little victory gardens in urban back-lots in order to stem imports of costly foreign food. Corruption among border police ran rampant as truckloads of Ghana's cocoa crossed into neighboring Togo and the Ivory Coast where farmers could find much higher prices than those offered by Ghana's one legal purchaser, the Cocoa Marketing Board. Long-justified as insurance against the wild fluctuations of the world price, the Board effectively imposed a regressive 50 percent tax on all cocoa sales, money that went almost exclusively to the "development" projects of the largest urban areas where, at that time, a relatively small minority of Ghanaians lived.

Poor farmers (those working only a few hundred square feet or, at most, a few acres) and farm laborers suffered the most. Their unions had been banned by a government bent on quelling dissent and egged-on by the economists who advised the major international lenders. (After all, "Unions are anti-competitive.") Yet, union leaders were willing to risk further prison and possible torture to meet with a naive nineteen-year-old American undergraduate in the hope that some part of their story might get to people whose decisions mattered.

Had the Cocoa Agreement been signed in 1963, the story might have been different. A more stable and higher price may have prevented Ghana's *first* coup in 1966, the one engineered by officers connected to the country's cocoa aristocracy, against the central figure in Africa's struggle for independence, Kwame Nkrumah. The price stability provided by the international agreement might have helped wean Nkrumah from the colonial government's dependence for development funds on the hypocrisy of the regressive Marketing Board. A local cocoa market would have removed the need for smuggling; the seeds of the culture of corruption that affected the country for a generation might never have been sown. Almost certainly, civilian governments would have allowed unions and producers' associations to remain above ground, legal, and more capable of reminding the powerful of the needs and demands of the country's vast, rural underclass.

Sadly, similar things took place in other cocoa countries—Nigeria's Western Yorubaland, Northeast Brazil, and parts of Indonesia and the Caribbean. The lack of attentiveness of a few men in a British Cabinet meeting meant unnecessary suffering for tens of millions. In fact, the failings of even fewer privileged men may have been enough to stop the agreement: many of my informants were convinced that the US "policy" that prevented British agreement for ten years was really just the reflection of the ideological predilections of the rarely supervised civil servants who negotiated on the country's behalf. The major American manufacturer was alternately indifferent to or supportive of the agreement. As one American cocoa buyer put it, "There are lots of Quakers in Hershey, Pennsylvania, too." More significantly, Hershey was, then, another family firm, and the Hersheys were Mennonites, another dissenter, pacifist denomination with an even stronger paternalistic commitment to the Third World than the Friends had. The

Kennedy and Johnson administrations had no ideological opposition to interventions in global commodity markets. Yet, at least one of the long-serving, and rarely overseen, American negotiators was, as described by his British counterpart, "A true believer," who felt that all such interventions were deeply, morally suspect.

At age nineteen, I believed that that American negotiator might have been right. Nonetheless, after accepting hospitality from dozens of farmers and union leaders who patiently told me why they believed something very different, I became repelled by a system that allowed one man's unshakable convictions, the ill-considered views of a dozen British Cabinet members, and the serendipitous persistence of a bored civil servant looking for a more interesting job, to count so much more. The political marginalization of the tens of millions of people directly affected by the proposed cocoa agreement seemed unconscionable to me. It still does. John A. Hobson (1965 [1902]: 15–27) was astute to define "imperialism" first in *political* terms before he described its economic taproot; for Hobson, imperialism was the vast extension of the direct control over foreign peoples and territories that marked the end of the nineteenth century. For me, as well, "imperialism" became fundamentally a matter of power; its larger manifestations include all the ways that people are excluded from the collective decisions that affect their lives. Since I first went to Ghana, I have wanted to amplify the voices of the politically marginalized and to imagine what the world would be like if their views really counted.

Development

Most political economists would say that "marginalization" is a political consequence of a lack of "development." I agree, but just as my understanding of "marginalization" has a political cast, my understanding of "development" has a social and psychological one. I would like to live in a world where each of us can become all that he or she can, a world where, (to use Abraham Maslow's [1968] inadequate word) "self-actualization" is possible for everyone. Gandhian ecologist Arne Næss (1989) chooses the Norwegian gerund, "*selvrealisering*," self-realizing, to emphasize an active condition rather than a destination, and Maslow's self-actualizing subjects were actively involved in something outside themselves, devoted to a calling or vocation, as well as emotionally strong, creative, and wise.

In recent years, a group of visionary scholars, many associated with the UN Development Programme, notably Amartya Sen (1999) and Martha Nussbaum (2000, 2002) have articulated what they call the "human capabilities approach" to development, whose basic premise is similar. Nussbaum (2002: 123) writes:

> The central question of the capabilities approach is not, "How satisfied is this woman?" [or] "How much in way of resources is she able

to command?" It is, instead, "What is she actually able to do and to be?" The core idea seems to be that of the human being as a dignified free being who shapes his or her own life, rather than being passively shaped or pushed around the world in manner of a flock or herd animal.

Nussbaum's epigraph, reinforcing the point, comes from Marx's *Economic and Philosophical Manuscripts*, "In place of the *wealth* and *poverty* of political economy come the *rich human being* and *rich human need*. The rich human being is . . . the human being *in need of* a totality of human life-activities."

There are, of course, political and economic preconditions for the flourishing of humanity, but they are not the gross accumulation of material wealth that Adam Smith's culturally constricted vision saw as the only sure means for being treated with dignity. As Ashis Nandy (2002) argues, most societies, at most times, have seen poverty—self-chosen, dignified poverty—as contributing to the deepest kind of humanity. The material enemy of development is not poverty; it is *destitution*, the absolute misery of not meeting our basic physiological needs.

Closely linked to destitution, and the next most basic level of human need identified by Maslow, is *insecurity*. Of course, many communities tell themselves wonderful stories about the extraordinary compassion and heroism of average women and men in times of war, but for most of us, most of the time, war—like famine, and like disease—only stunts and deadens our humanity.

Maslow's next most fundamental level of human need becomes even more purely psychological and social. Maslow writes of needs for "esteem," for a stable and high level of self-respect and respect from others, without which we feel weak, helpless, and worthless. These needs relate to the capabilities approach concern that people have a well-founded sense of control over their own lives.

There is a political and economic corollary here: *inequality* is the enemy of esteem, the enemy of development. As Sen (1999: 146–159) emphasizes, political equality, democracy, gives us control over our lives; ending political marginalization, bringing the voices of all those affected into the process of collective decision making, is at the core of real development.

Equally, to the extent to which we have turned-over collective decision making to the market rather than the ballot box, *economic inequality* is the enemy of development. The Cadburys and Rowntrees who ran the giant British chocolate firms in the 1970s were gentle and compassionate women and men, but the fact that their wealth, their market-power, dwarfed that of the women and men who grew their cocoa, contributed to the farmers' weakness, helplessness, and lack of sense of worth.

Today, the predominant approaches to economic development do not share these concerns. For example, the World Bank, which works consciously and somewhat successfully to place itself in a position of ideological hegemony over the discourse of development professionals worldwide (Cammack 2002), recognizes growing world economic inequality, but sees poverty rather than inequality as the central challenge to development. Without question, the Bank's current, at least hortatory, focus on poverty is progressive as compared to the exclusive focus on growth in national income through industrialization that dominated the original discussions of "development" fifty or sixty years ago (Murphy 1984: 48–52). However, for the development professional, it still leaves "development" as, primarily, a problem "out there," a problem for other people whose material conditions, perversely, have just never become like those that typify the industrial West. In contrast, if "development" is about all the richness of human being, and the richness of human need, it is very much about things right here, among the world's privileged. It is about the inequalities in wealth that make the Quaker chocolate manufacturers' compassion so ineffectual. It is about the persistence of the justifiable contempt with which much of the world treats the privileged West. It is about the consumerism that diverts us from living more humane lives, and about all the ways that the insecurity, inhos-pitableness, and indignity of our materially "rich" societies prevent us from becoming all we could be.

Peace research, institutional economics, Gramscian International Relations

The field of International Relations is a great borrower of methods and approaches from other social sciences. In trying to understand global insti-tutions, marginalization, and development, my borrowings have been a little different from those of most of my contemporaries who study inter-national organization and international political economy. Typically, my colleagues have looked to neoclassical economics and strategic game theory to amend and give a more rigorous form to a related tradition of scholarship that is also rooted in the classical liberal political economy of England and Scotland at the beginning of the Industrial Revolution: the functionalist tradition of international organization studies.

I, too, have been greatly influenced by the functionalists, especially those, such as Mary Parker Follett, whose approaches overlap with social psy-chology and organizational studies. Even so, I came to these "International Relations" methods late. Both as an undergraduate and as a graduate stu-dent my greatest exposure was to multidisciplinary approaches to conflict resolution and to Institutionalist and Marxist analysis of the role of ideas in the unfolding of modern economies.

Lynn Mather's freshman seminar gave me a glimpse of the systematic peace studies scholarship of the 1960s and 1970s. The central focus of my research has been to understand institutional innovations aimed at mitigat-ing or resolving what peace researchers call "asymmetric" (Rapoport 1979) or "unbalanced" (Curle 1971) international conflicts, like those between colonizers and the colonized. I have been influenced by Johan Galtung's (1971) communication-based analysis of imperialism, which sees patterns of inclusion and exclusion from networks of potential collective decision making as the defining characteristic of the hierarchies that create structural violence and that require the particular analysis and particular conflict resolution techniques that peace researchers have identified as essential to asymmetric conflicts. In addition, I see Herbert Kelman (1979) and others' practical attempts to resolve protracted social conflicts of identity (which are analytically similar to asymmetric conflicts) as one of the best, nonviolent models of how to overcome the social problems that most interest me.

If there is a single lesson from peace research that I wish every student of international organization and international political economy could learn, it is the practical distinction between symmetric and asymmetric conflicts. As early as the early 1960s, Anatol Rapoport pointed out that asymmetric conflicts, including North–South conflicts over creating "development" institutions, could not be adequately understood if they are treated as if they were strategic games:

> A revolt of slaves against their status as slaves cannot be "settled" by a compromise whereby the slaves are accorded better treatment, or whatever. Once the *structure of the system* becomes the real issue, offers of this sort will be seen only as attempts to preserve the structure.
>
> (Rapoport 1979: 236)

These peace research foundations make my approach similar to that of J. Ann Tickner. Tickner has great sympathy with Gandhi's philosophy of self-development and self-reliance and she recognizes, as Galtung does, that a radical form of collective self-reliance, if practical, would dissolve the networks of structural violence that keep so many on the margins. Her first major study explained the failure of the Gandhian vision in India, comparing it to the similar failure of Jefferson's hope for the United States of self-reliant (and, today, we might say "self-actualized") small holders (Tickner 1987). In her later work, when she came to focus on the particular marginalization within the global political economy, Tickner (1992) identified Kelman's dialogic approach to resolving fundamental conflicts as analogous to a non-violent, feminist method of confronting structural inequities.

Tickner's explanation of the failure of the Gandhian and Jeffersonian visions rests upon her understanding of the security dilemmas faced by modern states, the technological demands of their militaries, and the internal logic of the industrial system. Similar conclusions about the security system led me to rely on the work of scholars who address questions of war and technology while remaining in dialogue with peace researchers (see Chapter 6), but the bulk of my original research has been on the unfolding of the industrial system. In that work, I was influenced by the classical Institutionalist Economics taught at Grinnell College when I was undergraduate, and by its leading figures of the early twentieth century including Hobson, Thorstein Veblen, John R. Commons, John Maurice Clark, and Wesley Mitchell.

The Institutionalists tried to understand the evolution of the "habits of thought and action" guiding human interaction with the rest of the material world. Their approach was profoundly and unabashedly historical. Hobson (1912), Veblen (1966), and Commons (1924) gave me a better understanding of the origins of capitalist industry than that gained by most of my American and British contemporaries who were educated in more conventional economics programs. More significantly, John Maurice Clark's (1923) analysis of overhead costs made me aware of the fundamental role of economies of scale in the pressure for the geographic expansion of industrial economies. This insight had disappeared from the standard international trade economics because it was too difficult to formalize, until Paul Krugman (1986) and his colleagues cracked the problem in the 1980s.

Perhaps unfortunately, in exchange for learning the forgotten and still valid insights of an older economics, I never gained the mathematical sophistication that Krugman's work exemplifies. I did learn to value statistics, but not formal theory. My teachers' example taught that research meant reading all the relevant documents, questioning any of the participants still living, and, following the examples of Wesley Mitchell, the founder of the National Bureau of Economic Research, and Edward Azar, one of my graduate professors, trying to make the resulting information as systemic and easy to manipulate as possible.

The Institutionalists' concern with the specificity of the habits of thought that guide actors served me well in my first serious research, the study of the Cocoa Agreement. Had I been willing to assume the interests of the parties involved, I would not have learned about the paternalism of some chocolate manufacturers or the importance of some civil servants being so captivated by market economics. That success increased my attraction to understanding the role of beliefs and values in shaping social life.

That cocoa study also taught me to love field research, not just the challenge of trying to look at an issue though the eyes of those with different values, language, and life-worlds, but also just the pleasure of figuring out how to get hard-to-find answers to specific questions: the thrill of the chase.

The breakthrough in that first project had come when I noticed an advertisement in *The Economist* placed by Oxfam. It emphasized how little cocoa farmers received of the small change we spend when we buy a chocolate bar. I wrote to Oxfam and asked if there had been any corporate reactions to the advertisement. The reply came back that there was one very strong one, from Sir Michael Rowntree, an Oxfam board member, who accepted part of the advertisement's argument, but did not welcome its publication. In fact, he seemed to take the issue almost personally, given his family's long philanthropic record.

My interviews with members of the paternalistic chocolate families triggered a continuing interest in the role of philanthropy in the origin of significant regulatory institutions, (see Chapters 3, 10, and 12), at the same time that it further reinforced my conviction that political change could only be understood if we recognized the power of ideology and of group identity. It is true that over time the philanthropic cocoa companies have become more and more like the simple profit maximizers assumed by rational choice theories (Swift 1998); over time, "ideology" does approach "interest." Nevertheless, at any particular time, as the Institutionalists recognized, the behavior of all conscious social actors, including the most powerful, is better predicted by the goals and worldviews that they then hold. Moreover, we can understand the story of global governance only when we recognize the roles that aristocratic philanthropists played in the nineteenth century and that bourgeois philanthropists (including the cocoa families) played in the twentieth.

To pay attention to ideology and identity requires conceptual frameworks that emphasize the role of our habits of thought in shaping the consequences of our actions. My concepts initially came from the Institutionalists, especially from Veblen, who saw habits of thought and action evolving through a process of "selective elimination" of institutional innovations.

Veblen is not widely cited by contemporary International Relations scholars. Yet, historian of American social science, Dorothy Ross (1991: 207) aptly calls Veblen "the American Gramsci," a thinker who is now much more central to the field. Veblen, like Gramsci, was someone, "drawn to the problem of false consciousness and training in idealist philosophy into a revision of Marx's theory of history." Not surprisingly, the more I encountered questions about global institutions and the marginalization of the South that could be answered only by taking lived ideas into account, the more I was drawn to Gramsci as well (see Murphy 1998b).

There is, by now, an identifiable Gramscian approach to International Relations that loosely links a school of which I am happy to be considered a part. Nonetheless, a focus on the distinctions between schools may lead us to overstate differences among scholars working on relatively similar problems, and Gramscians who study international institutions are not that different from others who are not "Gramscian."

The most distinctive claim I have made is that the degree to which global institutions actually can serve the least advantaged is heavily influenced by the way the world is understood by the institutions' powerful makers. At the beginning of the twenty-first century, when a fundamentalist kind of liberal ideology remains triumphant, it may be particularly important to remember that, while liberal fundamentalism has had other periods of temporary triumph, it has never really served the long-term interests of the powerful, let alone those of the marginalized.

This insight does not, in fact, contradict conclusions of approaches to the study of global institutions that are dominant, at least in the United States. The institutional theory of Robert O. Keohane (2002) and the international regimes literature out of which it developed (including Keohane 1984) tells us that national leaders and political elites construct international institutions to serve their understanding of national and domestic needs. Thus, most global institutions meet the needs and advance the interests of the most powerful national governments and the corporate sectors that have significant influence over them. The literature on embedded liberalism and multilateralism (Ruggie 1998) emphasizes that these same institutions serve the needs and advance the interests of several nations and business interests by enhancing cooperation centered upon a shared set of liberal political and economic values. "Multilateralism," the coordination of relations among three or more states, has been the primary means of such liberal collaboration since the Second World War.

The focus of my research has been broader. I have linked the longer-lasting innovations in international cooperation, the major institutions of institutionalized international relations to the regulatory needs of an expanding, "globalizing" capitalism and asked whether those institutions can also serve the marginalized, as their champions have always claimed. Yes, most of the long-lasting international political and economic institutions are, indeed, "liberal," and, yes, we can freeze the history of global governance at certain points and argue that the existing network of institutions unambiguously serve the cooperative interests of relatively powerful member governments. However, if we are interested in questions of marginalization and development—questions about those who *are not* served by the array of regulatory institutions that exist at any time—we also need to ask additional questions. We need, for example, to look for *proposed* institutional innovations that would have served the interests of the powerful just as well as those that came into being, yet, at the same time, would have better served the interests of the marginalized. What prevented those that better served the marginalized to be chosen? Conversely, have there been proposed institutions that would have served the marginalized less well than those were selected? What allowed the better institutions to be chosen?

Thus, my specific research questions have included: What delayed the Cocoa Agreement, (even though the major cocoa companies did not oppose it)? Why, in the 1970s, did the North fail to accept any of the South's proposals for a "New International Economic Order," even though almost all those proposals were reflections of the same Keynesian liberal analysis that underlay the embedded liberalism of the postwar, Western multilateral order? Why, throughout the history of capitalist industrialism, have some previously marginalized groups gained from the institution of new political and economic regimes over wider market areas, while others have lost? Why, today, have innovations in international organization seemed to favor women (in many parts of the world) and some previously marginalized ethnic groups, while industrial workers (who, arguably, benefited from the waves of innovation at the end of the World Wars) have gained so little?

Other Gramscian International Relations scholars have been less focused than I have been on the complexity of what has happened and is happening with different groups of the disadvantaged as a consequence of economic globalization and its governance. They emphasize the way today's global institutions have become "transmission belts" for neoliberalism, part of the process of the "internationalization" or "transnationalization" of the state. They emphasize the Marxian identity in the final instance between the state and the interests of the capitalist class, now a transnationalized, perhaps even, global, capitalist class (Gill 2003: 86, compare Schechter 2002: 15–16).

I prefer to recognize that identity between capitalist interests and global governance as something that is very much "in the long run," a "long run" that may never arrive, especially if a more humane means of organizing the global political economy can be developed in the meantime. We can learn something relevant to that goal from the concrete improvements that specific marginalized groups have gained through the politics of global governance since the Industrial Revolution.

To be clear, though: to look for strategic insights from the partial victories of some of the marginalized is not the same as uncritically embracing liberal fundamentalism. It is not to argue, along with sociologists of the "World Polity School" (Boli and Thomas 1999; Luo 2000), that globalization and global governance are the material manifestation of the unfolding of a (presumably progressive) liberal internationalism. It is certainly not to overlook the ethical consequences of the internationalization of neoliberalism, the failing more typical of so much of the literature on global institutions.

To critically analyze the liberal worldview underlying global institutions requires articulating an alternative. That is the purpose of Chapter 2, "World Organizations and Human Needs." It considers the 150-year history of the most inclusive intergovernmental organizations in light of the needs-centered idea of development.

That history represents a series of approximations to global governance incorporating ever-larger human communities and multiple states. Most of these governance innovations have been informed by versions of liberalism. This is the subject of Chapter 3, "The Dialectic of Liberal Internationalism."

Chapter 4, "Social Movements and Liberal World Orders," considers the learning about effective governance beyond the state that has gone on since the early nineteenth century. It is ironic that egalitarian social movements have played a central role in this learning despite the fact that, so far at least, industrialism has, looked at globally, only increased inequality.

Nonetheless, critical thinkers within the liberal tradition have developed ever more sophisticated analyses that reasonably promise a more egalitarian world. Learning has led to progress—to political development—in global governance.

Yet, that progress is far from simple. Relatively effective governance guided by increasingly sophisticated and critical strands of liberal internationalism has alternated with ineffective governance guided by an uncritical liberal fundamentalism. "Liberal learning" may be a central dynamic in global political development throughout the industrial era, but so is "liberal forgetting." Chapter 5, "The Promise of Democratic Functionalism," considers both dynamics, including the contemporary consequences of forgetting some of the origins of the most progressive liberal internationalist thought of the twentieth century.

Chapters 6 through 9 argue we are at a point of transition when thoughts and plans about global governance—what we remember from earlier eras and what we have forgotten—truly make a difference. Chapter 6, "International Institutions, Decolonization, and 'Development'," considers the origins of the governance structures that are, today, the least effective. "What the Third World Wanted: The Meaning of the NIEO," Chapter 7, examines the fate of the egalitarian liberal ideas underlying the proposals for a New International Economic Order that were at the center of discussions about reforming global institutions almost a generation ago.

The NIEO failed for many reasons, but one reason is sufficient to explain why the program has largely been forgotten: the collapse of the Soviet industrial model and its abandonment by China led to the most recent of many temporary triumphs of liberal fundamentalism, the neoliberalism of the last two decades. Since the 1980s, the whole range of Keynesian projects, including that of the Third World alliance, have been forgotten. Chapter 8, "Freezing the North–South Bloc after the East–West Thaw," considers the consequences of the current era for people in the marginalized parts of Africa, Asia, and Latin America. Chapter 9, "Global Governance: Poorly Done and Poorly Understood" returns to the idea of needs-oriented development, evaluates the consequences of today's global governance, and considers how little we understand about how to move forward.

Chapter 10, "Political Consequences of the New Inequality," begins to consider the other side of the dialectic: the political opportunities created as a consequence of this current moment of economic and political globalization. "Leadership and Global Governance for the Information Age," Chapter 11, returns to the process through which effective global institutions have been created in the past. It considers some of the intractable contemporary issues of global governance, environmental and labor issues that divide North and South and that divide an increasingly unilateralist and hegemonic United States from the rest of the world.

The concluding chapter, 12, "To Mingle, Meet, and Know: Marginal-ization and the Privileged," comes back to the larger issue of mitigating the fundamental, asymmetric conflicts that divide the world. I argue that meaningful development can be fostered when the privileged learn from the marginalized, and that this can be understood as a fundamental concern of the world's privileged, even those in its most powerful state, as well as a fundamental concern of the scholarly field of International Relations.

2 World organizations and human needs

In 1995, the Commission on Global Governance brought worldwide attention to a new concept. Shortly thereafter, Susan Strange wrote:

> [T]he search is on for better ways of managing society and economy than has so far been achieved through the unaided efforts of the individual nation-states. Foundations have readily provided the resources for research into "global governance"—often without any clear idea of what it may mean. New journals and a great many conferences with similar titles have proliferated. At the same time, there has been a parallel revival of interest among policymakers as well as academics in the possibilities for reform of existing international organizations from the United Nations to the World Bank and the International Monetary Fund.
>
> (1996: 183)

The last sentence clarifies the real source of the debate over global governance. It is not about creating something fundamentally new, nor is it really about completely transcending "the unaided efforts of the individual nation-states." Rather, it is about creating *effective* intergovernmental organizations at a global level, effective world organizations.

Effective for what? Is it just a matter of international political economy? Modern intergovernmental organizations go back to the first decades after the Industrial Revolution. Promoters of that fundamentally new economic system found that some form of international governance was needed simply because it is the nature of industrial economies to grow beyond their original political boundaries. Yet, neither the Global Governance Commission nor all those academic reformers to whom Strange refers have limited their concerns to promoting this project of industrialism. Their implicit focus is on human needs.

That is the concern of this chapter, too. However, I am concerned with effectiveness of those institutions that existed in the past, the giants (or dwarves) on whose shoulders any new, twenty-first century system of global governance will have to stand. Formal, bureaucratic, global institutions, world organizations—those intergovernmental and quasi-governmental agencies open to any independent state, even though all states may not have joined—have existed since the 1860s, the result of diplomatic efforts that began more than a decade before. Some world organizations have contributed to substantive regulation of world society. Others have pointed to the existence of governance exercised elsewhere, for example, through the widespread adoption of similar national regulations, the enforcement of formal international agreements by a few powerful states, and the global imposition of rules by private, transnational associations. Others, the smallest number, have just been reflections of utopian dreams, although they are often aspirations that let us see the human needs that the utopians yearned to see met.

Thus, a focus on human needs is not new to the study and practice of international organization. It has been central to speculative analysis of international organization since its beginning and, starting in the 1970s, many studies began to take what was called a "basic needs" approach, emphasizing the importance of satisfying the physical requirements for daily living (compare Galtung 1988).

Yet, human needs go well beyond the physiological. We certainly need air, water, food, shelter, and clothing, but we also have socially constructed material needs. In many societies, most adults cannot gain access to material necessities without wage employment, and to get that, in some places, including my own country, may require secondary education, access to an automobile and a phone, and a wardrobe that would be considered extravagant to half of humanity.

We also have equally salient, equally fundamental, security needs, needs felt by adults during natural disasters, humanitarian emergencies, periods of social crisis, and war. Children feel these needs more frequently and acutely than adults do, because children (perhaps wisely) doubt the power of the adults in their world to make it always safe.

Every parent recognizes that children also have fundamental needs for affection and for a sense of belonging—needs to escape loneliness and alienation, and needs to give love as well as to receive it. Yet, the realization that these childhood needs remain with us throughout our lives may be Abraham Maslow's (1968) greatest contribution. The simple reciprocal exchange of affection is the basic building block of the communities that nurture us as social beings, and that keep us sane.

Linked to our needs for belonging are our needs for self-respect and for respect from others, without which we feel inferior, weak, helpless, or worthless. Moreover, when our basic physiological needs and our equally fundamental social-psychological needs are met, we are better able to do the truly worthwhile, essentially human work of self-realization, of following that takes us beyond ourselves.

Maslow originally believed that human beings faced a strict hierarchy of human needs, that we worked first to meet those that are physiologically basic, then concerned ourselves with security, belonging, recognition, and, finally, self-actualization. Gandhi and those inspired by his life and thought, more accurately recognize that we concern ourselves with all these needs (Weber 1999). A strict hierarchy cannot be found in the habits of any contemporary human community. In part, this is because what we must have to meet our physiological needs seems insignificant in comparison to the abundance that industrial economies can create. In part, it is because the social-psychological task of building community and the personal task of self-realization are, in fact, one. Violence against oneself makes self-realization impossible and violence against a living being is violence against oneself. The real enemies of self-realization remain destitution, insecurity, and the political inequality that leave so many without control over the major decisions that affect their lives.

Here, in this chapter, the major focus is on the basic, physiological needs that, when unmet, leave us destitute, and the fundamental social-psychological needs that, when unmet, may lead to great violence. To what extent have the major intergovernmental organizations worked to meet those needs?

The UN system and its predecessors have done a great deal: promoting decolonization, caring for refugees, furthering public health, improving the overall material standard of living of many societies, and even alerting humanity to the fact that we share basic needs. This is an important record to recognize at the beginning of a book that ultimately portrays global governance, or "what world government we have actually had," in a harsh light.

Basic physiological needs and related human rights

That the world organizations actually do help meet both kinds of needs was one of the conclusions of my research into the coevolution of modern intergovernmental organizations and capitalist industry. I began the research in the mid-1980s by creating a list of world organizations, adding autonomous secretariat divisions identified by Robert H. Manley (1978) to Harold K. Jacobson's (1984) then standard list of such entities. I also added organizations disbanded before 1985 but found on Michael D. Wallace and J. David Singer's (1970) historical compilation. To identify sources covering the entire history of each organization I consulted standard bibliographies and the subject catalogs of the New York Public Library, which has had a policy of collecting works on international institutions and has maintained a subject catalog, including citations to articles, throughout most of the almost 150-year history of the world organizations. I read each of the sources and recorded what they reported to be the ongoing activities of each organization, coding all of the active statements in which an organization was the subject that referred to an externally directed action repeated over at least a five-year period. I then cleaned the resulting data set, removing multiple references to the same activity, and data on the same activity that came from different sources. With some modifications, I later updated the data to reflect the many changes in the 1990s.

In the end, each record of an activity included the five-year period in which the organization carried out the activity, a standard organization identity number, the verb found in the source statement, and the rest of the source statement, which could be considered detailed description of the issue area of activity. In addition, I recorded the more general political-economic issue area the activity most immediately affected. Initially, I considered these to be attempts to influence (1) international markets for goods, (2) international factor markets, (3) economic relations between industrialized and less-industrialize states, (4) interstate politico-military relations, and (5) relations between individuals and their national governments, including activities that help meet basic needs.

Some observations can be made with respect to the importance of human needs in each of these five areas, especially the link between activities in the first four issue areas and the emergence of intergovernmental attention to the basic needs of individuals.

Commerce

Over half of the activities in the original data set immediately affected commercial relation. These activities helped liberalize the global economy by standardizing and lowering costs of shipping and communication, making trade restrictions transparent, and encouraging intergovernmental agreements to reduce trade barriers.

The first health-related activities arose along with commercial responsibilities. Governments aimed to confine West Asian and tropical diseases so that international trade would be less subject to unpredictable quarantines and less suspect as a carrier of exotic infections. As medical science changed its focus from quarantine, to treatment, to prevention, intergovernmental organizations responded. They became concerned with improving individual health (Jacobson 1974). Still today, whenever intergovernmental organizations propose programs to free all individuals from an infectious disease, they find strong allies in those whose livelihood depends on the international flow of goods and people, as the recent SARS crisis demonstrated. Goldman Sachs Vice Chair, Robert Hormats, characteristically argued that the crisis was an object lesson of what was wrong with the US's recent retreat from multilateralism, "This is not multilateralism for multilateralism's sake," he said, "It's not ideological. It's pragmatic. You need broad coalitions for international trade and commerce to work smoothly" (Gray 2003).

Labor

About 15 percent of the activities have affected factor markets. The bulk involve world organizations promoting international standards for labor and promoting ways to shift the cost of maintaining those standards to the economy as a whole. Many of the labor standard-setting exercises contribute to the fulfillment of basic human needs. While the International Labor Organization's meager autonomous powers, by themselves, cannot enforce international labor standards effectively, labor and employers in leading sectors have an interest in having standards apply in all competing industrial economies. They, in turn, often convince governments throughout the industrialized world to enforce standards like maximum hours of work in factories and offices and bans on child labor in factories. Even in newly industrializing nations, local standards often begin to converge with global norms due to the local pressure of newly powerful, industrial workers alongside the international pressure from more industrialized countries.

Third World development

Another 15 percent of the cases are development activities immediately affecting relationships between the industrialized world and its far-flung economic peripheries. World organizations help expand the industrial and export agricultural sectors of the Third World and, much less frequently, help maintain the coherence of traditional economies. The fundamental intergovernmental role, and the World Bank's original purpose, is to "greenline" some traditional economies by encouraging long-term capital investment. In many cities, banks "redline" (encircle on their company map) neighborhoods of the marginalized to warn loan officers against extending credit to businesses or homeowners within those communities, a practice that quickly leads to neighborhood decline. The World Bank does the opposite for the countries it favors. It offers low interest loans and technical assistance to a few international "neighborhoods," thus suggesting that these are fine places for investment.

As is the case with activities affecting labor and commerce, activities in this issue serve highly mobile international capital, the leading sectors that may be interested in the enforcement of labor standards, and the investors who most profit from international commerce. However, states gave world organizations responsibilities for development not only to protect capital, but also in response to nationalist demands. In the 1920s, the committees monitoring the League of Nations' Mandates (Wright 1930) promulgated what might be called "modernization rights" of individuals, including the rights of children to basic education and the rights of workers to decent conditions, remuneration, and the ability to refuse any job, human rights standards that pointed to, and beyond, basic physiological needs.

Relations between states

Half of the data set's remaining cases (a total of ten percent) involve conflict management, peacekeeping, and all those things that journalists and historians tend to focus on when they write about the UN. Since the days of the League, the international community has claimed to protect political refugees and disadvantaged minorities within any nation-state. The League of Nations and the UN established standards of service for all refugees— minimum physical standards of nutrition and shelter. These standards, in turn, became operational definitions of "basic needs," caloric requirements and the like (Holborn 1975: 32–36). Moreover, advocates for refugees quickly came to see meeting their basic needs as a matter of human rights. The day-to-day work of caring for refugees revealed other rights as well, including the labor, educational, and cultural rights declared for those who live under League Mandates. In fact, here is where the world organizations may have had their greatest impact on meeting human needs: by pointing to their practical, cross-cultural reality in the day-to-day work of deciding what must, at minimum, be provided to those displaced by war.

Fundamental social and psychological needs

To understand what world organizations have done to meet the wider range of human needs, it is important to consider what we know about the connection between war and "basic needs." The destitute rarely are able to fight, but peace researcher John Burton (1979: 1), argues that instead of asking, "Will people fight when certain (already specified) needs are not met?" social scientists should ask, "For what needs (to be determined empirically) will people sometimes be willing even to fight?" The set of needs Burton and his colleagues identify resemble those identified both by Maslow and by Gandhi. They are the social and psychological conditions we must have to survive, develop, and cope with change. Meeting such needs maintains the key attributes of what political scientist Karl Deutsch (1966) called a "cybernetic actor," (or we could just say a "human being"). Security, a sense of belonging and self-worth, and even a belief in the possibility of self-realization are prerequisites for memory, a coherent sense of self, and the possibility of learning. Burton focuses on the social psychology of learning itself (1979: 78–80): All of us need the security and recognition needed to reinforce learning (by linking new information back to images that include a coherent and positive image of self). We also need a sense of identity itself, including personal hopes, fears, and expectations. Burton claims that there is overwhelming evidence that humans will act to meet these needs, even if they will die in the struggle to do so.

Here are two examples of people who will meet such needs, come what may. I took them from field notes made for a study that had a very different purpose (Murphy 1987), but they speak to Burton's central point.

A Nigerian

An African university student, about to fail at the end of his second year, doubts his own abilities but is unsure of the source of his problems because of the seemingly random feedback coming from a university so under-staffed that overworked professors explain grades with the first thing that pops into their heads. They may never have read the student's exam anyway. Some professors accept bribes. Assigned books fail to appear in the library. Supplies are scarce. Student stipends are paid months late in devalued currency, forcing the student to work long hours far from campus because he was told by one professor, who later failed him, that to work during a term was "unscholarly." ("Did he see me at my job across town?") The student cuts through all the randomness by noticing that he is the only Northerner in his class, and the only classmate to have failed. He has failed because "they" will not let Northerners succeed. All the sepa-rately inexplicable, seemingly random insults he has experienced for two years now form a consistent background to this new "information."

An Assimilado

A Portuguese shopkeeper living on one of the Cape Verde islands in 1975, saving money to send his son to the university in Lisbon learns from the radio that the government in the capital has decided to turn the island over to the revolutionaries who have been fighting the Portuguese army hun-dreds of miles away in Africa. Not only are these foreigners to take over, Lisbon has also declared that no one in Cape Verde is Portuguese any longer. They are now all "African." Portuguese universities will be much more selective about letting these "foreigners" in. His son, who has never been the best in his class, will have no chance. Crushed, the shopkeeper tells his brother, visiting from America, "What is this! I am no poor black! I am no communist! I am no African! But they tell me I am no Portuguese, too!"

"True," says his brother, "you are not Portuguese. In America, we have known that all along. Here the Portuguese treat us like dirt and the blacks do too, even though they want us to say we are black like them. We just say we are 'Cape Verdeans.' You are Cape Verdean. Your son is Cape Verdean. He shouldn't be going to university in Lisbon with Portuguese, or becoming an African communist; he should go to university with other Cape Verdeans, in Massachusetts or Rhode Island." Denied one part of a coherent identity, and denied recognition by an old govern-ment in which he put his faith and a new one that will completely deny his identity, as he understands it, the shopkeeper accepts the recommenda-tion of a brother who recognizes his most important dreams, and "becomes" a Cape Verdean.

These fundamental needs are not merely the needs of individuals. They have implications for groups and for the relationship between groups and governments. When individuals cannot meet fundamental needs by maintaining relationships to existing institutions, they will break those relationships and find new identities. They "become," for example, "Northerners" or "Cape Verdeans." As Deutsch (1966) demonstrated, modern nationalism arose in large part as a way that people in modernizing societies, confronting great political and economic change, could meet their fundamental needs for identity and recognition.

In some cases, the power of identity groups defined in opposition to the existing social order means civil war. Place the failing university student of the first example in Nigeria in 1965 and you have the makings of a staunch supporter of the anti-Ibo counter-coup and the crushing of Biafra.

Perhaps much less frequently, the emergence of new identity groups can mean that an established government will have incentive to join with the group itself, declare itself the government of the disaffected, and allow enough participation by them that their personal hopes and expectations become bound up with the hopes and expectations of the rulers. By 1980, many of the revolutionaries who had returned to Cape Verde in 1975 had seen their comrades who had been born in the islands kicked-out of the former Portuguese "sister republics" on the African mainland that they had helped to liberate. The government stopped calling itself first an "African" or "liberation" government and started to call itself "Cape Verdean." It contacted people born in the islands and living abroad, especially in New England, set up a sort of "law of return," and opened channels for widespread participation and dissent. Events had forced political leaders to find their own identity among the people they governed.

The leader of Cape Verde's liberation struggle, Amilcar Cabral, who was assassinated in 1973, would have understood his comrades' actions a decade later. Cabral was a student of Frantz Fanon, and Fanon's (1961) clinical reports of the dreams of hegemony, strength, and control reported by the most victimized people in colonial Algeria dramatically demonstrate that even under the must crushing denial of security and community, people *will* make sense of the world, even if it is only in the world of fantasy. They will find their identity within it, even when an incoherent world gives them no anchor, even when an indifferent world denies them any human existence.

The argument here is not that the denial of fundamental needs inevitably results in delusion, suicide, or war. Far from it, there are many alternative ways in which people can make sense of a rapidly changing world that allows them no secure sense of self. The argument is that it is within communities denied these social and psychological anchors that violent conflict is the most likely to erupt. Moreover, as Fanon documented, irrational violence arising out of fractured identity is as much a problem for the colonizer as the colonized.

Ashis Nandy (1983) suggests that Gandhi deeply understood this connection. For Gandhi, the violence that could result from the loss of identity in a rapidly changing world—like all violence—was ultimately self-destructive. (Here, of course, the contrast with Fanon's views could not be starker.) Violence against others was, to Gandhi, as irrational a way to deal with the terrifying incoherence of colonialism as violence against oneself. His genius was to form a political movement that found a way to make sense of the fractured identities of many Indians under colonialism without making it *essential* that they try to remove from themselves (from their person and from their communities) those parts that were incompatible with a new, more coherent view of themselves. Indians did have to remove the "British" parts and "Muslim" parts of themselves and of their communities in order to transform colonialism.

Of course, violence against what Nandy calls those "intimate enemies" did erupt with the partition of India and Pakistan, and it continues to plague the subcontinent. Yet, it is likely that Gandhi's movement averted greater violence because it aimed at not only the liberation of India, but also, "liberation of the British from the history and psychology of British colonialism" (Nandy 1983: 48–49).

Fundamental needs, conflict management, and conflict resolution

What have world organizations done to meet this set of needs? Surprisingly little. Burton and his colleagues trace a great deal of the violence since the Second World War to attempts to meet fundamental needs for identity and recognition. Groups form in conflict with existing authorities and then lash out, violently, against the "intimate enemies"—their colonizers, other identity groups—who are incompatible with the oppressed's new view of themselves. Even though the world organizations have directed many of their "security" activities toward the same conflicts, the UN's focus is not these fundamental needs; rather, its goal has been, as the title of one study puts it, *Moderation Through Management* (Butterworth 1978).

We can distinguish between *resolving* conflicts and merely *managing* them. Parties involved in conflict resolution treat their conflict as a joint problem arising out of the ways they have met needs for recognition, identity, and order in the past. "Conflict management," as practiced by global intergovernmental organizations, merely involves moderating the effects of conflicts on the world order, the order that consists of, at minimum, the relations of dominance of government over the governed, the maintenance of boundaries of sovereignty between states, and the maintenance of the global hierarchy of autonomous states.

Historically, the range of means used by world organizations to manage conflicts has been wide. They have intervened on the side of one party, usually that of the national or colonial governments confronting a rebellion. The world organizations have placed neutral troops between warring parties. Backed by regional powers or by superpower agreement, intergovernmental organizations have invoked and enforced prior agreements between warring parties. The UN has also facilitated direct bargaining between parties over scarce goods—land, water rights, and so forth—at issue in various conflicts. Finally, the UN and its predecessors have even proposed and helped maintain cultural, economic, social, and political boundaries between states.

None of these means of conflict management addresses the fundamental socio-psychological needs of the groups in conflict. Subject people can still maintain their identity, and through it, their conflict with those who have subjected them. Even if they have full autonomy within their own boundaries, people isolated from each other by troops or by international agreements can retain memories of past victimization. The oppressors across the border can remain enemies. Moreover, the social-psychological states that would fill these needs cannot be divided among warring parties; they are not the kind of things that can be bargained over. Just as masters and slaves cannot "resolve" their conflict by bargaining over the rules of slavery, groups whose identities require that they deny the identity of some "other" have no way to "bargain" over who each other will be.

Conflict resolution as practiced in a few labor-management settings (see Chapter 5), in some community development practices, and in a particular type of international conflict resolution workshops, focuses on fundamental needs. The mutuality of working together itself helps meet the need for recognition. The act of focusing on the conflict as an identifiable problem makes it easier for all parties to learn from the past. Moreover, because the process treats human needs for security and identity as fundamental and nonnegotiable, conflict-protracting challenges to the self-identities of the parties can be avoided.[1]

Burton (1979: 121) argues, that to accept the possibility of conflict resolution we must also accept that, "parties to a conflict are responding to the situation in the ways that appear most beneficial to them in light of the knowledge that they have." The irrational behavior of adherents to all-encompassing ideologies is just, "behavior not understood or approved by others." At the very least, someone who entertains the assumptions that underlie this approach to conflict would want to know, for example, what made Bin Laden's followers identify with a messianic and peculiarly violent Islamism and what made Hitler's followers identify with Aryan imperialism.

In fact, it was reflection on the political economic sources of fascism's appeal to its followers that influenced what responsibilities states gave to post-Second World War international *economic* institutions, but not the responsibilities they gave to the UN's security institutions. Many interwar economists, especially John Maynard Keynes (1971 [1920]), believed that the harsh conditions imposed upon Germany by the victors at the end of the First World War contributed to Hitler's rise. In the 1930s, creative *ad hoc* multilateral public and private diplomacy eased those conditions by funneling credit to Europe and establishing robust new international economic institutions, but that did not happen rapidly enough to prevent the Nazi's electoral victories and their successful, unilateral experiment in ending the Depression. The more benign peace imposed in 1945 and Germany's inclusion in the Marshall Plan, reflected the lessons learned.

If the founders of the UN system had paid as much attention to contemporary work on the *social psychology* of that linkage—the work of Wilhelm Reich (1970) and, more significantly, that of the Frankfurt School (Adorno *et al.* 1950, Fromm 1973)—the postwar security system might have been different. Such reflection would take us back to complex histories of what Burton's colleagues, Edward E. Azar and Nadia Farah (1981) call the "structural victimization" that typifies the rapidly changing societies where events force people to shift their identities. Faced with limited options, people in rapidly changing societies often identify with groups whose "action scripts" turn the former victims of oppression into victimizers— deniers of fundamental needs—of others whose subsequent search for new ways to meet their own socio-psychological needs may continue the process. Some Germans, battered by the impossible terms of the Versailles Treaty, become the anti-Semitic perpetrators of the Holocaust; some Zionists, ripped apart by that incomparable horror, become intransient rulers over millions of Palestinians. Perhaps the entire nineteenth- and twentieth-century histories of the geographic centers of international crises—East and Central Europe, Southwest and Southeast Asia, North and Central Africa—can be told as that of one complex chain of victimization.

Today's global intergovernmental organizations are not equipped to consider that view of history any more than they are able to trust in the long-term rationality of adherents to all-encompassing ideologies. Victorious states created the current global system for managing conflicts after long struggles against revolutionary states (fascist and later Leninist) whose behavior appeared to confirm every assumption of the traditional Realist paradigm. The genesis of the contemporary system would be reason enough for its practice to affirm a key Realist conclusion: "The interests of the greater powers and world society as a whole must sometimes be placed before the interests of the parties [in the conflict]," (Burton 1979: 121). In contrast, to resolve rather than manage conflicts rooted in chains of victimization, Burton argues we must let, "the relations of the parties most directly concerned take precedence." The interests of the great power and the maintenance of the global status quo must be secondary. Yet, because their founders designed world organizations to protect the current order, we cannot expect them to grant an equal hearing to those who oppose it. We cannot expect them to facilitate the participation of challengers in fundamental decisions about the future, even if that is what resolution of violent protracted conflicts would require.

Nonetheless, for a time, parts of the UN system promoted a kind of real conflict resolution, during the years when a balance of power prevailed between those who refused to let colonizing states and colonists have any say in the process of decolonization and those who would refuse to let dependent people have any part (see Chapter 6). Because of this tenuous balance of power, the world organizations could occasionally act as a conflict resolver, bringing all parties into a process of solving the problem of colonization. The UN especially had this role in the decolonization of the many African states that were so poor and out of the way that civil servants could often consider the needs of the parties involved rather than the interests of the superpowers.

Eventually, the very success of decolonization undermined this role. By the time that most of the former African colonies gained their independence, in the mid-1960s, UN debates about decolonization had become pro-forma. The UN continued to play a role reinforcing the power of the anti-apartheid movement and allying with anti-apartheid and anti-Portuguese forces within the US and European governments, but new groups demanding separation or regional autonomy were less and less welcome within the world organizations (compare Haas 1983).

The future: basic needs

World organizations have played a larger role in satisfying basic physiological needs than in meeting fundamental needs for identity and security.

Most of the activities that help meet basic needs have been added to the intergovernmental agenda as an adjunct to activities that serve the economic interests of powerful states and their most powerful citizens. These activities reduce the transaction costs of intergovernmental co-operation by, for example, providing conference services and maintaining international accounts, in the way that Robert O. Keohane's (1984) theory of international institutions would predict. Labor standard-setting is also enforced by reporting procedures and retaliation, but again, these powers imply little challenge to the status quo, except, perhaps, in newly industrializing countries.

Beyond providing information and reducing transaction costs of intergovernmental cooperation, some of the world organizations' "development" activities empower some groups within privileged Third World countries against the government and against traditional economic forces. Throughout most of their history, the development organizations have tilted toward "modernizing" elites. In time, perhaps, more organizations will tilt toward the economically marginalized as well. Under Robert S. McNamara, the World Bank provided a forum for those who argued that development required alleviating poverty or meeting basic needs (Chenery *et al.* 1974). It even moved in the direction of focusing on poverty (Streeten with Jolly 1981). In the 1980s, UNICEF (the UN Children's Fund) and the UN Development Programme promulgated needs-oriented alternatives to the neoliberal economic consensus that dominated the other development agencies of the UN family and, by the end of the 1990s, the World Bank and even the

International Monetary Fund placed the alleviation of poverty at the top of their hortatory agendas (Thérien 1999).

Mahbub ul Haq (1976), the World Bank's vice president under McNamara and later the intellectual leader behind the UNDP's needs-oriented *Human Development Reports*, believed that the world organizations were evolving toward a global system of basic needs fulfillment. He saw a parallel between the trajectory of domestic and international economic policy. While at the national level, most states have taken measures to meet basic needs—public ownership of basic industries, redistributive income taxes, welfare schemes, social insurance, and so on—nothing similar has happened internationally, even though the same moral arguments for the welfare state can be applied to people beyond one's borders. The power of those ideas, ul Haq argued, is great enough that we may eventually see international redistributive taxation and global institutions that assure the material needs of all humanity are met.

I am skeptical. The UN family's rhetorical consensus about the significance of basic needs emerged at the same time that the material commitments of the major powers to any international redistribution shrank (Thérien and Lloyd 2000, and see Chapter 8). Yet, to give ul Haq's argument its due, we have every reason to believe that as long as pressures for the integrated expansion of international economy remain and as long as the forces underlying modern nationalism continue, intergovernmental organizations will develop new responsibilities toward individuals, even if they only do so incoherently and haphazardly. Moreover, as long as the international system creates stateless people for whom the UN system is given responsibility, the world organizations will have to continue to define individual basic needs and minimal human rights and, thus, contribute to the power of the ideas that ul Haq highlighted.

New roles in meeting fundamental needs: modernization, rebellion, democracy

Arguably, world organizations do at least a little to meet fundamental needs whenever they help individuals cope with change. To illustrate, we turn to the question of rebellion, one that McNamara raised as his initial justification for anti-poverty development aid. What little we know about rebellion suggests that the best way to avoid it is to make the governed as active and equal participants in government as possible (Tilly 1978). The rebellions that challenge social order are less consequences of unmet basic physiological needs than they are consequences of unmet fundamental social and psychological needs. Unmet fundamental needs make us apt to identify with a group that challenges those with coercive authority over us. We cannot rebel if our identity requires continuation of the government as it is, and a government can only assure that its continuation is fundamental to the identity of those it governs by ceasing to be separate from them.

Just because a government allows little participation, does not mean that the governed will rebel. People can meet their fundamental needs yet treat demands from government only as one obnoxious aspect of their environment. The people Goran Hyden (1980) calls the "uncaptured" peasantry of Africa are case in point. Living within a so-called "premodern" mode of production, an "economy of affection," where production relies on human energy and distribution is based on non-market expectations within a local, family-like community, some African farmers have a culture resilient enough to have thwarted government modernization efforts. Yet they do not rebel, even when governments violate what the global community would say are fundamental human rights. For example, despite the horrors of Tanzania's failed 1970s experiment of modernizing agriculture by relocating most farming communities, many Tanzanian farmers continued to have a certain affection for their government. Most treated it like a natural phenomenon, as if bureaucrats and floods that dislocate villages were much the same thing.[2]

Nonparticipatory governments need only worry about rebellion when any one, or a combination, of four factors make it more likely that the governed will meet their fundamental needs by identifying with groups that challenge the political status quo:

1   when government actions thwart the reasonable hopes of the governed, forcing them to change that part of their sense of self that relates to who they will be in the future.

For example, if the Tanzanian government had actually succeeded in its relocation efforts and shattered local communities, farmers would no longer have been able to expect the material relief from any disaster that the local traditions of reciprocity assured them. They might then organize against the government through new groups formed to make sense out of this unexpected distress.

Nonparticipatory governments need not actually be the agents that thwart the governed's reasonable expectations. The probability that people will meet fundamental needs though identity groups in conflict with their government increase:

2   when hopes are thwarted by any cause;
3   when a country already contains identity groups opposed to the government (this point relates to one of most frequent ways that the Cold War superpowers protracted conflicts in the Third World, by encouraging competing oppositions to nonparticipatory governments); and
4   when the government stands out as the only differentiated, easily identifiable institution in the country.

In countries where people have little information about other institutions, nonparticipatory governments become lightning rods for criticism. People *will* make sense out of their world. If government appears to be the only powerful institution when hopes are dashed, people in government should not be surprised to be blamed.

Today, the place where each of these four conditions is most likely to occur is the Third World. We might want to argue that the UN system helps avoid disorder whenever it helps assure that the reasonable aspirations of Third World people will be fulfilled. Nonetheless, hard evidence of the degree to which world organizations have helped prevent the dashing of reasonable hopes may be difficult to find. In addition to knowing what intergovernmental organizations do, we would have to know people's hopes and few people in the world are ever asked about their aspirations, by their governments or by anyone else (see Chapter 12).

We can posit one set of aspirations that most people share due both to the penetration of modern market economies into the traditional economies of affection and to the defenses that those economies of affection have maintained. In most societies, our closest relations have great meaning for us, in part because they remain divorced from the challenges of the impersonal market. As Christopher Lasch (1977) puts it, the family becomes the individual's haven in the heartless, modern world. As a result, almost everywhere, people hope that relatives in the next generation (the people in our remaining economies of affection) will have more material advantages than we did. Moreover, in many parts of the world, people's lives are materially better than those of their immediate relatives in the last generation.[3] Have the world organizations contributed to this? I would be reluctant to say that they have not. The evidence of the real role of the UN system in meeting basic physiological needs, or at least in reminding governments of those needs by elevating them to the status of right, is too great. If world organizations have played a role improving the material prospects for the next generation, then in that sense, they have also helped many of our parents meet a fundamental identity need.

Yet, for people in some parts of the world, even material conditions have worsened over the last generation, while insecurity has grown and inequality has increased (see Chapter 10). Moreover, the world organizations sometimes force governments to thwart even the material aspirations of the governed (for example, when the IMF requires austerity programs in exchange for help with balance of payments problems) and globally sponsored development programs can crush traditional identities. Even at the very margins of human existence, when UN relief efforts allow people to meet their fundamental needs through something more than deathbed fantasy, the result can be the unification of the formerly destitute into an identity group actively opposed to those who claim authority over them. As Abdel Monheim Al-Mashat (1985) argues in his extensive cross-national study of basic needs fulfillment and the security of national governments, we should not be surprised that some of the most secure governments, and some of the most "peaceful" parts of the world, are in states where people are the poorest. Therefore, he concludes, if and when those governments come under pressure to institute policies for basic needs development, the state's security will require that they grant the public an increasing voice in government, as well.

Until recently, many who worked for the world organizations did not see the logic of this argument. Instead, they gave governments in countries where people were the most deprived this advice: give bread to avoid civil war, but do not worry about continuing political repression. One of the most important, if under-remarked, changes in international institutions that took place at the end of the Cold War was a significant shift in the views of policy-makers who worked with and within the UN system about the role of democracy within global and national governance. In 1995, Secretary General Boutros-Ghali (who, not incidentally, had been one of Al-Mashat's teachers), inaugurated the new journal, *Global Governance*, with an article, "Democracy, a Newly Recognized Imperative," that made the same argument as Al-Mashat's book. In the same issue, Michael Barnett (1995) documented the rapid adoption of the view that democracy was good for international security in general. Post-Cold War leaders believed the research that said democracies rarely fought democracies and they looked to the UN to promote democracy globally.

Has the UN become a successful promoter of what Barnet calls "empirical sovereignty," that is, that democratic situation in which governments are close enough to the governed that they share an identity? Perhaps it is too soon to know, but this has certainly become the political utopian vision of the trajectory of global governance that corresponds to the economic vision articulated by Mahbub ul Haq and the UNDP.

Yet, even if the world organizations develop along this trajectory, it is worth remembering that what most of us wish for our children (and for ourselves) is more than freedom from the destitution, violence, and the kind of political inequality that robs us of control over our own lives. We look for community, for meaningful work, for love. For these things, most of us do not look to political institutions. We look to governments only to protect the social space in which we can meet these fundamental human needs in their apposite ways.

3 The dialectic of liberal internationalism

What explains the record of the world organizations relative to human needs?

Global governance has emerged in fits and starts, and the crises of international institutions coincide with the world's political and economic crises. Moreover, it is not just one version of liberalism that has come to dominate the emergent world polity. "Effective" international institutions have existed when relatively complex liberal ideas have been dominant. Crises of international institutions correlate with the dominance of a relative unreflective liberal fundamentalism, including the neoliberal ideas that have been so prominent over the last two decades.

Table 3.1 begins to fill in the outline of the roles of world organizations presented in the last chapter. It lists the one or two organizations with the largest staffs and budgets in each policy area.

Perhaps the greatest impact of these organizations has been on the industrial economy. They have facilitated the periodic replacement of lead industries for over a century.

By the mid-1800s, the early industrial economy of cotton mills had yielded to that of railroads and steel and then to an economy dominated by the mass production of consumer products by the electrical, chemical, and food-processing industries of the turn-of-the-century Second Industrial Revolution. The Automobile and Jet Age of the twentieth century followed. Now, we have entered another industrial era led by the information industries—computers and telecommunications—and the financial and leisure service sectors they have fostered. The scale of capitalism changed with each new set of lead industries. Firms grew. Their markets grew. The industrial world expanded.

World organizations facilitated all these changes in scale. By helping to secure ever-larger market areas for industrial goods, international institutions made it profitable for firms to invest in new technologies. At the same time, the world organizations helped mitigate conflicts that go along with the expansion of the industrial system; they privileged some workers in the industrialized nations, insured investment in previously less developed countries, and strengthened the states of the less industrialized world.

Table 3.1 Major world organizations in 2004

	Abbreviation	Location	Main area of responsibility
Food and Agriculture Organization of the UN	FAO	Rome	Agriculture
International Atomic Energy Agency	IAEA	Vienna	Arms control
International Civil Aviation Organization	ICAO	Montreal	Transportation infrastructure
International Criminal Police Organization	Interpol	Lyons	Public safety
International Labor Organization	ILO	Geneva	Labor
International Monetary Fund	IMF	Washington	Public finance
International Organization for Standardization	ISO	Geneva	Industrial standards
International Telecommunication Union	ITU	Geneva	Communication infrastructure
International Telecommunications Satellite Organization	Intelsat	Washington	Communication infrastructure
United Nations	UN	New York	General purpose
UN Development Program	UNDP	New York	Development
Office of the UN Disaster Relief Coordinator	UNDRO	Geneva	Relief and welfare
UN Educational, Scientific, and Cultural Organization	UNESCO	Paris	Education and research
UN Environmental Program	UNEP	Nairobi	Environmental issues
UN High Commissioner for Refugees	UNHCR	Geneva	Refugees
UN Human Rights Commission		Geneva	Human rights
World Bank		Washington	Development
World Health Organization	WHO	Geneva	Health
World Intellectual Property Organization	WIPO	Geneva	Intellectual property
World Trade Organization	WTO	Geneva	Trade

The agencies have also helped perfect the state system itself by extending it to all parts of the globe and mitigating some of its terror. In strengthening the nation-state and the state system, the UN era institutions also helped encapsulate the major challengers to industrial capitalism, the Soviet and Chinese communist systems, for more than a generation. Today, the same agencies help reincorporate the post-communist states into the capitalist world order.

While world organizations may have acted as part of the superstructure of the capitalist world economy, they have by no means simply been institutions functional to capitalism, some sort of inevitable result of the workings of capitalism itself. Their history is part of the dialectic between capitalism and the alternative ways of organizing economic and political life. In helping encapsulate antagonistic social systems, the world organizations also helped those social systems thrive, at least for a time. In helping to create privileged labor markets in the industrial capitalist world, the agencies also helped secure the power of part of the industrial working class. Moreover, and perhaps most significantly, in seeking the legitimacy needed to carry out their other activities, they have strengthened social movements that hope to replace today's states with universal institutions securing human rights, meeting basic human needs, and preserving the global environment.

Yet, while global governance may sometimes contribute to forces undermining capitalist industrialism, it also has become necessary for its success. Consider the last generation when both the network of world organizations and the global economy have been in trouble. First, in the early 1970s, conflict between industrialized capitalist nations and their poorer partners began to split the UN. Then price-fixing by Third World oil producers sent an already weak world economy into a tailspin. Liberal internationalist observers of the simultaneous crises began to argue that the crisis in the world economy would end only when the crisis in international institutions ended. Sociologist Daniel Bell contended that the nation-state had become "an ineffective instrument for dealing with the scale of major economic problems" (1977: 134). The business and government leaders of the Club of Rome (Tinbergen 1976) argued for a global kind of Keynesian liberalism under which world organizations would be given the task of boosting production and assuring ever-higher standards of living. In the 1980s and 1990s, a dozen similar commissions made essentially the same case.

Thirty years after the first OPEC (Organisation of Petroleum Exporting Countries) oil crisis, most of the world continues to experience the major or minor hardships of what Paul Krugman (1990) has called the "age of diminished expectations" which began in the 1970s. The real wages of many industrial workers in the United States were no higher in the 1990s than they were in the 1970s, while people in the former communist states and much of the Third World face more dismal prospects. Similarly, the chronically under-funded central organs of the UN still can barely make ends meet, while even the better-endowed IMF and World Bank do not have what it takes to fulfill their new commitments to eliminating poverty and meeting basic needs. The argument that we need fundamental changes in international institutions before the return of anything like the postwar boom years remains relevant.

The venerable liberal internationalist case that such institutions can create widespread and long-lasting prosperity is at the center of the story of global governance. We can see the best evidence for the liberal argument only if we divide the history of world organizations a little differently than most liberal analysts do. Instead of treating the nineteenth-century Public International Unions, the League of Nations system, and the postwar UN system as the three successive generations of world organizations, we need to link their history to that of industry by noting that each new generation begins when an agency regulating a revolutionary new communication technology appears. In 1865, the agency was the International Telegraph Union (ITU), the first major Public International Union. In 1906, it was the Radiotelegraph Union (RTU), designed to regulate the airwaves. In 1964, it was Intelsat, the International Telecommunications Satellite Organization, and a new kind of world organization—a global public utility, outside the UN system, providing part of the world communications infrastructure instead of just regulating services provided by others.

Further experiments in international organization quickly followed each of these three beginnings. The Universal Postal Union and a half-dozen other organizations all appeared before 1890. Agencies serving some of the other new industries of the early twentieth century—the chemical, electrical, and automobile industries—succeeded the RTU, as did the peace organizations created at the 1907 Hague Conference and its successor of 1919, the League of Nations. Similarly, despite recent fears about the future of the UN system, new global agencies have been created in every year since 1965, most of them still inside the UN system, although perhaps the most significant, like Intelsat and the World Trade Organization, institutions outside the UN family that were designed to promote the new industries of the twenty-first century.

The recent crises of international institutions and of the world economy also have their earlier analogues. Each generation of world organizations began a decade or so before a long period of crisis, and its key economic institutions appeared only at the end of the crisis, often after years of war involving the great powers and after years of economic malaise. In the late nineteenth century, the crisis began with the Austro-Prussian and Franco-Prussian wars and continued through the Long Depression. The Public International Unions that helped boost the world economy after the Long Depression were established only in the last five years of the century. The League of Nations operated in an era of crisis that began with the First World War, ended with the Second World War, and had the Great Depression in between. The economic agencies of the UN era were created as the crisis ended: the IMF and the World Bank at the 1944 Bretton Woods Conference and the General Agreement on Tariffs and Trade (GATT) within three years of the end of the war.

In the first two generations of world organizations, international transportation agreements immediately preceded the key economic pacts: the European Rail Union (the Central Office for International Rail Transport) in 1890 and the International Civil Aviation Organization (ICAO), the first of the UN specialized agencies, in 1943. Both agencies eventually worked with the earlier communication agency to provide the infrastructure for a larger market in which industrial goods could be traded. The ITU and the Rail Union allowed a Europe-wide market for industrial goods to emerge, while the radio and aviation agencies created a potentially global market.

The actual turn-of-the-century trading area that the Public International Unions helped regulate extended the continent to the overseas dependencies of the European empires. In contrast, the actual trading area partly governed by the UN family after the Second World War remained smaller than the world linked by radio and the airplane. It covered the Organization for Economic Cooperation and Development (OECD), the club of wealthy market countries (linking Western Europe, Canada, the US, Japan, Australia, and New Zealand), and all their economic dependencies in Africa, Asia, the Caribbean, and the Pacific, but excluded China and the Soviet bloc.

Within these geographic limits appeared successive "world orders," concrete historical political and economic systems, the turn-of-the-century *Interimperial Order* and the postwar *"Free World" Order* (originally the world of Franklin Roosevelt's "Four Freedoms"—freedom of speech and religion and freedom from want and fear—the goals of the wartime "United and Associated Nations," the anti-fascist alliance). These "interrelated trading areas" provide what W. W. Rostow's earliest work on economic development calls, "the optimum unit for the study of economic history . . . the frame within which many of the most important national, regional, or even international problems must be placed if they are to be fully understood" (Rostow 1948: 12–23).

The limits of these trading areas were the result of economic agreements that followed the Rail Union and the ICAO. The Brussels-based International Union for the Publication of Customs Tariffs of 1890 signaled the beginning of a wave of European trade liberalization in the 1890s. The GATT marked the beginning of a similar wave throughout the postwar Free World.

Liberal internationalists argue that the wider markets created in Europe in the 1890s and throughout the capitalist world after the World Wars were the keys to the subsequent eras of unprecedented economic growth: Europe's Second Industrial Revolution and the Free World's boom years.

If we accept the liberal argument about the earlier eras, we should expect that a new wave of trade liberalization could assure another era of unprecedented prosperity within the global larger trading area, including China and the post-communist states, united under the WTO.

The designers of global governance have always believed that liberal international institutions could create an increasingly prosperous and peaceful world, a conviction that is older than the oldest of the world organizations. This chapter examines the justifications for that conviction in light of an equally venerable, but more pessimistic tradition that also links industry and international affairs. It shows how Gramsci's social theory allows us to combine insights from both traditions in a more complete account that steps beyond the liberals' simplified concept of human motivation and recognizes sites of regulation of the world economy at levels other than those of the nation-state and the state system.

The liberal vision and conflicts it can obscure

Both liberal internationalism and world organizations are things of the industrial age. Although liberalism appeared a century before the first modern factories, liberal internationalists honor men of the generation that built those factories, Adam Smith and Immanuel Kant, as their founders.

Three characteristics of the industrial age convince the followers of Smith and Kant that some form of global governance will be needed to realize peace and prosperity. First, and most significantly, is the propensity of capitalist industry to outgrow any government. The most efficient factories produce more than can be sold in a single country. They fuel desire for that abundance in countries without factories, and combine with the need of competing industrialists to find wider and wider markets. The *Communist Manifesto* put it that the industrial bourgeoisie's new economy, "batters down all Chinese walls . . . [and] creates a world after its own image" (Marx and Engels 1932 [1848]: 13).

Second is the link between capitalist industrialism and a republican polity. Industrialism emerged in a society divided among lords, peasants, yeoman farmers, free wage earners, and the bourgeoisie. Early liberals argued that it would remain dynamic only in a society where classes share power. As Adam Smith put it in 1776, the interests of those who gain their income from land and those who gain their income from wages are "strictly connected with the interest of the society," while the bourgeois merchant and manufacturer have immediate interests opposed to those of society as a whole.

> Profit does not, like rent and wages, rise with the prosperity, and fall with the declension of the society. On the contrary, it is naturally low in rich, and high in poor countries, and it is always the highest in the countries that are going the fastest to ruin.
>
> (1982 [1776]: 265–266)

A state controlled only by capitalists would destroy the commonwealth by impoverishing the wage earner and despoiling the land.

Yet, third, the division of the early European industrial world among sovereign aristocrats could have thwarted its advance. Capitalists might have faced excessive demands for investment from political leaders who were preparing for war and pursuing mercantilist policies. As Smith worried, sovereigns were often more interested in extending the limits of their rule than in assuring the prosperity of the people and their lands. Therefore, champions of the industrial system have tended to promote consensual institutions that transcended the narrow interests of the separate sovereigns.

Liberals have always had more than mere prosperity in mind when they championed the industrial system. Marx may have seen industry's promise as the generalization of the pride and self-respect that comes from employing our full potential in productive and unalienated work, but Adam Smith's earlier formulation differs only slightly. For Smith, the ultimate goal of statecraft was to secure and enhance the dignity of a nation and its people. Wealth was just a means to that end. Likewise, for Smith, the factory system—or, to be more precise, anything that contributed to increased productivity (including freer international trade)—was simply a further means to this end, not an end in itself.

In *The Wealth of Nations* Smith celebrates the increasing division of labor— within factories, within societies, and across societies—as the key feature of the new economic system he observed in his pin factory. He argued that the introduction of further industrial innovations would depend on the progressive expansion of the realm of unrestricted trade. As the title of Smith's key third chapter put it, "the Division of Labor [even within the factory] is limited by the Extent of the Market." Economic growth, the generalization of prosperity, would follow.

In 1795, in *Perpetual Peace*, Kant completed the link between industry and international organization by arguing the complement, that the desire to secure these benefits of expanding international commerce would guarantee the ultimate victory of "world citizenship" over the tradition of warring states. With Kant, the institutionalization of a peaceful and prosperous world order became defined as a project of the progressive part of the bourgeoisie (motivated by more than the concerns of immediate profit) and as a natural extension of both bourgeois republicanism and of the norms of the hospitality extended to foreign merchants. The emergence of formal intergovernmental institutions would simply be an extension of an emerging cosmopolitan civil society, which was itself the real, ultimate guarantor of peace.

Yet, neither Kant nor Smith was willing to rely on the cosmopolitan bourgeoisie to achieve this happy result by itself. Even if, as Kant said, "The spirit of commerce . . . is incompatible with war" (1957[1795]: 32), liberals had to guard against placing governments and international agreements solely in the hands of the merchant and industrial classes. They would simply use a monopoly of state power to create and protect real monopolies, as the East India Company (Smith 1982: 630–634). Luckily, the republicanism then embraced by the bourgeoisie could prevent businessmen from gaining too great an influence over government. Kant and Smith both understood republican constitutions as those incorporating a division of power. In their day, republicanism could only mean counterbalancing the power of the bourgeoisie with that of the older ruling class, the aristocracy, and that of the nascent state class of professionals working in government and the modernizing universities.

In the generation that followed, the new political and intellectual disciplines that grew out of Kant's and Smith's own field of moral philosophy kept this new liberal internationalist vision alive. Fred Parkinson (1977) gives equal credit for the resulting "functionalist" tradition to Jeremy Bentham and Auguste Comte. Functionalists support the establishment of governmental and intergovernmental institutions to carry out specific, limited activities, the "functions" needed to assure that the promise of a liberal world order will be fulfilled. In Comte's lifetime, functionalist arguments became the justifications for proposed Public International Unions, which later influenced the designers of the League and the UN.

Liberal internationalism also gave rise to a scholarly tradition that analyzes those international institutions that have actually been created. Early studies included Paul S. Reinsch's *The Public International Unions* (1911) and Leonard Woolf's *International Government* (1916), as well as a fundamentally new genre of studies on managing conflict at all levels, from the local to the global, pioneered by Mary Parker Follett in 1918 (see Chapter 5). Follett's and Woolf's ideas were reflected in those of David Mitrany, who in turn inspired the postwar neofunctionalists, most notably, Ernst Haas (1958, 1964). Finally, the neofunctionalists have inspired the contemporary generation of liberal analysts of international institutions who still identify with the larger liberal tradition that affirms "at least the possibility of human progress," while rejecting the simple myths linking peace and free trade that have, from time to time, been propagated (Keohane 1989: 10–11).

The liberal vision of universal peace and prosperity achieved through industry and international organization, remains a powerful social myth, a vision that only can become reality if specific people come to believe in it and act upon it. Gramsci wrote that in such myths, "political ideology and political science are fused in the dramatic form" (Forgacs 1988: 238). This is a fusion we still see in today's neoliberal defenses of the peace and prosperity promised by a universal WTO and a hoped-for new openness of Americans, Europeans, and Japanese to goods from the farms and factories of the Third World.

Gramsci recognized that the line between "ideology" and "science," the line between what we wish were true for all time and what is now true at this one moment, is never fixed. Ideological commitments only become a problem when we allow our hopes to veil our understanding of the things that thwart their realization. The liberal internationalists' major blindspot of this sort obscures conflicts generated by the development and geographical extension of the industrial system itself.

Thomas Pynchon (1984: 41), pinpoints what liberals tend to miss:

> By 1945, the factory system—which more than any piece of machinery, was the real and major result of the Industrial Revolution—had been extended to include the Manhattan Project, the German long-range bomber program and the death camps, such as Auschwitz. It has taken no major gift of prophecy to see how these three curves of development might plausibly converge.

Gandhi shared Pynchon's skepticism about the liberal project. He believed that no clever institutional reforms "would succeed in eliminating conditions that enslave man as long as technologically induced economic growth remained the major instrument of need gratification" (Roy 1988: 74, recall Chapter 2). Many Western commentators on international affairs have shared this view. Oswald Spengler's *Decline of the West* of 1923 inspired many in the generation of realists who came to dominate the field after the World Wars (Farrenkopf 1991: 269). Pitrim Sorokin, who some peace researchers claim as a founder (Eckhardt 1987: 187), felt Pynchon's pessimism in 1906, long before the nuclear age began (Sorokin 1937). And the earliest systematic analyses of patterns of war between great powers (for example, Wright 1942) start with the assumption that the application of science to the techniques of violence made each of the state system's great periodic struggles for predominance potentially more destructive than the last.

Grounds for pessimism have remained as the systematic analysis of great-power war has matured. When Nazli Choucri and Robert North (1975) studied the wars that bracketed the Interimperial Order, they concluded that some basic dynamics of industrial society were "master variables" that move the great industrial powers to use their constantly growing capacities to destroy. Both technological change (which appears to be self-reinforcing) and population growth (which in the industrial age has been encouraged by advances in medicine) accelerate demand for resources and for further economic growth. This creates, "lateral pressure [a.k.a., imperialism] the tendency of a social unit to expand its geographic compass, to push outward the boundaries that partition reality between the 'external' environment and the unit itself, and to draw an ever greater expanse of reality within itself" (Ashley 1980: 14).

When Richard Ashley extended this analysis to the postwar Chinese–Soviet–US triangle, the same patterns appeared. To Ashley they pointed toward a more fundamental conclusion about the industrial age, "Technical-rational action has brought progress—progress toward destruction of all it has built" (1980: 214); if we remain subservient to technical rationality in our pursuit of economic growth, we can only end where Pynchon's three curves of development plausibly converge.

Of course, even some of those who have seen great promise in the industrial system have also warned against making a fetish of technical rationality. Adam Smith worried about the numbing effects that the division of labor could have on the minds and spirit of working men and women (Hirschman 1977: 105–108). At the first appearance of the modern machine, an even more revolutionary and alienating power, acute observers immediately recognized its potential. Charles Babbage, the early Victorian mathematician who designed most of the elements of the modern computer a century before its production would become technically feasible, commented, "The most singular advantages we derive from machinery is in the check which it affords against the inattention, the idleness, or the knavery of human agents" (quoted in Hobson 1912: 74). Not only were factory workers perfectly subject to discipline automatically meted out by the factory's machines, machines even eliminated the need to consult with workers before changing processes of production. Thus, they allowed for a much more complete application of science to production than Smith had observed in his pin factory. As a result, as Engels and Marx recognized, technological innovation became a much more powerful social force than it had ever been before, an anti-democratic force, and an alienating force. Hobson argued that these two effects combined to create a "new economy of force and knowledge" (1912: 74), promising expansion of production limited only by human ability to understand and control the physical world, but requiring most men and women to give up hope of ever acting with complete autonomy and responsibility.

With industrial workers

Conceivably, of course, every application of science to production could be made contingent on the agreement of those who work with the machines, conserving the revolutionary potential of the "economy of knowledge" while discarding the "economy of force" along with the alienation and disempowerment it entails. This has been the vision of the many socialists from Robert Owen to Herbert Marcuse who recognized that a human need to act with authority cannot be met by what industrial capitalism is best able to provide: prosperity for some. It is the vision that Richard Ashley's studies of lateral pressure led him to embrace.

Liberal internationalists from Smith to Hobson, and even to John Maynard Keynes have held out little hope that such a radically democratic society could emerge without destroying capitalist industrialism's capacity to create wealth. Their best hope has been that the eventual world of plenty created by the industrial system would allow all to experience some of the dignity and humanizing pleasures now enjoyed only by those who most benefit from the machine's economy of force and know-ledge. In 1920, Keynes introduced his *Economic Consequences of the Peace* by reminding readers of the "Eldorado" privileged Europeans enjoyed before the Great War (1971 [1920]: 10). Continent-wide prosperity had been maintained by what Keynes called "the delicate organization" of inter-national institutions that he feared the Treaty of Versailles had doomed. In lamenting that lost world, Keynes repeated the liberal rationalization for the profound inequality on which the social order was based:

> If only the cake were not cut but allowed to grow . . . perhaps a day might come when . . . overwork, overcrowding, and underfeeding would have come to an end, and men, secure of the comforts and neces-sities of the body, could proceed to the nobler exercises of their faculties.
>
> (Keynes 1971: 21)

More recently, when Keynesians discussed reforming international insti-tutions in one of the early Club of Rome reports, they repeated Herbert Marcuse's argument that collective decisions about technological change should be taken democratically by all who would be affected (Tinbergen 1976: 82), but they did not explain how that could happen without under-mining the system's ability to produce wealth. They did not confront the deeper issue that capitalist industrialism rests on inequalities in power: for the system to work, a few must have the ability to change the processes of production, while most must simply submit to the logic of the machine. This contradiction between the demands of industrial system and the demand for democratic control (something that liberals have also long championed) creates the first of the fundamental conflicts liberal internationalists tend to ignore.

With older social orders

A second appears because even if Adam Smith were correct that all of us pursue honor and esteem above all other values, we do not all pursue them in the same way. Traditional social relations threatened by the intro-duction of industrial capitalism remain sources of honor and esteem within societies recently brought into the industrial world. Despite the compen-sation offered by economic growth, people may fight when technology threatens to transform their lives. Because liberals rarely consider the funda-mental socio-psychological needs outlined in Chapter 2, they tend to ignore this range of conflicts, as well.

With the less-industrialized world

Similar conflicts can appear with the geographic extension of the indus-trial system. Representatives of a preindustrial order will fight to retain their positions within newly industrializing societies, while other social movements demand the introduction of the industrial system and become frustrated by the slow pace of capitalist investment in industry. Fortunately or unfortunately, as Nigel Harris (1987) argues, capitalist industrialism, even with all its proven dynamism, has been able to expand only so far and so fast. Industrialism has always left vast regions behind. The resentment both of those who come from countries which have recently entered a regional, imperial, or global manufacturing system, and of those who cannot do so even if they want to, creates the third kind of conflict that most liberal internationalists overlook.

Among the powers

Uneven development occurs within the core of the world industrial economy as well as between its core and its periphery. One industrialized society can resent another country that develops some new industries first. Similarly, the ever increasing prosperity promised by liberal internationalists cannot stop the leaders of expanding industrial states—each internally united by its own sense of national identity—from seeing the peaceful international integration necessary to achieve that vision as a threat to the power of the traditional interests to which national identity and the state have both been linked. Alternative visions of empire—to assure that the sun never sets or to provide *Lebensraum*—may suggest a future in which both the demands of national identity and the needs of an ever-expanding economic system can be served. In fact, the coincidence of desires to preserve an older social order who with conflicts arising from uneven development among the industrial powers provides the best explanation for the apparent connection between lateral pressure and great-power war in the nineteenth and twentieth centuries.

Liberal learning and the critical tradition

When liberal internationalists do recognize one or more of these conflicts they tend to see them as temporary: conflicts over democratic control of the industrial system and conflicts with the less industrial world will be put aside as long as prosperity is assured. Conflicts with the old order and conflicts among unevenly developing industrial powers will be overcome as the traditional nation-state withers away, something that is bound to happen as necessary functions of government become supranational (compare Mitrany 1943: 2).

A few liberals in every generation have gone further by recognizing that opportunities for reasserting a more local sovereignty also grow with international integration, and such reassertions can solve the conflicts that the industrial system promotes. Partially delinking from the world economy can promote industrialization and in later struggles to develop new technologies,

something the leaders of newly industrializing countries have long understood (Tickner 1990). Even that iconoclastic sympathizer with the movement
to integrate the world economy, Thorstein Veblen, argued in 1915 that
a temporary delinking from the world economy played an essential role
in the industrialization of nineteenth-century Germany (Veblen 1966). Only
England, the first country to industrialize, had had the opportunity to enter
the Industrial Revolution under laissez-faire.

A century later, even Britain had an industrial policy. In the late nineteenth century, both the British and German governments fostered national
industries and both tried to assure that private capitalists would become
increasingly dependent on the state; by 1900 a seeming "retrograde"
ideology of official nationalism, rooted in justifications for the old order,
became as typical of the industrial order in Britain as it was in Germany.
Yet, while late Victorian capitalists may have become, as the great pros-
elytizer of free trade, Richard Cobden, put it, "toadies of a clod-pole
aristocracy" (Jones 1987: 194), their investments also continued to provide
Britain with the wealth and prestige that Adam Smith considered the ultimate justification of laissez-faire. Their Tory nationalism even served the
laboring poor in being used as a justification for the first laws that alleviated
some of their "overwork, overcrowding, and underfeeding," something
that the Cobdenite liberal internationalists had only promised.

Later, when Keynesian liberals finally kept that promise, they could do
so only by allowing a new form of economic nationalism to develop
throughout the industrialized core of the Free World (Mayall 1990:
88–110). Keynes not only supported the strong states needed to give large
slices of the economic cake to the disempowered, he advocated minimizing
the uneven development of the powers, encouraging rapid development
in the less-industrialized world, and compensating those parts of the world
where such development would remain unlikely.

The history of the critical tradition reveals a process of learning more and
more of the conflicts that the larger liberal internationalist vision can
obscure. Each generation notices more of the conflicts. Each generation has
proposed more effective means for coping with them. The changing content of these critical theories suggests a broad, evolutionary explanation of
both liberal internationalism and the world organizations based on it.

As with all evolutionary explanations, it identifies two processes: one that
generates institutional innovations, and another that selects some to survive. The critical tradition in liberal internationalism itself has provided
the innovations. Long before Keynes, the nineteenth-century liberals constantly found new "necessary" functions for international institutions to perform. As James Mayall argues, John Stuart Mill constantly "expanded his
chapter on the 'limits of laissez-faire' when he realized that only the state
could finance a system of universal education and provide other public
goods" (Mayall 1990: 98–99). Keohane (1984) identifies a key attribute of
the process that has selected only some of these experimental institutional

innovations to survive: they do so if a sufficiently powerful coalition of national governments learn that they benefit from the state-to-state cooperation that the institutions encourage.

Keohane's work focuses only on the last thirty years. The longer history of global governance demonstrates not just national governments must benefit. In addition, in fact, *primarily*, a sufficiently powerful coalition of social forces must gain from the new institutions. The changing audiences that successful critical liberal internationalists have addressed reveal the content of those coalitions. From Kant's day and throughout the nineteenth century the audience was Europe's aristocracy as well as the cosmopolitan bourgeoisie whose interests were to be served by the proposed international institutions. After the turn of the last century, critical liberal internationalists such as John A. Hobson and Leonard Wolf also addressed "enlightened" businessmen and the traditional state class, which, in many cases, grew out of the aristocracy. However, they also addressed the newly powerful social democratic parties and the newer class of state functionaries responsible for bringing the masses into the new industrial state. Mary Parker Follett focused on another new class: professional managers operating within the giant industrial firms that first appeared between 1880 and 1920. From the 1920s until the 1980s, reformers focused on the business, government, and labor elites of one industrial nation in particular, the United States. These coalitions of powerful states and social forces become a Darwinian mechanism that "selects" surviving international institutions by remaining parties to agreements and by continuing to finance them even during the fiscal and political crises that come with worldwide depressions and great-power wars.

Gramsci and world order

This description of the selection mechanism and the evidence we have of continuing liberal innovation still leaves many things unexplained. We do not know whether the process of selection will continue to assure evolution along the liberal path or what exactly the process of innovation really is. Antonio Gramsci's synthesis of liberal, Marxist, and Realist social theories both helps fill the gaps in this evolutionary explanation and takes us beyond it. It helps us understand the mythic element in liberal internationalist thought, the reasons that effective, critical liberal internationalists have always appealed to the kinds of "higher" aspirations that other liberals ignore. Gramsci lets us understand the role of coercive and noncoercive structures at all levels—from the factory floor to the boardrooms of the world organizations—in successive world orders. When we consider these many levels, we can better see how seemingly illiberal developments like the reassertion of economic nationalism by the postwar welfare states have contributed to realizing the liberal vision, and why they are likely to be part of any new world order.

Historic blocs

Gramsci's idea of a *historic bloc*—a complex of economic, political, and cultural institutions which permits the normal social development characteristic of a particular period and a particular economic system—helps us combine the most instructive elements of the liberal tradition with theories that account for the wider sources of conflict in the world economy. Gramsci used this concept to overcome some of the misunderstandings arising from the traditional Marxist architectural metaphor for society— with its contingent political and cultural "superstructures" resting on a determining foundation or "base." Gramsci recognized the reciprocal determination of base and superstructure. He argued that ideas, culture, politics, and laws are more than simple functions of economic interests and the powers granted to people by their roles in production; these super-structures have an independent existence and force. Moreover, Gramsci believed that no economic system can fully develop—not even the contra-dictions within its inner logic can fully develop—outside of a conducive political and cultural environment. "A historic bloc is the dialectical unity of base and superstructure, theory and practice, of intellectuals and masses" (Forgacs 1988: 424) that makes such development possible.

A historic bloc is the kind of social formation or social order in which normal processes of social, economic, political, and intellectual development can go on. A historic bloc is not a social order in crisis. It is not a society experiencing a "time of troubles" (Lih 1990). It is not a social formation at the cusp between two dominant modes of production or poised between two industrial epochs. It is certainly not a society at war with itself.

It is easiest to understand Gramsci's concept by recognizing that it, like the older superstructure-base distinction, was developed through metaphor, using analogies to articulate something that observers had not recognized in quite the same way before. Thus at various places in Gramsci's work he suggests a whole series of ways in which specific aspects of social life are like a *blocco*.

In one sense, a historic bloc is simply an alliance—a "bloc" of those whose interests are served and whose aspirations are fulfilled by this economic and social system. In this sense, the cosmopolitan bourgeoisie has always been part of the historic blocs that have partially fulfilled the liberal internationalist vision, but the allies of this class have changed. In 1920, Keynes considered much of the European working class as outside the prewar continental social order whose passing he so regretted. While after the war, with some help from the Keynesians, industrial labor entered the historic bloc *qua* alliance in most parts of the industrial world.

But a historic bloc is more than just an alliance. *Blocco* in Italian can also mean "block," and Gramsci seems to play with the meanings of that word as well. In one sense, a historic bloc is a social order that must be looked at in different ways in order to be understood completely. Its different faces must be examined the way we might examine a child's building block or a Rubik's cube. Only when we have looked at all of the faces of a historic bloc—its biological-material face, its economic face, its political face, and its cultural and ideological face—can we begin to understand the ways they are internally connected one to another, and therefore begin to understand what makes the characteristic form of its overall social development possible. To understand periods when the champions of industrial capitalism say it has worked best (the quarter-century before the First World War and the quarter-century after the Second), we need to examine the economic relations characteristic of the period as well as the dominant political institutions and the governing ideas and look for the interconnections among them.

Considering Gramsci's concept as an architectural metaphor per se can make the same point. A historic bloc is like a complex urban multi-use "block," perhaps one of those massive sets of shops and flats of seven or eight stories centered on a large courtyard built in the boom years before the First World War, when Gramsci first came to industrial Turin. The depth of the block's foundation, the base, like the mode of production, establishes "limits of the possible" for what is above. (Builders can raise more than seven or eight floors on foundations of concrete and stone.) Moreover, to be useful, the whole "structure of the superstructure," the building above ground, has to be coherent. Coercive structures (walls, floors, ceilings) have to work with enabling structures (rooms, halls, stairways) in the same way that the institutions of political society must work with those of civil society.

Gramsci's purpose in developing this concept was to emphasize that only within such a coherent ensemble of coercive and enabling institutions—linked to a particular base of technologies and relations of production—can the normal development of society occur. Such a bloc becomes the framework for history. When a historic bloc is stable, life goes on "as it should," following its own inner logic, like the normal day-to-day lives of people sharing the same block of flats. When a society is in crisis, when a historic bloc is crumbling or partially deserted, like a house in a city under siege, normal life cannot go on until the bloc is rebuilt, reclaimed, or other structures found.

Crises, organizing within civil society, and the emergence of new social orders

Gramsci used Marx's political economy and insights from the Italian tradition of Realism to identify the sources of social conflict that could undo a historic bloc. Gramsci recognized that *organic crises*—times when something tears the social alliance, economic and political relations, and the ideological glue of a historic bloc asunder—can originate in regional, sectoral, and ideological conflicts as much as in class conflicts (Gramsci 1971: 210–218).

Nevertheless, like Marx, Gramsci emphasized that all social crises were subjects of a historical dialectic; they arose from the *normal* development of a social order. The disempowerment of the workers within the factory was a normal consequence of capitalism when it worked as it should, but at the same time, so was the growing social significance of the working class. Together, the trends set up the possibility of a social conflict that could transform the social order. Similarly, we can see lateral pressure, different rates of economic development, and the increasing allegiance of both capitalists and workers to the nation-state as normal consequences of international social orders fulfilling the liberal internationalist vision.

Much of Gramsci's work focused on the politics that ended such crises. Most significantly, Gramsci would have us look at the relation of political forces, "the degree of homogeneity, self-awareness, and organization obtained by various social groups" (Forgacs 1988: 204), all of them functions of both intellectual and political leadership, especially within *civil society*. In normal times, Gramsci argued, this realm of non-coercive institutions of social order works alongside the coercive institutions of what he called the *state proper* or *political society* (Forgacs 1988: 235), to give a coherent "structure to the superstructure." In times of crisis, in the societies in which liberal internationalism has played its historical role, civil society has remained as the primary site of the cohesion of the political forces that can create a new order.

Gramsci's civil society is the social realm in which abstract economic interests (those the observer can infer as inherent to individuals or groups occupying particular positions within the systems of production and reproduction) take on their concrete forms as specific aspirations linked to specific worldviews. It is the realm of voluntary associations, of the norms and practices that make them possible, and of the collective identities they form. It is the realm where "I" becomes "we." As such, it is the level of the superstructure typified by active consent and cooperation, not by coercion and force. It is the realm where ideology and intellectual leaders have their greatest impact (Augelli and Murphy 1988: 129–134).

Industrial societies have support an increasingly articulated civil society. As a result, much of the political struggle that accompanies the periodic crises of capitalist industrialism takes place within the realm of voluntary association and it takes place about the boundaries of that realm. It is the politics of parties, trade unions, and business associations, as well as the politics of churches, private philanthropies, and pluralist interest groups.

It is a politics operating on many levels. In the late 1970s, Robert W. Cox began to use Gramsci's concepts to reach conclusions about contemporary international institutions. He argued that the stable configuration of UN agencies had helped crystallize the supremacy of the worldviews and social forces that governed the Western world since 1945. At the same time, and of necessity, the global agencies provided political space in which opposing social forces could articulate their own worldviews and develop counter-hegemonic alliances (Cox 1980: 374).

Gramsci recognized similar developments in previous world order crises. In the notebooks he compiled from 1929 through 1935, while a prisoner under fascism, he included memoranda on what he called "international institutions" (Gramsci 1991: 291). He was interested in transportation organizations such as the International Road Conference, which reflected the new craze for superhighways (p. 325) and the Maritime Conference where labor played a growing role (p. 358). Equally intriguing were attempts to establish international responsibility for social welfare (p. 284) and the growing role of US businessmen and the US government in international cooperation through the International Chamber of Commerce (p. 291). The changing array of American proposals for institutions to help resolve the continuing conflicts between Germany and the European victors of the First World War (p. 343) also concerned him. Gramsci wrote, "In the period since 1870 . . . the international organizational relations of the state [have] become more complex and massive," pointing out that this had happened at the same time that domestic civil society had become more complex and more closely linked to the state proper (Forgacs 1988: 233).

Liberal internationalists as intellectual leaders

Gramsci never systematized his notes on the changing international order and the crisis he observed in the 1930s, but, as with his analysis of crises *within* industrial societies, his starting point was the role of *intellectual leadership*, the kind of leadership that liberal internationalists have provided in each crisis of industry and international organization. Thus, Smith saw mercantilism and the limits imposed by narrow national markets as barriers to industrial innovation and recommended policies to expand the geographical scope of the social order. Nineteenth-century functionalists recognized that states would have to cooperate to build the infrastructure of wider international markets. Both Hobson and Keynes, for slightly different reasons, argued that policies designed to increase the wages of the working class would spur demand, and then investment, and thus resolve the periodic crises to which capitalist economies are prone. David Mitrany recognized that statism could doom an expanding capitalist economy and urged the piecemeal transfer of sovereignty to international institutions.

Intellectual leaders do more than come up with ideas about the institutions of the next world order. To go back to the image of a historic bloc as a puzzle, as a Rubik's cube, or one of those wooden block puzzles that Gramsci might have played with as a boy: those trying to reconstruct a historic bloc need to work on all of its faces at once. They must put together the ideology of the new order with its political institutions, define its economic base, and, of course, build coalition of social forces that constitute the historic bloc qua alliance.

The changing audiences to whom the liberal internationalists have addressed their appeals have been the social forces that they have hoped to bind together in alliances at the center of the new historic bloc. While the political processes in which successful liberal internationalists have taken part have been just as painstaking as the manipulations needed to solve any complex, three-dimensional conundrum.

Perhaps the architectural metaphor is even more telling. Building the international institutions of a world order in an industrial age is a bit like building a cathedral in late medieval Europe. While the aims of liberal internationalism provide designers with a single general plan—the way that the rituals of the medieval Church demanded structural similarity among all diocesan seats—the final form of the institutions of the prewar Interimperial Order and the postwar world order of the Free World differed as greatly as Salisbury and Chartres. Like most gothic cathedrals, the institutions of each of the successive world orders have been built sporadically over many years as the interest of the community to be served waxed and waned and as different sponsors and benefactors were found to realize one or another part of the originally imagined project. As a result, if we look closely at the completed edifices we see a host of ill-assorted parts. At no point during their construction did their designers have any real assurance the final structures would be as pleasing as Chartres with its mismatched but harmonious towers, or Salisbury, rising triumphantly to defy its inadequate foundations.

Initially, the successful liberal internationalist designers of world organizations have focused on mobilizing the *political leadership* of national governments and powerful philanthropists willing to act as *sponsors* and *benefactors* of new international institutions (see Chapter 11). Throughout each of the world order crises, liberal internationalists have led transnational coalitions that pressed governments to call international conferences, establish international agreements, and create experimental intergovernmental organizations to carry out the two *primary tasks* essential to fulfilling the liberal vision.

The first has been to *foster new lead industries* by creating and securing international markets for industrial goods. International agreements transportation and communication agreements help complete this task, as do agreements defining tradable goods through industrial standards, rules protecting intellectual property, and rules directly governing international trade.

The second has been to *manage conflicts* with organized social forces potentially opposed to the further extension of the industrial system: workers subject to the discipline of new industries, people whose interests are tied to older economies, and those in the less industrialized world.

After convincing political leaders to establish institutions carrying out these tasks, liberal internationalists have relied on the institutions themselves to help develop powerful constituencies for their maintenance. Surviving agencies gain the support of major investors who bet on the new opportunities created by the wider markets and of interest groups that have come to depend on the benefits that the international institutions confer.

Accounting for the liberal trajectory

The historical social orders which liberal internationalists helped to create each lasted through 20 or more years of the relative prosperity and relative peace their designers had promised. Nevertheless, so far at least, the normal development of a capitalist industrial economy has also had undesired consequences not anticipated by designers of past world orders. The boom years have always ended and a decade or more of conflict, both international and domestic, has followed.

Capital accumulation and the capacity to build new world orders

The power that liberals have always relied on to create new social orders—the power of private investors—has also tended to prolong world order crises. After years of war or weak profits due to industrial strife, it can appear as if the whole capitalist class has gone on a gambling binge, pulling money from long-term investments and betting on short-term financial maneuvers with high stakes and little connection to the real economy of jobs and production. Moreover, when the casino economy finally goes bust, as it did at the beginning of Long Depression in the 1870s and after the crash of the New York stock market in 1929, a decade of unproductive hoarding can follow. Investors put their funds into precious metals, jewels, or anything rather than gambling on fundamentally new industries.

Yet, even during a world order crisis that capitalists have protracted by gambling and hoarding, liberal internationalists have had rational hopes for the future. Even in the process of prolonging the crisis, capitalists prove that they still have the investment power needed to build the new industrial era of the next international social order. So far, each era of rapid industrial growth (with its institutions encouraging capitalists to put their money into long-term productive investments) has left capitalists in a better position than they were at the beginning of the era. When liberal internationalists have succeeded in convincing a bloc of "progressive" investors to lend a hand in creating a new industrial era, the larger historical process of capital accumulation has already provided them with the capacity to make the necessary contribution of investment in new industries.

The state class and the reproduction of critical liberal internationalism

Similarly, even if today's critical liberal internationalists feel isolated in an era of fundamentalist neoliberalism, they can look to the past for evidence they will have successors whose vision may triumph. Much of the intellectual leadership needed to reform international institutions has come from thinkers linked to the growing industrial state. This is the group that some scholars influenced by Gramsci have called the "cadre class" of "salaried functionaries who are in one way or another engaged in operating the reproductive and normative structures that unify . . . social class relations . . . state managers, teachers, trade union bureaucrats, social workers and others" (Pijl 1990: 301; Markovitz 1977: 325–341, 1987: 233–321). This state class is in no more danger of disappearing than is the growing link between civil society and the state proper within the industrial world.

Political leadership and the role of the liberal myth

Nevertheless, liberal fundamentalists thrive in the early years of the world order crises when the power of private investors is at its peak. The fundamentalists provide the intellectual leadership needed to justify the era of gambling and hoarding; they provide justification for a kind of governance of the world economy by capitalists alone, unencumbered by necessary alliances with other social forces. As a result, we should not understand the past triumphs of the critical strain of liberal internationalism as consequences of an inevitable evolutionary process; they have been the particular historical consequence of social struggles that could have had very different outcomes.

This becomes especially clear when we consider the political leadership necessary to create the Interimperial Order and the Free World Order. A host of aristocratic philanthropists played the central role in the nineteenth century, and the United States government led the move toward the postwar order. Liberal internationalists had to mobilize that leadership and they did so, in great part, with the mythic elements of their philosophy. They did so by appeals to the kind of higher aspirations about which they, as liberals, have always been skeptical.

Both at the beginning of the Long Depression and during the interwar years many liberal internationalists were, at first, narrowly realistic about appeals to such aspirations. They first appealed to the self-interest of leading military powers. In the 1870s, they turned to the German empire, the victor in the recent great-power wars, and to Great Britain, the dominant maritime power. In the early interwar years, it was the United States, the decisive victor in the First World War, which received much of the attention. While the US eventually played a key role in creating the UN system, and Germany played a smaller role in establishing the Interimperial Order, Britain played a very small role in establishing the institutions that facilitated the Second Industrial Revolution and, until Pearl Harbor, isolationism and unilateralism dominated US policy.

When the liberal intellectual leaders could not rely on the preponderant powers, they could find less powerful states, aristocratic benefactors, and private philanthropists to sponsor the necessary conferences and act as benefactors to the original agencies. Altruism, *noblesse oblige*, or other of those higher aspirations explain the action of these political leaders. In the nineteenth century, liberals appealed to a sense of *noblesse oblige* on the part of princes. Similarly, in the twentieth century, world-order advocates made successful appeals to wealthy philanthropists and leaders of less-powerful democratic societies. In virtually every case, the successful appeals used the rosy future of a liberal world of greater peace and prosperity, the liberal internationalist social myth, to motivate immediate sacrifices. Nineteenth-century princes endowed the precursors to today's ITU, WIPO, WTO, ILO, FAO, Interpol, and UNESCO because liberal intellectuals convinced them that what they gave up today, would lead to a better world tomorrow (Murphy 1994: 76–81).

Gramsci understood the power of such appeals. They tap something deeper than the possessive individualism that liberal theorists see at the base of all human action; they tap a social group's collective aspirations to remake society in their own image. Moreover, Gramsci understood that our interests and aspirations never motivate our actions *directly*; our actions stem from the concrete goals and views of the world we have learned. Our interests and aspirations shape our learning to the extent that our concrete goals may asymptotically approach our interests, but, contrary to liberal social theorists, Gramsci argued that interests, by themselves, poorly predict what we will do (Augelli and Murphy 1988: 122–126).

It is ironic that the power of the liberal internationalist vision has depended on practical men and women whom other, more dogmatic, liberals have derided as "statists." The liberal systems-builders of nineteenth-century European states played a more significant role in creating the prewar European "economic Eldorado" than any Cobdenite true believers. The Keynesians who championed the welfare state and development co-operation had more to do with establishing the Free World Order than any of the Depression-era champions of liberal orthodoxy. Similarly, we should expect that today's globalist Keynesians are more likely to carry the liberal internationalist vision forward than any of today's neoliberal fundamentalists. This is the most important practical lesson of immediate importance that the history of global governance should teach us.

4 Social movements and liberal world orders

This chapter develops some further lessons from the history of liberal internationalism. It takes the story backward, before the formation of the world organizations, to the politics within the countries that initially tried to follow Britain's lead into the industrial age. More significantly, it takes the argument forward, to current attempts to reform international institutions and to create a world order more supportive of human development, more responsive to the whole range of human needs. I emphasize that in every transition period like the present, there has always been more than one liberal internationalist vision, just as there are, today, global Keynesians like Joseph Stiglitz (2002) and deeply compassionate utilitarians like Peter Singer (1999, 2002) in competition with the liberal fundamentalists in Washington. In the past, the liberals who have succeeded are those who were able to convince the powerful that their version of liberalism best reflected the interests and aspirations of those connected to the new lead sectors. This is not surprising.

We are more likely to overlook that the successful intellectual leaders also reached out to, and were nurtured and informed by, egalitarian social movements that opposed the first phase of each previous step-wise wave of globalization. These were the vocal critics of the great historical economic and political crises overseen by liberal fundamentalists. To exaggerate only slightly, the key ideas of the successful critical liberal internationalist intellectual leaders of each era, the ideas that distinguished them from liberal fundamentalists of their day, come from the ideology and practice of social movements of the Left.

As I said at the beginning, I am interested in what the history of international institutions since the Industrial Revolution can tell us about the current prospects for creating a global polity that can contribute to real development. This chapter summarizes some of those lessons in the context of the programs of political action in response to globalization that have interested many of my students over the last few years.

To be concerned with development, as I have described it, is to be concerned with substantive democracy, with helping shape a global polity *without* political privilege, a world where institutions of governance marginalize no one. While I would not claim that this is the aim of all of my students, I do argue that they are representative of many relatively privileged people throughout the world who recognize a set of moral dilemmas that the late Susan Strange argued we all face, given the nature of contemporary, unregulated globalization.

The late twentieth-century decades of relatively slow global economic growth, rapid marketization, and the relative retreat of the state may be a stage in the development of a wider, socially progressive, liberal world order. If an earlier pattern holds, the prospects for the next phase will depend on the relative success of the whole range of political practices that currently energize a generation of students that an older generation often considers alienated and politically passive. Moreover, given the political opportunities open at this particular stage in the development of the global polity, it may very well be that the women's movements and human rights that attract many students will be the only egalitarian forces with significant influence on the shape of the emerging global order.

Pinocchio's problem

I teach at an elite college for women in the United States. Although we grant only about 600 bachelor's degrees each year, the College's graduates include a disproportionate percentage of the women in high public office in the US (including the Senator from New York, the former Secretary of State, and the former US Executive Director of the World Bank) and the majority of women anchors and lead correspondents on national television and radio networks.

While the majority of our students are middle-class or working-class women on scholarship, the rest tend to be unusually well-connected politically. At the end of one recent semester, for example, when questions about the US's off-again, on-again support of China's entry into the WTO came up in class, one student brought her father, the White House Chief of Staff, to "clear things up."

Increasingly, our students, whether already well-connected or not, come from outside the United States; among the twenty women in the class to whom Chief of Staff spoke were citizens of Bhutan, Bulgaria, China, Costa Rica, France, Korea, Pakistan, the Philippines, South Africa, Taiwan, and Thailand.

Given this background, it is surprising to many on the Wellesley faculty that our students' political attitudes and actions so closely mirror those of the average young adult in the United States. Before the 2004 election, most were deeply alienated from contemporary politics and, at best, seem indifferent to many of the domestic social issues that interested their parents' generation. At Wellesley, as throughout the US, the number of students majoring in political science or preparing for careers in social work, education, or even law has been declining for almost a decade.

Yet, at the same time, the number of students studying international affairs has been climbing. Moreover, in the last five years, the anti-sweatshop movement and the protests at the WTO meetings in Seattle and Cancun and the joint World Bank–IMF meeting have energized students around the world. In addition, every year a very large number of our students seek out dangerous and poorly paid jobs in refugee camps and relocation centers in Eastern Europe, Latin America, and Africa. Even many of those who choose to climb the corporate ladder claim that similar moral convictions have led them to choose their own sixty-hour workweeks and six-figure salaries.

On occasion faculty colleagues from outside of International Relations ask me if there is anything that International Relations can tell them about our students' political attitudes and actions. Lately I have provided an answer taken from Susan Strange's reflections on the ethical dilemmas all of us confront in the current phase of the "internationalization," "globalization," or "increasing paradigmatic scale," of industrial capitalism.[1] I argue that our students share the egalitarian goals honored by their baby-boom parents and teachers, but that the women in their twenties recognize better than most of us do the sorts of things that Strange was trying to tell us about the changed world in which we now live.

In *The Retreat of the State* (Strange 1996) and her subsequent publications, Strange worried about a *specific*, and, I believe, incontestable way in which state institutions have become weaker in the face of processes of globalization. (Strange readily admitted that those processes were set in motion, in part, by powerful states themselves, but the consequences for all states remained.) What worried Strange was the decreasing ability of all states—not just "failed states" or "new democracies" but also "welfare states" and "development states"—to do anything about growing economic inequality across occupational classes, regions, races and ethnic groups, and even generations both within nations and across the world.

If there remained any question about the reality of increasing global inequality and about its connection to the weakening of state capacity, recent work completed by the World Bank's Development Research Group should put it to rest (Milanovic 1999). To put it in its starkest terms: some analysts argue that income inequality between the world's households grew more in the twenty years that an average undergraduate student has lived than in the 200 years before. Moreover, as most economic historians would argue, the two centuries of rising global income inequality since the Industrial Revolution were, themselves, unprecedented (Bairoch 1993, and see Chapter 10).

Progressive social movements created the development state and the welfare state to slow or reverse that process. Until something like 20 years ago, within many countries, they did. Now, as Strange argues, individual states, by themselves, cannot. This gives us what Strange calls "Pinocchio's problem." Moral men and women of Strange's generation, the generation raised in the Depression, who fought for decolonization and against fascism, knew the welfare state and the development state (for all their flaws) as moral agents. These states lessened the growing inequality that is an inherent product of industrial capitalism. Thus, moral women and men of Strange's generation and of the baby-boom generation had reason to be loyal to the state; we had the luxury of being able to rely on the welfare state and the development state as a moral compass (however biased). Now, when it seems that no state, by itself, is capable of confronting what theorists long-called "the social problem," none of us have that moral luxury. We are like Pinocchio at the end of the story: without strings; we have to make up our own minds about "what to do and whose authority to respect and whose to challenge and resist" (Strange 1996: 199).

Strange insisted that now the responsibility for dealing with "the social problem," the problem of reversing growing inequality, rested with all of us, those in universities and private firms, as much as those in philan-thropic foundations and governments. Our students' words and actions suggest that they agree. They try to act morally within the entire range of human institutions that have some impact on growing inequality. We can summarize their strategies under three headings:

1   creating stronger states;
2   making private institutions more accountable;
3   working for cosmopolitan democracy.

Each strategy has its limits.

Creating stronger states

In recent years, I have been struck by the fact that the most frequently men-tioned alumna hero of Wellesley's International Relations majors is not Madeline Albright or Hillary Rodham Clinton, but Lori Wallach. She is the public-interest lawyer who masterminded the Seattle protests against the WTO after earlier working to remove the US President's ability to "fast-track" trade liberalization and to scuttle the Multilateral Agreement on Investment (Lori's War 2000). Some American students strive to emulate her by promoting the American labor agenda—taking active part in the AFL-CIO's training programs directed toward college students and sup-porting the unions' legislative program. Its major points include: (1) limit-ing US involvement in multilateral and bilateral arrangements designed to foster ever freer trade and investment; and (2) increasing public responsi-bility in support of nationally oriented welfare and health policies. Similarly, some European students work for a more independent, and a more inwardly focused European Union. Both sets of students worry that the policies they support may serve to marginalize Third World economies even further.

A stronger US or European state, their African, Asian, and Latin American friends tell them, is simply a stronger center of imperialism.

Some students from outside the OECD also try to overcome Pinocchio's problem by working for stronger states. Yet many accept the position articulated by Susan Strange and her collaborators that the successful contemporary development state, carefully following plans to improve "human capital," is really just in the business of attracting global businesses, which, together, have much more of the social power than ever before.[2]

Making private institutions more accountable

Firms The power of business deeply influences a group of students for whom another Wellesley alumna, Alice Tepper-Marlin, is the hero. She is the inventor of socially responsible investment funds and founder and head of the Council on Economic Priorities (CEP), an organization that gives a series of awards for corporate responsibility. More recently, Tepper-Marlin has successfully developed a set of monitored international private labor standards, SA8000, modeled on the environmental standards created by the International Organization for Standardization (ISO). The CEP (2001) describes this initiative as enabling "organizations to be socially accountable by convening key stakeholders to develop voluntary standards, accrediting qualified organizations to verify compliance and promoting understanding and encouraging implementation of such standards worldwide." Students who champion the CEP's work see it as marshaling the power of firms that have decided to address Pinocchio's problem in the way that Strange believed that all firms should.

They, too, worry about their strategy. Despite the demonstrated impact of Tepper Marlin's earlier innovations that rely on the interest that firms that have made socially responsible bulky investments have in forcing others to make similar investments (see Chapter 11), one can question whether it is sufficient to transform an institution—global capitalism—whose fundamental principle of profit maximization seems antithetical to the notion of universal corporate responsibility.

Non-governmental organizations Matters of principle attract other students to organizations whose core beliefs seem to be closer to egalitarian norms, organizations like the Red Cross, Worldwatch, Oxfam, and the other charities who increasingly carry out the welfare work of the state in areas of humanitarian crisis.

Again, the flaws in a program to universalize that strategy are easy to find. As the charities themselves recognize, they have increasingly become merely conduits for funds from Northern governments trying to maintain international order on the cheap. The 1997 International Federation of Red Cross and Red Crescent Societies *Annual Report* refers to the resulting "NGO colonialism" and the "pimp talk" that pervades NGOs seeking to satisfy the shifting charitable whims of Northern donors (IFRC 1997: 14, 21).

Working for cosmopolitan democracy

Some more reflective students, including many of those who protested in Seattle and Washington, try to go beyond the moral dilemmas faced by the dependent NGOs by envisioning a world of international public institutions with greater power and with greater democratic accountability to their ultimate clients. For these students, David Held's (1997) theory of cosmopolitan democracy is the moral guide. Yet, even a student who has worked in the field with local activists trying to block one of the World Bank's massive dam projects, and who led a group from her country who actually had access to Bank decision-makers through its environmental review process,[3] complained of the "excessive idealism" of Held's approach, at least in the short-term. Pinocchio's problem may exist because states, by themselves, cannot reverse growing social inequalities. However, the same is even truer of today's international institutions, even the most powerful.

The double movement

We can make sense of the limits of these strategies by first recognizing that globalization takes place through the market/economic then social/political process that Karl Polanyi called the "double movement." By "globalization," I mean here simply the tendency for successful industrial economies to outgrow their political boundaries. As discussed in Chapter 3, in Adam Smith's (1982 [1776] : 265–266, 630–634) terms, a successful economy is one in which there is an ever-increasing division of labor. This growth in the division of labor—not growth in the amount of money that is following through the market, but growth in the number of workers (or even more precisely the labor power) united within a single economy (a single "market area," in Rostow's [1948] terms)—is a long-term requirement of capitalism. Smith's insight ultimately is not one about markets, per se, it is one about the *technical* division of labor.

When Marx and Engels translated the same insight into their own terms, Smith's intuition became the basis for the Marxian image of the bourgeoisie progressively turning the entire world into a single productive machine. Marx's key idea, Kees van der Pijl (1998) writes, is that of the incremental, ultimately global, *socialization* of labor via the inherently asocial processes of the market. Capitalists need markets to expand beyond the social and political boundaries that once contained them and despite the support that any current set of bounded political entities might have given to industrial capitalism in the past.

Stepwise globalization

Globalization, understood in this sense, has never been smooth or continuous. It has occurred in a stepwise fashion in response to political changes, resulting in the periodic development of new, larger social orders. Political coalitions among capitalists are needed to support such "new orders" since no individual capitalist industrial or financial sector reflects the general interest of capital per se and there are always more- or less-powerful sectors that benefit from the current, less-than-global, social order. Similarly, there always will be more- or less-powerful, socially protected non-capitalist forces opposing the next phase of globalization.

The large steps in the step-wise process of globalization have occurred in conjunction with the periodic changes in lead industries. Large investments have initiated each era. Those investments, in turn, have typically required market areas larger than the ones that typified the lead industries of the waning industrial era. The early nineteenth-century Industrial Revolution involved large, often public investments in the power systems for mills. The mid-century Railway Age involved large investments in railway networks. The turn-of-the-century Second Industrial Revolution required network investments in electrical power systems and telephone systems. The mid- to late twentieth-century Automobile Age involved even larger investments in roads, modern railway networks, airports, the modern mega-factories, and the marketing and research facilities typical of twentieth-century industry. The Information Age has required the even larger investments in the internet and in the computerized design and factory systems, such as for the Boeing 777 or the planned new generation of super jumbo jets.[4]

As has been the case with the internet (and as was the case with US railroads), individuals and governments sometimes can make these bulky investments piecemeal. Nonetheless, since the Industrial Revolution, those network-building investments at the beginning of an industrial era always have taken place over a larger geographic scale than the network investments of the previous era. There is an evolutionary logic to this. The network investments create larger market areas and the larger market areas make possible the ever-larger scale investments required by each succeeding generation of lead industries. Those large investments—such as those needed to build power plants or to fund the costly research operations of a modern chemical firm, or to build the factories to create the new generation of airplanes—require secure, large market areas to assure the economies of scale that will make investment in the new industries profitable (Murphy 1994: 123–127, 229–231, 234).

In theory, natural growth in population and imperialism could increase the size of the community over which the division of labor takes place just as easily as the integration of industrial societies can. In fact, integration has proven to be the best solution. Human populations cannot grow as rapidly as "potential productivity"—that is to say, human invention of new ways to do things with seemingly less labor input—will allow economies to grow and imperialism is a relatively costly endeavor. To assure industrial growth via imperialism in less-industrialized societies (the British strategy of the late nineteenth century and the strategy of Italy and

France in the first half of the twentieth century) adds the cost of political control to the cost of the investments in infrastructure and human capital needed to make the strategy successful. To assure industrial growth via imperial control of other core societies (the Nazi strategy in Europe) requires antagonizing other industrial powers, powers that, in combination, are likely to be able to defeat you. Figure 4.1 illustrates this perspective on globalization by highlighting the growth and integration of the market areas of lead industries since the Industrial Revolution.

Despite the fact that integration rather than imperialism is the characteristic mode of globalization, the process does not occur without conflict. Students of International Relations immediately recognize that many of the blank spaces in Figure 4.1 cover periods of great conflict: the American Civil War, the Franco-Prussian War, the World Wars. The rise of global level intergovernmental organizations (see Chapter 3) and histories of the United Kingdom, Germany, the Northeastern United States, and Japan (Murphy 1995, 1998a), show successful industrial societies have had to deal with the four conflicts between those who benefit most from the emergence of new industrial eras and the following opponents (as outlined in Chapter 3):

1   Industrial *labor*, ultimately over democratic control of production.
2   All those who have received political-economic advantage from the current order, *older economies* and *older sectors* (for example, agriculture and older lead sectors).
3   Citizens and local rulers of the *"Third World"*; that is, those regions within the market area that will not experience all the benefits of the new lead industries, regions whose economic roles will be limited to

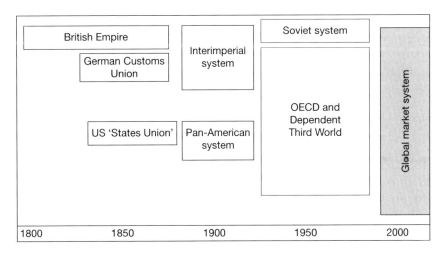

Figure 4.1 Economic areas of successive world orders

providing low-wage labor and resources (natural and agricultural) for the industrial core.
4   *Rival industrial centers* (other core powers within the same system) or *other industrial systems* especially those based on alternative forms of industrialism or proto-industrialism, for example, the southern slave system, German and Italian fascism, or Soviet socialism in contrast to what van der Pijl calls the "Lockean" systems of the industrial powers that have so far been the most successful.

While managing these four types of conflict is the central, fundamental new task of modern statecraft, the fundamental conflicts of pre-industrial civilizations remain:

5   Conflicts between humanity and the rest of the living world, the *"environment,"* that are rooted in our incomplete transition to a settled form of life.
6   Conflicts over *gender* inequality rooted in the gendered origin of the state.
7   Conflicts between privileged and less-privileged *ethnic groups* that are rooted in the characteristic response of settled societies to their vulnerability to raiding/warrior societies.

The intensity of all of these conflicts changes over time and is linked to the regular pattern of transition from one industrial era to the next in what can be summarized as a *build, thrive, clash-grab-hoard cycle*.

The *build* phase involves the formation of a new historic bloc, reflected in a mix of governance strategies of firms, states, international institutions, and popular social forces. The social calm thus established encourages the relatively large fixed investments that fuel the take-off of new leading industries. These lead to a period of relative prosperity (*thrive*), also characterized by the mitigation of the social conflicts inherent to capitalist industrialism. A kind of high cosmopolitanism, a widespread willingness of governments to risk resources in new liberal internationalist projects is apt to mark the last years of this period. This is the phase in which the first of the new market-expanding international institutions that become relevant to the *next* phase of industrial growth are established. For example, Intelsat, established in 1965, provides essential infrastructure for today's Information Age.

However, almost simultaneously with this high cosmopolitanism, some of the inherent conflicts re-emerge: conflicts with labor, conflicts with those on the periphery of the privileged capitalist core, conflicts between different industrial centers of the core, especially conflicts with other social models governing parts of the world economy. These *clash*es mark the beginning of a long period of reduced prosperity, the next (*hoard*) phase of which begins with the reassertion of capitalist power in a profit-grabbing mode that may include cost-cutting globalization.

The temporary triumph of finance and Pinocchio's problem

As Henk Overbeek (1990: 28) argues, the clash-grab-hoard half of the cycle is one in which productive capital is in crisis and the "concept of money capital 'presents itself' as the obvious, rational solution." Governments adopt cost-cutting policies and begin to focus on issues of international competitiveness, and the institutions responsible for the stability of the international financial system begin to impose liberal fundamentalist policies on states that are increasingly desperate for such international or transnational support. In the current manifestation of this phase Robert W. Cox (2002: 33–34) has noted the "internationalization of the state," the creation of global policy networks deeply embedded in most national governments and bent upon "giving priority to competitiveness in the global economy and precluding interventions by whatever authority that are not consistent with this aim."

While this phase of reassertion by financial capital may be marked by significant economic activity, much of it is apt to be speculative, and of little lasting importance. Moreover, when speculative bubbles burst, the habit of under-investment in production is likely to continue, leading to the stagnation of the hoard phase of even more defensive strategies and greater political parochialism.

In slightly different ways, Cox (1992), Kees van der Pijl (1990), and I have described the transitions that take place at this point as involving the second half of Polanyi's double movement against the extreme market logic of the liberal fundamentalism that becomes so predominant in the grab phase. That movement involves the intellectual leadership of members of the cadre class, critical liberal "system-builders" who see a larger role for government. These intellectual leaders have marshaled both political leaders and industrial leaders (most often, of the new potential leading sectors) in what Gramsci called passive revolutions, comprehensive reformist projects that, nonetheless, require no "fundamental reordering of social relations," (Forgacs 1988: 428).

Historical sociologists of the World Polity School argue that the liberal internationalism that has characterized a wider and wider sphere of state and civil society institutions, is, itself, the force propelling the development of a global polity (Boli and Thomas 1999; Luo 2000). However, liberal reformism was behind many, but not all, of the "new world orders" that have emerged from periods of crisis. There certainly have been illiberal experiments championed by illiberal systems-builders—fascist Italy, Nazi Germany—which Polanyi understood as part of the double movement. Some—the Soviet and Communist Chinese systems—lasted throughout an entire industrial era. Nonetheless, the power of international capital has always eventually sided with liberal reformism, hence, perhaps, its triumph.

World order crises and openings to previously marginalized social forces

As the sequence of bursting bubbles (perhaps, in recent years: the Japanese real estate and banking crisis, the East Asian and Russian financial crises, and the threatened deflation of the post 9/11 US economy) increases, the political space for egalitarian social forces increases. It is this political potential that, I believe, many people with egalitarian urges sense today. They hope to be part of the creators of a double movement, a move back toward a reformed social order. Yet, although history tells us that such a potential exists, history also tells us that it probably exists only for some social forces. In particular, it may exist for social forces that have not been implicated or blamed by the powerful for the economic doldrums of the last generation.

In similar periods in the past, the increasing inequality engendered by unregulated capitalism (under the hegemony of finance) began to become more tractable as new forms of social regulation emerged. These were, most often, forms consistent with the long-term liberal internationalist project.

Some social movements do not become innovators

When one thinks of the historical links between egalitarian social movements and industrial cycles what immediately comes to mind is not this hypothesized link to the construction of new industrial orders, but the clear connection between egalitarian politics and the social conflicts that mark periods of relatively slow economic growth. Labor movements, anti-colonial movements, development movements, women's movements, movements for ethnic and racial equality, and more comprehensive movements for democracy and human rights all serve to identify and articulate fundamental conflicts that emerge within industrial societies.

Much of the most persuasive literature on social movements has emphasized the modernity of social movements, their "modular" (replicable and replicated) character, and the way in which they are facilitated and limited by the political opportunities created by modern nation-states (Tarrow 1998). Nonetheless, these findings should not obscure the connection between economic and social conditions and the likelihood that egalitarian movements will form and act. Eighteenth-century settlers in Britain's American colonies organized their anti-colonial republican movement in response to the increasingly harsh direct rule necessitated by the long (if successful) British hegemonic conflict with France as well as to the political opening created by an increasingly distracted imperial power. The British Chartist and factory-hours movements responded both to the harshness of the labor regime in the early mills as well as to the political opportunities created by proximity and by the opportunity for alliances with embattled Tory interests. Turn-of-the-century labor and anti-colonial movements tried to expand the limits of the possible in an era when unprecedented prosperity and relative peace promised a more fundamentally democratic future. Similar economic and social conditions influenced the civil rights movements, development movements, and new social movements of the 1950s and 1960s.

Standard arguments about the frequency and intensity of domestic conflict should lead us to expect that social movements will become active during periods of relative peace and prosperity. We should also expect that those periods will become intensely contentious if the high expectations that social movements have during those "good times" are frustrated by more powerful social forces bent on maintaining the inegalitarian status quo. The histories of the United Kingdom, the US, Germany, and Japan reveal the role of specific egalitarian movements in the early clashes that marked each of the ends of periods of relative prosperity.

At a more inclusive level of analysis—that is not at nation-states or sub-national units but at the level of the geographic units in which the leading industries of industrial economies have developed (as outlined in Figure 4.1)—the dominant conflicts of each clash period have often been between alternative economic centers and alternative social orders. These include the conflict between industrial north and slave south in the United States, the series of brief wars between Prussia and Denmark, Austria, and France that helped unify the German Empire while securing its specific geographic class structure, and the World Wars that bracketed thirty years of this century.

It is commonplace, and relatively accurate, to conclude that the political-economic models of the social forces that lost these "international" conflicts bridging the periods between industrial eras played no role in the historic blocs that defined the new industrial era. The social model of the American slave Confederacy played little part in the social order of the Gilded Age and Progressive Era United States and its new empire in the Caribbean and Central American "near abroad" and in the Pacific. The Austro-Hungarian vision of Germany and Napoleon III's vision of Europe played little role in the new Prussian German Empire or in the European Inter-Imperial System that provided German firms with the market area needed to be part of the Second Industrial Revolution. The Fascist vision of Eurasia and Africa and the idea of an Asian Co-Prosperity Sphere played little role in the Free World Order established under US hegemony after The Second World War.

Something similar may be the case when the dominant conflict preceding an industrial era is "domestic," or, at least one contained within the older economic unit. The social forces that "lose" play little role in the next world order. For example, when Chartists and early industrial labor movements challenged the early nineteenth-century social orders of Britain and New England, that may have helped assure that the Railway Age would, in both regions, remain a period of little concrete improvement for wage workers. When the Indian revolutionaries of 1857 failed, they nonetheless raised the perceived long-term costs of maintaining the economically crucial empire, and that may have contributed to Britain's commitment to an increasingly coercive imperialism throughout the rest of the century. When Vietnamese Communists, OPEC oil barons, and other elements of the diverse Third World reaction to American hegemony contributed mightily to the end of the post-Second World War "Golden Years," but failed to create a New International Economic Order, they may have helped assure that the Information Age would be particularly harsh on the societies condemned to be providers of resources, low-wage products, and cheap labor (see Augelli and Murphy 1988, and Chapter 7).

Nevertheless, others do

Some may find this thesis neither interesting nor surprising. Why should we find it remarkable that social movements of those who suffer from persistent marginalization play no role in the development of new social orders? It is only surprising when we recognize that *some* movements of that sort have played such a role as part of the double movements that have marked the transitions from one industrial era to the next.

For the most part, the relevant movements have been "domestic," labor and progressive parties, suffragists, anti-slavery movements in the US and the UK, and anti-colonial movements within empires. Yet, there has long been a transnational character to many of the most successful egalitarian movements. The anti-slavery movement in the US originated in trans-national (often Quaker or Jacobin; that is, French-Revolution-inspired) associations, was fostered and transformed by world associations of the African Diaspora who opposed the Anglo-American solution of resettling all black slaves in Africa, and helped nurture and maintain the social movements that fought for the end to slavery in Latin America (Charnovitz 1997: 192–193; Goodman 1998; Keck and Sikkink 1998: 41–51). Anti-colonial movements have relied upon strong transnational links that transcended the realms of individual colonial powers, throughout this century (Nyerere 1980; MacFarlane 1985; Ansprenger 1989). The modern movements for women's suffrage and women's rights have always been transnational (Keck and Sikkink 1998: 51–72). In addition, of course, in the beginning "internationalism" was simply "labor internationalism" (Waterman 1998: 14–44; Lynch 1999).

In the current period of transition, egalitarian social movements, now almost always involving transnational links, have played demonstrably significant roles in the development of the social order connecting the industrialized OECD core to the dependent Third World and to semi-peripheral societies in Latin America, Eastern Europe, the Middle East, and Southeast Asia. Democracy movements and human rights movements, transnationally linked and often supported by core governments (especially since the mid-1980s) have played a central role in the transformation of Latin American, African, and East European societies, and continue to play significant roles in the remaining large states that have not made movement toward liberal democracy (Chilton 1995; Gaer 1995; Robinson 1996). Similarly, transnationally linked women's movements have been instrumental in transforming the "development" agenda of intergovernmental agencies to one that emphasizes the empowerment of women. At the same time women's movements have linked national struggles for gender equity allowing lessons learned in one area to be applied in others and contributing to the rapid diminution of legal gender discrimination as well as to substantive gains in women's access to income, wealth, job opportunities, and political positions (Chen 1995; Higer 1997).

Social movements and the "Information Age" double movement

The influence of these social movements on the verbal commitments of governments and intergovernmental agencies, on the allocation of international aid funds, and on domestic legislation (whether enforced or not) is clear from a number of regional studies. However, it is equally clear that neither these movements, nor the less successful movements promoting the interests of labor and the Third World have been able to reverse trends toward widening income gaps within and across societies. Moreover, as the recent global financial crisis demonstrates, outside the United States and the European Union conditions hardly encourage the pattern of bulky investments needed to build the Information Age global economy. In large parts of the semi-periphery and the periphery, the Former Soviet Union, parts of Latin America and South Asia, and much of Sub-Saharan Africa, a kind of kleptocratic anarchy remains (Murphy 2002).

Nonetheless, even today the outlines of the social compromises at the center of the next world order may be visible. Temporary resolutions of the fundamental conflicts of industrial societies may emerge from the small victories of the egalitarian social movements that have found political opportunities in the 1980s and 1990s. Many of us who live in industrialized societies are, for example, aware that the entrance of women into the wage labor force has allowed household incomes to remain stable or shrink less dramatically despite the fact that most of the economic growth of the past decades has gone to the top five percent of wage earners (Larin and McNichol 1997). In this context, the slightly rising incomes and protections for dual income working families associated with the "Third Way" economic policies of Bill Clinton, Tony Blair, Gerhard Schroeder, and Italy's Democratic Party of the Left governments created a surprisingly strong and broad sense of social legitimacy (Murphy 1999). As a result, someday we may look back on this period as one in which the victories of women's movements in the industrialized world helped temporarily resolve the fundamental labor conflicts that would otherwise have impeded the complete emergence of the Information Age.

Similarly, empirical studies of gender-based small-scale lending, primary education for girls, and other elements of the emerging global consensus on development that have been fostered by transnationally connected women's movements suggest that some aspects of "the Third World problem" may, without conscious strategic decision, end up being managed by low-cost gender-related changes in North–South relations (Evans 1998; Mayoux 1998). The recent wave of "democratization without development" in Latin America, Africa, and Eastern Europe has been more consciously supported by some Northern governments (especially the Reagan administration) as a strategy to manage the increasingly fraught North–South relationship. We may someday also look back on it as part of the historic bloc that maintained the period of relative peace and prosperity associated with the Information Age (Robinson 1996).

Lessons for today's egalitarian social movements

The previous sections argue that one important constraint on the influence of transnational egalitarian social movements may be their perceived role as a primary source of the conflicts that destabilized the earlier period of relative peace and prosperity. The relevant perception is, of course, that of the more powerful social forces—the ruling classes and ruling states—or, to be more operationally specific, the groups that serve as "political parties" (in Gramsci's sense) for the dominant economic interests and states, the groups that effectively articulate the worldviews and political programs followed by powerful nations, international institutions, and individuals. These include both the liberal internationalist intellectual leaders who initiate the reformist programs for a new world order, as well as the larger communities of discourse of which they are a part, those Cox (2002: 33) identifies in the current Information Age transition as:

> the official and unofficial transnational and international networks of state and corporate representatives and intellectuals who work towards the formulation of a policy consensus for global capitalism . . . a *nébleuse*—something that has no fixed and authoritative institutional structure, but which has emerged out of discussions in bodies like the Trilateral Commission, the World Economic Forum meetings in Davos, the regular meetings of central bankers, of the OECD, IMF, World Bank, and the G7 and G8 summit conferences and their preparatory meetings.

The perceptions about egalitarian social movements that matter are the perceptions of the powerful. Table 4.1 takes each of the liberal industrial systems that are precursors to the emerging "Global" Market System of the Information Age and gives a shorthand reference to the political movements, or Gramscian "parties" of the powerful who provided the primary set of innovations for each era. The sources for Table 4.1 include my own work on the major powers and on the international organization system (Murphy 1995, 1998a), Woodrow Wilson's (1898), J. Ann Tickner's (1987) and Daniel Deudney's (1996) analyses of the antebellum United States, and Amsterdam School analysts Henk Overbeek (1990) and Kees van der Pijl's (1998) accounts of British, European, and trans-Atlantic social movements in relation to the emergence of industrial orders.

These social movements of the powerful acted as political leaders, promoting institutional innovations articulated by liberal internationalist intellectual leaders, often "cadre class" civil servants and their political parties or party factions. However, the periodic need for social conflict-resolving and globalizing institutional innovation also creates political opportunities for social movements that are more firmly connected to egalitarian goals than the critical liberal internationalist, left-sympathetic "experts in government" may be. To act effectively within this arena the history of successful egalitarian social movements suggest that they need to include at least five elements in their strategic mix:

1 model mongering
2 elite–radical cooperation
3 a transnational leadership cadre
4 cross-regional learning
5 using international institutions

Model mongering

First, movements need to be dedicated to what John Braithwaite and Peter Drahos (2000: 588–590) call model mongering, meaning the constant,

Table 4.1 Innovators associated with liberal industrial orders

Industrial system ("world order")	Primary innovators
Late Industrial Revolution Britain	William Pitt the Younger's Conservatives
Railway Age British Empire	Disraeli's Conservatives
Railway Age German Customs Union	List's German Nationalists
Railway Age American "states Union"	"Hamiltonian" Jeffersonians
Second Industrial Revolution Inter-Imperial System	Large-enterprise German liberals, Cecil Rhodes's liberal imperialists
Second Industrial Revolution Pan-American System	American Republican "Progressives," McKinley, Theodore Roosevelt
Automobile Age "Free World" System (OECD and dependent Third World)	New Deal Liberals, Ford, Keynes, Monnet

experimental promotion of an ever-growing array of possible (egalitarian) solutions to the conflicts and globalization problems faced by governments and powerful social forces. For example, small-scale gender-based lending, reproductive freedom, primary education for women, and other elements of a thirty-year-old Women in Development agenda have been well marketed across a host of institutions whose primary concerns are not gender equality, but who have become convinced that these programs will reduce poverty, minimize costs of development assistance, placate an increasingly powerful Northern women's constituency, and help clean up the environment.

The general point is that liberal internationalist intellectual leaders have to find their new world order ideas from somewhere, and most often, the somewhere is further Left.

Elite-radical cooperation

Second, to be able to both successfully innovate in the interests of less advantaged groups and to sell those innovations to status quo-oriented institutions requires a division of labor within the social movement into more and less radical elements *that maintain active cooperation with one another.* Amy Higer (1997) notes the importance of this element in the success of the International Women's Health Movement and historians reach similar conclusions about nineteenth-century anti-slavery movements (Goodman 1998). Elite-radical cooperation provides the transmission belt for learning from the model-mongering egalitarian groups to the liberal intellectual leaders, the experts in government who have the ear of the powerful.

A transnational leadership cadre

Third, effective movements need a unified central cadre of activists operating across the regional lines separating the emerging, more global industrial system. Again Higer's (1997) account of the International Women's Health Movement, historical accounts of anti-slavery movements, and the experience of nineteenth-century labor internationalism and twentieth-century anti-colonialism make this point. To go back even further to the very beginning of the social movement era, one might argue that any successful movement needs its Thomas Paines, i.e. men and women who act in relation to a number of states and who can temporarily help protect the egalitarian activists of one society by offering sanctuary or marshaling diplomatic pressure from another.

Cross-regional learning

Fourth, a willingness and ability of local movements in one part of the new "globalized" region to learn from the experience of local movements in other regions. Again, this seems to be a key element of the success of contemporary women's, democracy, and human rights movements. This is in sharp contrast to labor and Third World movements. They have been riven by regional differences and by perceptions that fundamental differences in interests exist, for example, between industrial workers in Bangladesh and industrial workers in the US or between destitute Africa and industrializing South Asia. Such differences make cooperation very difficult (Murphy 2002).

One of the strongest pieces of evidence supporting both the third and fourth points comes from the response of status-quo powers to the international conference system and especially to the nongovernmental (NGO) forums that now regularly take place alongside the intergovernmental meetings on the rotating list of major topics (for example, human rights, the environment, women, population, social development). There is a widespread belief among NGO participants that the NGO forums serve as a major venue for inter-regional learning as well as the primary locus for the development of a transnational cadre linking various regional social movements. In fact, the belief in the efficacy of the NGO conferences for exactly that purpose has been a primary motivation for the work of conservative forces within the United States to end the global conference system (Fomerand 1996).

Using international organizations

The fifth and final issue is related: successful egalitarian social movements have been those willing to marshal the powers of intergovernmental organizations to promote and test the movements' proposed institutional reforms. Again, contemporary democracy and human rights movements, which have added forms of political conditionality to intergovernmental development assistance and have convinced the central organs of the UN to be service providers to almost every state involved in a democratic transition, illustrate the point (Joyner 1999).

Lessons for my students

Returning to the small group of the world's seemingly alienated and politically disengaged students that I know, I am struck by the degree to which the political actions that do engage them are consistent with the lessons of the longer history of the development of the global polity. I see among Wellesley students and alumna a part of a transnational leadership cadre of women concerned with what is ultimately a reformist project of developing a more socially accountable system of international governance to accord with the larger market area of the Information Age.

To promote that project some have become familiar with the political spaces offered by existing international organizations, and they have worked to both strengthen and democratize those institutions. Other women have become mass organizers and model mongers, like Lori Wallach.[5] Others have become corporate executives or advocates of innovative forms of business self-regulation.

What they—and the other creators of the next world order—have, perhaps, not yet learned is the importance of cooperation across those two groups of organizers (elite and mass). Nor, perhaps, have they come to understand the significance of constantly passing the lessons of state-strengthening strategies in one part of the world to another. Finally, let me reiterate the possible significance of the links between this part of the emergent leadership cadre and the modern international women's movement. Recall that prior eras of a more socially responsible international liberal order have to pass as a coalition between privileged capitalist social forces and *some* of those that have not been privileged: (1) industrial labor; (2) groups and regions relying on older sectors; (3) the Third World; (4) states championing other industrial systems; (5) champions of the environment; (6) women; and (7) less-privileged ethnic groups. In the past, groups that the privileged have considered "responsible" for the breakdown of the last era of "peace and prosperity" rarely have become allies in the creation of the new.

A recent in-depth study of the perceptions and attitudes of a small sample of highly privileged but "socially responsible" American men revealed a tendency to consider the demands of industrial workers, the Third World, and American minorities, and the costs of fighting the former Soviet system as responsible for the economic doldrums of the mid-1970s through the mid-1990s. Despite the relative gains of women and environmentalists over the same period, they were seen more as allies or as justified claimants rather than as enemies (Kelley 2000). There may be no better place to look for the outlines of the emerging world polity than among activist women. Unfortunately, given those who the powerful still perceived as "to blame" for the world's economic problems, it is unlikely that the global polity will be able to resolve the social issue at the core of Pinocchio's problem, the problem of income inequality within and between countries.

5 The promise of democratic functionalism

Chapter 4 closed with the argument that activist women will play a central role in shaping the next world order. This chapter discusses women activists playing similar roles before, within the movement for democratic functionalism in the first half of the twentieth century. The full promise of that movement was never fulfilled, and, in fact, some of the women at its center were long forgotten by policy-makers and scholars involved in international affairs. Here I explore why, and consider whether the story of democratic functionalism in the twentieth century has any lessons for those attempting to shape the world order that is emerging today.

Most accounts of twentieth-century functionalism conclude that British debates over "guild socialism and pluralism" provided the most important intellectual foundation for the approach to international relations developed by David Mitrany in the 1930s and 1940s (Haas 1964: 8). Yet, a comparison of Mitrany's innovative theory to international affairs with contemporary innovations in the study of public and private organizations suggests another inspiration: the similar functional approach to organization studies that had been spurred by the rapid growth of modern corporations (especially in the United States) and subsequently of the state throughout the industrialized world.

Historians of the liberal tradition in International Relations will find the connection between Mitrany's ideas and those of the founders of organization theory interesting simply because those links help clarify how an approach seemingly so at odds with the then current theories of diplomacy and international law could have arisen and gained ground so quickly. But for most scholars in the field the more important reasons for uncovering the links between Mitrany's approach and early management theory have to do with the growing sense that the functional approach, for all its known weaknesses, is, once again, very relevant to today's core issues of world politics. By borrowing from the organization theory developed by Mitrany's contemporaries we may further increase the relevance of the functional approach to today's problems of international governance.

Some early organization theorists provide more coherent and plausible responses to the criticisms regularly leveled at Mitrany, especially Mary

Parker Follett, who died in 1933, the year of publication of Mitrany's *Progress of International Government.* (Thus, it is unlikely that Mitrany influenced her remarkably similar ideas, although Mitrany probably knew her work, including her studies of international functional organizations in Geneva.) The organization theorists provide better answers to questions about how functionalist cooperation would overcome problems of fundamental conflict. Perhaps even more significantly, the better developed theories of the behavior of individuals and organizations allow more focused criticism that helps pinpoint exactly how far Mitrany's approach will take us in coping with contemporary problems of international governance. The pioneers in organization theory suggest that the problem with the functional approach is not its inattention to conflicts rooted in fundamental socio-psychological needs (for example, conflicts of identity such as those between viciously opposed ethnic groups, see Chapter 2). The problem is that the functional approach provides only a temporary way of managing the structural conflicts that divide classes and economic regions of wealth and poverty. Unfortunately, these ideas found no immediate home in International Relations and liberal internationalists forgot Follett for more than a generation, something that may happen again with new insights that women bring into an unusually male-dominated field.

Mitrany's early ambivalence toward functional government

Mitrany was far from the first to have developed a functional approach to international cooperation. Ernst Haas (1964: 8) points to the earlier work of Leonard Woolf and the turn-of-the-century American political scientist Paul Reinsch and Chapter 3 takes the story back to the mid-nineteenth-century European and American "systems builders" who inspired and later designed the late nineteenth-century Public International Unions that Woolf and Reinsch both saw as models for future functional cooperation. Yet, Mitrany's texts give us few clues about the immediate intellectual sources of his own functional approach. Given the exhaustive documentation in his 1930 book on land and peasants in Romania, his studies of functionalist government that immediately followed include surprisingly few citations. He mentions his colleague Woolf and fellow Fabian G. D. H. Cole—hence the usual attribution of Mitrany's concept to debates among guild socialists—but, as is the case with his pre-functionalist 1925 book on international sanctions, Mitrany's writings about international relations in the 1930s and 1940s are oriented toward issues of the day and have few academic trappings. For example, Mitrany gives later readers no way to track a critical reference in his *Progress of International Government.* The only empirical study he mentions that directly supports his analysis of functional governance at an international level is an unpublished paper by Gordon Shipman, a University of Arkansas sociologist.

Shipman's only indexed published work in the 1930s (Shipman 1931) was not on functional cooperation in the Geneva organizations (the subject mentioned by Mitrany), but on the non-verbal modeling techniques that social scientists need to develop if they are to live up to their claim to be scientific. Another American, Follett, did write about the Geneva organizations in between 1931 and 1933, and she made the argument that Mitrany attributes to Shipman (Follett 1937: 168–169).

Given the ideas for which Mitrany is most remembered, it is surprising that his early functionalist work seems, on the surface, to be less formal than his other scholarship conducted at the time. Perhaps even more surprising is the mixed attitude toward the expansion of functional government that Mitrany reveals throughout this, his most creative period.

Mitrany first proposed the centrality of the question of the functions of international government in *Progress of International Government.* In his 1934 article, "Political Consequences of Economic Planning," Mitrany made it clear that the problem for which he saw international functional cooperation as the emergent solution was the expansion of functional government *domestically* via the growth of public planning, and that, he argued, was a very mixed blessing.

Mitrany saw a teleology, a logic of spillover that assured planning would grow to encompass all aspects of the economy. While the immediate impetus for increased planning may have been the desire for economic stabilization as a consequence of depression in one or more industries, Mitrany argued that the experience of planning during the First World War proved that control of one industry would lead to the control of all. At the same time, the process of establishing public control would demand an equality of treatment not found in the private economy, and, therefore, the goal of planning would shift from mere stabilization to economic equalization.

This shift in goals—typically of planning in democratic societies—would help compensate for the inherently anti-democratic tendencies of functional government. About the shift to a planned society he asks:

> Does this mean the end of democracy or merely a redefinition of democracy . . . The transition will be awkward, but it need not be despotic. If planning were used merely as an attempt to give a new lease of life to our acquisitive society, then it would no doubt have to rely on coercive means. But if it be erected fairly and squarely upon a new social outlook, upon a "new deal" in which rights and rewards would flow from the giving of service rather than the holding of wealth, we have here ability and experience enough to create new political alloy in which the rigors of planning would be judiciously combined with the democratic principle of consent, and a democratic definition of purpose with the autonomy of technical execution.
>
> (Mitrany 1934: 32–33)

However, the teleology of planning in less democratic societies was very different. Mitrany's 1936 study of the economic consequences of the First World War in the Austro-Hungarian Empire and Southeastern Europe highlighted a case of the rise of functional government via wartime planning which had resulted in bloated bureaucracies lacking any democratic accountability. Even after the war, the institutional momentum of the wartime experience assured that functional government in the new, ostensibly democratic, successor states would remain unaccountable to the interests of the new popular majorities of peasants and workers (Mitrany 1936: 80–137).

In 1934, Mitrany argued that even among *democratic* societies the logic of functional government could become self-defeating. When he looked around himself in the early 1930s he saw the new planning-oriented democratic states bent on autarky, willing to throw aside the long-established inter-regional divisions of labor that provided the economies of scale needed to provide a decent life for the popular masses that the planners meant to serve. Mitrany worried that societies bent on autarky—whether democratic or authoritarian—would be driven to imperialism by the need to achieve that greater scale, and he worried that attempts to achieve international cooperative planning through the then existing international institutional means would fail. Such cooperation would require literally thousands of bilateral treaties and hundreds of specialized international agencies, all of which, lacking direct democratic oversight, would be likely to become corrupt, or, at the very least, captives of the interests they were supposed to regulate (Mitrany 1934: 337).

Mitrany averred:

> This is not an argument for or against planning. Nor is it a plea either for free trade or for a World State. It is merely a claim that the peaceful and rational progress of communal life will always depend on one essential principle: on our adopting for each period the structure, political and economic, which under existing conditions can produce the richest results with the smallest friction. At present, isolated national planning would clearly do violence to an international system that is active, highly developed, and patently indispensable.
>
> (Mitrany 1934: 342)

Nine years later Mitrany's *A Working Peace System* reflected a slightly different view: the Second World War had so changed conditions that international functional governance—the international transcendence of the national planning of the planning state—had finally become the one political structure under which the richest results could be produced with the least friction.

Mitrany's greater conviction about international functionalist solutions reflected a new recognition of the flaws of the prewar international systems that he had once considered so indispensable. Mitrany's certainty also reflected a new optimism about the prospects for democratic government now that an eventual Allied victory seemed likely. Equally important may have been the "consensus on global management, disagreement over national regulation of trade" that had begun to mark Allied discussions of the postwar order by 1943 (Murphy 1984: 13). Strong advocates of national planning, including Soviet officials and critical liberal internationalist Keynesians throughout the West, had come to accept Mitrany's kind of argument that, at the very least, active multilateral coordination of nationally planned economies was essential. At the same time American free trade fundamentalists, who were a very strong (and, ultimately, victorious) force in the Departments of State and Commerce, had come to recognize that intergovernmental management was needed in order to foster the more laissez-faire world they hoped to develop.

Later in life, Mitrany (1975: 24–29) argued that his functional approach developed not so much on the basis of elaborating a specific strain of liberal theory, but through reflection on the real, practical achievements of policy-makers facing the Depression and the World Wars. Mitrany's detailed scholarly analysis of the expansion of functional governance in Southeastern and Central Europe during the First World War triggered his recognition of its significance, but also led him to fear the impact on democratic governance of that development. His experience with New Deal era planning convinced him that the expansion of functional governance could be compatible with democratic values, but his caution about the autarkic bias of planning states remained. Nonetheless, by the time that the victory of the anti-fascist alliance became probable, Mitrany recognized conditions under which democratic planning-oriented states would be likely to turn toward a functionalist vision of international governance that would preserve both the democratic values of the New Deal and the advantages of the more integrated international economy and political system that existed before the First World War and during the brief, hopeful period in the mid-1920s when Mitrany had done his first activist scholarship aimed at strengthening institutionalized international cooperation.

The origins of organization theory

Even though the evidence supports the case that Mitrany's development of the functional approach did not involve the importation or elaboration of a well-developed theory of functional governance, such a theory—derived, in part, from reflection on some of the developments in national government about which Mitrany once was so ambivalent—did exist when Mitrany began to discuss the approach. Lucian Ashworth and David Long (1995: 24) point out that the most likely immediate source of Mitrany's idea of function was that of his mentor, L. T. Hobhouse, who taught that "a functionally ordered society . . . is necessary in order to combine democracy with planning," but it is equally true that "the use of function as the principle around which to order society was common currency of the first decades of the twentieth century" (Ashworth and Long 1995: 29). By the time Mitrany began to write about functional international governance in 1933, the functional approach to organization was at the center of well-developed theories of public and private management that reflected on the unprecedented growth of leading-sector firms throughout the turn-of-the-century Second Industrial Revolution.

Before the Second Industrial Revolution, the largest bureaucratically organized structures had been the Catholic Church and the military structures of expanding empires. Private firms remained relatively small affairs with few layers of hierarchy. Typically, family members or partners managed firms. In the second half of the nineteenth century first the railroads and then the leading industries of the Second Industrial Revolution changed all that. In the United States, and later in parts of Europe, giant chemical, electrical and consumer-goods industries expanded to serve continental markets. As Alfred D. Chandler (1962) was the first to demonstrate, continental markets were needed to assure the economies of scale that would make investment in the new industries profitable. Operation on that scale, in turn, dictated the formation of unprecedentedly large firms that began to dwarf all but the largest military establishments of the largest empires. The size of these firms demanded bureaucratic strategies of control, and, initially, the companies that were the most successful were those that adopted a policy of radical functional differentiation, creating relatively autonomous, task-oriented bureaucratic structures each responsible for meeting a single need in the company's overall business plan.[1]

However, by the time the United States entered the First World War the limits of the functional approach to business management were already becoming clear. Unified functionally divided structures became unwieldy across the entire continental (and, increasingly, intercontinental) markets of the new firms. The lack of competition among groups performing the same function allowed for efficiency, but it did not promote innovation. Moreover, the rigid application of scientific principles that led to the break-up of firms into efficient functional departments also created authoritarian structures that alienated workers and lower managers.

The continental market opportunities of the Second Industrial Revolution generated a kind of immediate, practical, often seat-of-the-pants management theory, but by the end of the First World War the problems of the early functional approach to business management had helped replace the first generation of theorizing with more reflective and academic scholarly practices, a developed organization theory. One result of that newer theory included replacement of the norm of the firm differentiated into simple functional departments with the norm of multiple, often competing functionally differentiated structures united as geographical or product-differentiated divisions of the same firm. Another result was the development of human relations approaches to management, approaches explicitly designed to restore some of the democratic control lost by workers and lower level managers (Guillén 1995: 22–28).

At the same time the rapid expansion of state functions, which had begun in some industrialized societies before the First World War, and which (as Mitrany's work notes) had become general throughout Europe during the war, led to a second kind of explicit theorizing in public administration. Much of this theoretical work attempted to apply what had been learned from the early scientific management practices of the growing American firms to the similar problems of governments attempting to plan for public welfare rather than private gain (Urwick 1937).

Both of these traditions of highly developed theorizing about the functional approach to government were available to Mitrany in the 1930s, but neither tradition was well developed within Britain itself. In large part, this is because, despite the economic advantages of the new organization forms that were so clearly demonstrated first in the US and then on the continent, Britain maintained its "continuing commitment to personal capitalism" (Chandler with Hikino 1990: 240–295). Few British firms arose in the leading sectors of the Second Industrial Revolution. Many of those that did, including the largest such as Unilever and Shell, found many of their markets and much of their management philosophy on the continent (Guillén 1995: 222–226).

Britain's few other lead-industry firms included the Quaker chocolate manufacturers Cadbury and Rowntree, which eventually became promoters of modern management theory, but in their case (as is partially true with the relatively progressive Unilever) an initially paternalist commitment to some level of workplace democracy made them suspicious of the earliest functional scholarship. The Quaker firms supported the newer "human relations" approaches of the 1920s. These approaches responded to the problems of worker alienation created by the first wave of American scientific management practice (Guillén 1995: 220–221). Rowntree became a major benefactor of the International Labor Organization's International Management Institute, the League of Nations era organization whose function was to expose European managers to the latest American theorizing (Murphy 1994: 175).

When it came to the application of the functional approach to problems in the public realm, the story was not that much different. France's expanding Third Republic with its new system for training professional administrators at the pinnacles of the functional bureaucracy created a host of organization theorists, including the innovative Henri Fayol (1937), who some claim to be the first to carefully articulate the main lessons of the functional differentiated government that held across traditional state bureaucracies and modern firms (Urwick 1937). In contrast, while Fayol used the experience of the growing French state to theorize the foundations of modern French planning, his British contemporaries theorized little about the expansion of state functions. When the next generation of British government managers began to think about the lessons of functional government in the 1930s they skipped over the early problems that challenged Fayol, and began their contributions to organization theory with reflection on the human relations problems that emerged in public as well as private bureaucracies (Lee 1937).

As a result, the most complex British scholarship employing the functional approach that was available to Mitrany in the 1930s really was contained in the limited reflections on functional governance of his mentor Hobhouse or his Fabian colleagues Woolf and Cole. Yet, this was far from the most complex theorizing using this approach that was widely discussed within Britain in the 1930s. Largely as a consequence of benefactors among the leaders of progressive British firms, a number of prominent American organization theorists began to play a leading role in elite discussions of management and government in the late 1920s. Ironically, and perhaps sadly, this was right at the moment that Mitrany was to move the center of his scholarly life to the United States.

Mary Parker Follett's democratic functionalism

One of the most prominent of the American management theorists attracted to Britain in the interwar years was Mary Parker Follett, an early political scientist who was regarded in the first half of the twentieth century as one of the founders of the fields of public administration and organization studies. Follett moved to London in 1929 and lived there until her death in 1933. She often traveled to Geneva to study organizational practices of the international functional bureaus and to lecture at the International Management Institute. In Britain Follett pioneered the profession of management consulting, working both for Second Industrial Revolution giants like Unilever and for progressive Quaker firms, over which she had a particularly significant influence (Metcalf and Urwick 1942). She also worked with colleagues at the Royal Institute of International Affairs who shared her interest in the experience of the Geneva organizations and she lectured in British universities, giving a widely publicized set of five lectures at the London School of Economics in 1933, shortly before her death.

For more than twenty years after her death, Follett's work remained widely known on both sides of the Atlantic. As late as 1954 the US Public Assistance Administration reissued one of her most popular essays in pamphlet form: "The Illusion of Final Authority: Authority must be Functional and Functional Authority Carries with it Functional Responsibility" (Follett 1954). Nevertheless, shortly afterward, as new research in the fields she helped found exploded, scholars and policy-makers forgot Follett's pioneering studies.

Even though both organization theorists and political scientists have rediscovered Follett in the last ten years,[2] the long eclipse of her work means that it is unfamiliar to the International Relations scholars who have recently begun to reassert the importance of Mitrany's analysis. This is unfortunate because Follett's analysis parallels Mitrany's so closely that the places where hers is more developed can give us some insight into ways in which Mitrany's functional approach might be applied to issues that he did not address.

The problem of reconciling democracy and planning is at the heart of Follett's work, as it is with Mitrany's work. Follett entitled her key 1918 book, *The New State: Group Organization, the Solution of Popular Government.* Like Mitrany, Follett began to look for that "solution" in relatively autonomous organizations whose purpose was to fulfill specific, identifiable human needs. Needs, for Follett, defined legitimate functions for collective organizations, functions that, within a democratic society, could be carried out relatively autonomously. She argued that within each functional realm, there should be legitimate, technical-rational authorities, but their authority would ultimately depend on their ability to actually carry out the function in question. That ability, Follett argued, certainly would change over time and probably it would only exist to the extent that democratic processes existed within the group designated to carry out the function.

Follett recognized, perhaps even more clearly than Mitrany did, that the invocation of human needs would not give us some final authoritative list of functions that we must perform collectively in order for humanity to thrive. Nor did Follett believe, any more than Mitrany, that some needs, and, hence, some functions, were inherently more significant than others (compare Chapter 2).

Nonetheless, Follett may have been slightly clearer about this point. As Long and Ashworth (1999: 17) point out, it is Inis Claude's understandable misreading of Mitrany as suggesting an inherent separability and hierarchy of needs that leads to Claude's most important criticism of the functional approach. It would be hard to have the same misreading of Follett because two of the issues that are absolutely central to her work are direct responses to the fact that needs-based issues are never really separable and that the hierarchy of what needs (and, hence, what functions) are the most important to a society will, in fact, change.

Because functions and their priority are bound to change, Follett (1918: 388) argued that no effective democracy could be based on the assumption that people could be sufficiently represented by their participation in a democratically organized functional group that plays some seemingly essential role within the society's division of labor. This was the claim made by Mussolini and other early champions of corporatism, including apologists for the wartime expansion of functional government in Eastern Europe of which Mitrany was so critical. Corporatist representation, Follett argued, would never be sufficient even within a society in which all people were fully convinced that that division of labor accurately reflected societal needs, despite the claims made for society-wide planning when it first appeared during the First World War. After that crisis, the relative importance of different functions changed, just as they were apt to change, at any point, in normal times. Therefore, Follett concluded, a system of democratic representation outside of the corporatist structure was needed to assure that each person's voice would be heard when the question of *which* functions were essential was raised.

Similarly, Follett provided a process-oriented answer to the question of how the efficient, functionally separated organizations should deal with the shifting boundaries of their functions on a *day-to-day* basis, in the time between what could only be periodic adjustment of boundaries by democratically chosen representative authorities. This was the basis for Follett's formula:

- coordination by direct contact of the responsible people;
- coordination in the early stages;
- coordination as a reciprocal relation of all features in a situation; and
- coordination as a continuing process.

It should not be surprising that Follett looked to the Geneva organizations to test the validity of this advice. Like today's UN agencies, the Geneva specialized agencies were highly autonomous from one another even though many of the tasks assigned to them (for example, rebuilding war-torn societies) required them to cooperate. Moreover, in most fields they could only carry out their mandates through cooperation with equally autonomous national governments and non-governmental organizations such as the Red Cross. In Follett's (1937: 161–169) last lectures she reported what she believed was convincing evidence that the international functional agencies were only effective to the extent that all parts of this formula for coordination were followed.

Follett's other major hypothesis about the relative effectiveness of different organizations focused on their adherence to a second process formula, in this case a democratic formula for finding out the "one best way" to carry out a task. The search for the "one best way" to do a job was a central theme of all management theory back to the very beginnings of "scientific management" in the generation before the First World War. The first management guru, Frederick W. Taylor, made his name by observing and clocking workers, analyzing the way that the most efficient workers did each task, and imposing those methods on all others. Taylor's process also was the target of much of the labor and lower-management strife that Follett began to analyze in the 1910s and 1920s.

Follett accepted Taylor's program of increasing efficiency by searching for the "one best way," but she rejected Taylor's method of searching for that one way. She argued that all that the first generation of management consultants discovered was the best way to do a job known so far, the way that had been figured out by one clever person by him or herself.

Follett argued that there were bound to be even better ways to any task that could only be discovered by people working out the problem creatively and collectively. Follett took it as a given that the heterogeneity of individual human experience created almost infinite opportunities for learning and that in any difference of opinion about what should be done lay the potential for discovering new efficiencies. She was convinced that she saw the value of this approach in practice in the few firms that experimented in co-management, including Cadbury in Britain and the Filene's department store chain in the United States (Follett 1918: 40, 118–119).

Finally, Follett's views on the importance of co-management as a way to discover new efficiencies leads to some clear conclusions about the preferable scale for functional agencies that seem to be very much in line with Mitrany's ideas. Follett believed that organizations should remain small enough, or internally differentiated enough, that collegial management could remain the norm. This is a position fully consistent with Mitrany's aversion to bureaucratic world government, or even for hierarchically organized national planning for that matter.

It is unfortunate that—because of her early death—Mitrany and Follett never had the opportunity to collaborate to develop the functional vision of international government that they were both investigating in 1933. Perhaps Follett would argue that they undoubtedly did collaborate, although at a distance, through the conversations of the many friends and colleagues they had in common including researchers at the Royal Institute such as Arthur Salter, Quaker businessmen and peace activists on both sides of the Atlantic, and American progressives including Felix Frankfurter and Emily Greene Balch.

Indeed, Mitrany's record of his own association with Balch suggests that more direct collaboration may not have been more fruitful. Balch was the Wellesley College economist who help found the Women's International League for Peace and Freedom and who received the 1946 Nobel Peace Prize for the work her organization did to convince the wartime allies to preserve the wide range of effective League of Nations specialized agencies under the new United Nations system. In Mitrany's memoir, published in 1975, he quotes a genuinely modest letter from Balch from the early 1950s in which she praises Mitrany's *Working Peace System*, notes the parallel lines on which their ideas have developed, and asks for his help in a planned volume employing the functional approach. Mitrany did not collaborate, and, in context, his motive for publishing Balch's letter contrasts poorly with hers for writing it. He uses the letter to show how widely he was recognized as the father of the functional approach; he does not mention Balch's Nobel Prize or the reason for which she received it (Mitrany 1975: 31). Perhaps because Mitrany was so much the intellectual loner within International Relations—and perhaps because he shared the sexism that marked the field throughout his generation—fruitful, direct collaboration with Mary Parker Follett would have been ruled out.

The functional approach and the resolution of fundamental conflicts

But the historical impossibility of direct collaboration between Mitrany and the pioneer organization theorists does not rule out the possibility of using Follett's work to help elaborate Mitrany's similar theory in light of criticism that makes us question its current applicability. Consider, for example, what might be thought of as the "rational core" of Inis Claude's critique. It is, as Ashworth and Long put it, "the argument that ideologically inspired conflicts or conflicts with a Cold War overlay were less susceptible to functional conflict management techniques." Ashworth and Long note that it was the end of the Cold War ideological conflict that made a reappraisal of Mitrany's approach seem timely. Yet, following from the rational core of Claude's argument, they conclude, "it might be argued that ethnic and other identity-based conflicts create other, perhaps even more serious challenges for Mitrany's views." Based on the fundamental similarities between Mitrany's and Follett's approaches, and on Follett's ability to provide a relatively persuasive account of how her approach would work to resolve conflicts of ideology or identity, I believe that such a conclusion would be wrong.

Anatol Rapoport (1960, 1979) has made all conflict researchers aware that acute conflicts over identity and ideas—like conflicts over the social structures that determine distributions of different social goods—are "fundamental" in the sense that they cannot be resolved through bargaining processes, the kind of processes that can be modeled by game theorists. Just as the conflict between master and slave cannot be resolved simply by readjusting material rewards received by slaves, but only by a social transformation of the structure of slavery, similarly, bargaining will fail to resolve conflicts over principles of identity or justice for which people are willing to die. These conflicts arise out of the thwarting of fundamental social and psychological needs (see Chapter 2).

Rapoport argues that the only possible way to resolve conflicts of ideas is for parties to communicate with each other openly and fully enough that both have an opportunity to change their views, a process Rapoport calls "debate." Follett began making essentially the same argument as early as 1918, but with an added fillip: while Rapoport has argued that debate was the only way conflicts of ideas could be resolved, he has offered no reason for believing that debate would lead to resolution in most cases; Follett provides a reason.

She rests her argument on her theory of learning that values heterogeneity of viewpoints. Follett assumes that people with fundamentally different views, acting together, will be more creative than people who share the same views. Follett's assumptions about the creative value of difference led her to believe that there was no inherent incompatibility between nationalism and internationalism. The same assumption led her to hypothesize that wars of identity or of ideas would tend to end with affirmations of the value of difference (Follett 1918: 344). She argued that all that needs to be done to harness the creativity that comes with difference (at whatever level of human organization) is to unite conflicting parties in the pursuit of a collective task. For parties in conflict—even if they are nations engaged in wars of ideas—the logically first collective task is somewhat obvious: working to come to a collective understanding of the nature of the conflict, a task that will make the second job that must be attacked collectively—inventing new means to live with one another—all that much easier (Follett 1942: 45).

Acting on the basis of her theory, Follett pioneered the modern kind of management consultancy that brings parties in fundamental conflicts together to come to a collective understanding of the problem and devise means to work with one another despite differences of identity or ideology. In international affairs, a similar approach has been followed by peace researchers who organize problem-solving workshops among parties to fundamental conflicts. Herbert Kelman's (1979) long series of private meetings among Israelis and Egyptians and then Israelis and Palestinians even mirrored Follett's (and many later management consultants') practice of focusing first on developing a joint understanding of the conflict itself. Moreover, Follett's expectations about the creativity generated by difference seem to be affirmed by the history of the workshop in which Kelman has been involved. Those workshops, and the interaction of Arab and Israeli scholars and policy-makers, developed a general theory of "protracted social conflict" that now influences the way many peace researchers understand identity conflicts throughout the world (Azar and Moon 1986).

Follett's theory would suggest that a key part of the "functionalist" solution to internationalized conflicts of identity and ideas would be the often long and difficult task of conducting problem-solving workshops, something that has been done the most effectively by relatively small groups that are beholden neither to powerful governments nor to intergovernmental organizations. In a recent analysis of knowledge cumulation in International Relations one of the most persuasive advocates of this problem-solving approach, A. J. R. Groom (1995) outlines its strengths directly after discussing Mitrany's functionalist theory and its limits when applied to international protracted social conflicts. Turning back to the management theory that first developed the functional approach, we might argue that the problem-solving approach is more than just a way of dealing with some issues that Mitrany did not address, it is the appropriate way, the way most in keeping with the logic of the functional approach that Mitrany brought to international affairs.

Structural conflicts and the limits of democratic functionalism

Follett's own work in helping resolve fundamental conflicts was not directed toward the resolution of conflicts of ideas, but toward the resolution of structural conflicts between workers and capitalists. Initially her approach proved attractive not only to progressive employers like Cadbury, Rowntree or Filene's, but also to companies that hoped only to figure out how to achieve their own high return on investment. Follett's ideas also proved popular among some labor leaders, like the International Labor Organization Director General who sponsored the founding of the International Management Institute in 1925 (Murphy 1994: 175).

Yet, even before Follett's death the shortcomings of her approach to industrial relations were becoming clear. Workers and capitalists always entered creative problem-solving workshops in a relationship of structural inequality. The owners and their agents could determine the agenda of issues that could be addressed with complete mutuality, and, in almost all companies at almost all times, the agenda excluded the issue of the structural source of the inequality: the issue of who owned the firm, who owned and controlled the means of production. The conflict with industrial labor over democratic control of new technology (recall Chapters 3 and 4) is a structural conflict.

Given that the fundamental source of conflict could not be addressed through Follett's means it became reasonable for workers to see the workshops, transaction groups and quality circles of the human relations approach as mere psychological palliatives or, even worse, as means for capitalists to extract even more from their employees: the output of their creative minds.

After the Depression Follett's approach to industrial relations once again thrived, but only in those industries where profits were relatively high and secure, and in those societies (such as the United Kingdom) in which an extensive welfare state and politically powerful labor movement provided alternative means to manage the fundamental structural conflict (Guillén 1995: 228–253).

Follett would have been disappointed with this outcome. She had imagined rational discussion leading to a snowballing of co-management and, eventually, to capitalists accepting something like what the anti-colonial leader, Amilcar Cabral (Chabal 1983: 177–180) had hoped for in post-independence Africa, the "class suicide" of the nationalist *petit bourgeoisie* as they became convinced of the needs of African workers and peasants. Follett, of course, imagined the most powerful sections of the global *bourgeoisie* coming to recognize that workers needed to have equal control over production, they needed to be equal stakeholders, in order to assure that industrial firms could carry out their function within society in the most productive way possible.

The flaw in Follett's analysis was a consequence of her idealism. By that, I do not mean the kind of "head in the clouds" attitude that constitutes "idealism" in International Relations (at least according to self-styled "Realists"). Follett's fault was a commitment to philosophical idealism that assumed that people would be guided by the outcome of rational argument rather than driven by the material logic of a social system that requires successful capitalists to act like capitalists as long as the structural basis for capitalist power remains (Cavallari 1990).

The work of Adam Curle, a later theorist whose approach is linked to the human relations school of industrial relations that Follett pioneered, helps pinpoint the precise difficulty with Follett's democratic functionalism. Curle agrees that the resolution—the agreement on how parties will work with each other in the future—of any structural conflict must come out of a Rapoport-style "debate" in which fundamentally different ideas are confronted and a creative synthesis emerges, albeit a synthesis that is likely to preserve difference (Curle 1971: 172–173). Nonetheless, Curle argues that as a first step in any structural or "unbalanced" conflict, the structurally weaker parties must unite to change the underlying power relationship and confront the (formerly) structurally superior party with the new level of equality before problem-solving negotiations can lead to anything more than temporary conflict management. It is the united power of the working class against the capitalists, the slaves and slave-free societies against the slavers, or the colonized against the colonizers, that can make the application of problem-solving techniques truly fruitful.

James Mayall has noted similar issues that arise when attempting to apply Mitrany's ideas about functional conflict resolution to problems of international economic inequality (1975). I agree that it is relative to structural conflicts in the global political economy that attempts to find guidance from Mitrany on today's problems of international governance are most likely to fail. Nevertheless, it may be useful to try to understand exactly why both Mitrany and early management theorists like Follett tended to ignore what today seem to be such clear structural conflicts.

This is one case where Mitrany's reasoning is superior to Follett's. Follett essentially ignored the possible existence of social structures that could not be bridged by the rational collective action of men and women of good will. She certainly expected conflict between workers and owners of industry, but she saw that instance of conflict as little different from other kinds of fundamental conflicts that divide societies into groups committed to incompatible ideas. Mitrany's position on the material basis of structural conflicts was more complex. His deep involvement in a democratic socialist intellectual milieu assured that he had given a serious hearing to Marxist arguments about the capitalist/worker divide, even if his critiques of Leninist practice vis-à-vis Eastern European peasant societies demonstrate his lack of sympathy for Leninist conclusions. More significantly, Mitrany, unlike Follett, provided a specific reason why he believed that the fundamental class division was ending, at least within democratic societies, in his argument that the process of public planning, once started, becomes inexorable, moving from one sector to the next, and, that within democratic societies, this process will shift focus from the simple problem of the stabilization of the economy to the problem of assuring equity.

Nonetheless, although Mitrany provides a clear argument for ignoring the problem of economic structural inequality there is a real problem with his position. In fact, Mitrany's implicit faith that real-world liberal democratic governments actually pursue equity does seem to reflect the sort of naivety that postwar "realists" found so troubling. Although, ironically, this particular naive faith in the representativeness of governments was shared by many postwar "realists."

To judge Mitrany less harshly, and, I believe, more accurately, it would be better simply to conclude that a major reason his theory may not be applicable in the post-Cold War world is that his expectations about the spillover of national planning have been confounded. We do not live in a world in which national planning to stabilize industries in the face of depression or war has spilled over into national planning to assure greater social equity. Instead, ours is a world in which 50 years of functionally oriented international cooperation among some states has led to ever wider and deeper international realms in which the market, rather than planning, rules economic life. We live in one of those eras, like the 1920s, when the lessons of critical liberal internationalists have been forgotten and the laissez-faire ideas, so attractive to mobile capital, rule. The immediate resolution of the crises that gave us the post-Cold War world further reduced the scope of planning, not only through the rapid dismantling of the Eastern European planning systems, but also through the cascading of liberal fundamentalist economic policies across the capitalist world as countries have tried to adjust to and succeed in the more competitive global economy created through international functionalist cooperation.

Arguably, in today's world, Mitrany's own fundamentally democratic goals could not readily be served by relying on the techniques that he championed from the Second World War onward. If promoting international functional cooperation simply means placing more and more of human life under the logic of the market, then it may simply reduce the efficacy of existing democratic institutions and expand the gap between the world's rich and poor. For this reason it might be concluded that Mitrany's (and Follett's) real heirs are not those who enthusiastically embrace the recent resurgence of (functional) multilateralism. Rather Mitrany might be an inspiration to those who see both opportunities and perils in recent moves toward international governance and who champion a "cosmopolitan democracy" that remains true to the egalitarian principles underlying early twentieth-century democratic functionalism.

Women's marginalization, liberal forgetting, and the thwarting of the liberal project

In Chapter 4, I introduced the range of political analyses and concerns that motivate many of my students when they think about the consequences of the current phase of globalization. Many identify with the project of creating cosmopolitan democracy. Most of these women would embrace the label "liberal," especially if it is understood that theirs is a liberalism at odds with the neoliberal fundamentalism emanating from Washington. Sadly, though, like many of their critical liberal colleagues over many generations, my students know little of the tradition of which they are a part; they have been forced to suffer amnesia; they have become subject to liberal forgetting.

My own field contributes to liberal forgetfulness. Many women at the center of important social movements made significant innovations in international relations, but were forced to leave the field, and were then forgotten by those who maintain the record of the discipline's past (Murphy 1996). This was the case with my predecessor at Wellesley, the College's first teacher of International Relations, Emily Greene Balch, the 1946 Nobel Peace Prize winner. In her day, she was certainly as important a figure, both intellectually and politically, as her male contemporaries who held similar views, played similar political roles, and whose names the field still remembers, men such as Norman Angell, John A. Hobson, and David Mitrany. The conventional explanation of the scholarly amnesia about Balch's role sees her exclusion from a standard academic career (being fired by Wellesley during the First World War), and, hence, the decision of the field to forget her, to be the result of her socialism and her pacifism, not her gender. Yet, Follett's career certainly suggests more field-specific gender biases at play. Like Balch, Follett never found a secure home teaching International Relations. She, too, encountered the discrimination against women that went with the masculine diplomatic culture maintained in the League of Nations (Miller 1991).

Today's women activists who are reshaping global politics—Lori Wallach, Alice Tepper-Marlin, the leaders of the International Women's Health Movement, the promoters of the Women in Development agenda— also may be forgotten by International Relations scholars a generation from now. That is, if the field's unusually masculine culture—linked to its special connection to the masculine realm of the military—remains. However, since the end of the Cold War, women within the armed forces of the industrialized countries, especially the United States, have been working an epochal change in the gender identity of the military (Katzenstein 1998).

Unfortunately, new security threats to the most powerful state appeared before the slow transformation of the gender identity of the military was completed. The prominent anti-feminist activist, Phyllis Schlafly (2002), wrote:

> One of the unintended consequences of the terrorist attack on the World Trade Center on September 11, 2001 was the dashing of feminist hopes to make America a gender-neutral or androgynous society . . . the feminists have been demanding that we terminate the discrimination that excludes women from "career advancement" in every

section of the US Armed Forces, assuring us that hand-to-hand combat is a relic of the past and that all our wars will now involve only pulling triggers and pushing buttons. Tell that to our troops who trudged over land mines and jagged rocks [in Afghanistan] where there are not even any roads.[3]

J. Ann Tickner (2002), with a great deal more analysis and better evidence, also concluded that the terrorist attacks would set back the transformations with the American military, and the culture at large.

If the marginalization of the voices of women concerned with transformation of international affairs goes further, if the voices of the critical liberal women activists who have been remaking the contemporary world order also become ignored, it will deeply undermine the larger historical project of liberal internationalism.

Follett would have understood the problem. The history of globalization and governance, of world institutions, is one that proves her argument about the creativity that can be generated by difference. Most of the new ideas that have "saved" capitalism, or, at least, that have advanced the liberal internationalist project of facilitating the step-wise globalization of capitalist industry, have been advocated by social movements of the previously marginalized and have been invented by men and women organically linked to those movements. Women's movements are providing that creativity for global governance in the Information Age, and the liberal internationalist project will suffer if they are ignored.

6 International institutions, decolonization, and "development"[1]

Liberal forgetting also happens with the contributions made by other movements of the marginalized including the movements of people in the less industrialized world. Decolonization contributed to the stability of the post-Second World War order in the "Free World," and movements for decolonization thus contributed to the liberal internationalist project. This chapter is concerned with the connections between international institutions and the political movements to end empire and to generalize the benefits of industrialization, in a world constrained by the dynamics of population growth, resource depletion, and technological change—and with why these perceived benefits have not emerged in the ways that these political movements expected.

Here, I treat modern international institutions as a means of regulating the "lateral pressure," the pressure toward empire, generated by the industrial system. Within the Third World, the involvement of international institutions in decolonization and development helped both to create, and constantly to reinforce, civil society at the national level. As a result, the recent crises in international institutions and those in much of the Third World are intimately linked.

International institutions as a partial answer to lateral pressure

Population, *resources*, and *technology* are the "master variables" in Nazli Choucri and Robert North's (1975; Choucri, North, and Yamakage 1992) studies that update the classical analyses of nineteenth-century imperialism; shifts in these variable explain the great power wars that bracket what I have called the "Interimperial Order" of the Second Industrial Revolution. Both technological change (which appears to be self-reinforcing) and population growth (which in the industrial age has been reinforced by technological change and advances in medicine) accelerate demands for resources, and for further economic growth, create lateral pressure, "that tendency of great power toward geographic expansion."

The term is useful for studies of center-periphery relations. It lets us see a similarity among cases of great-power expansions achieved by different means. Expansion can come through neocolonialism, informal empire, or the "humanitarian intervention" that allowed Britain to hold the Gold Coast throughout the first half of the twentieth century and which may allow the United States to control resource-rich parts of Africa and Southwest Asia for as many decades in this century (compare Sassen 2003). It can also come through the sort of economic integration championed by liberal internationalists since Adam Smith. Functionalist cooperation could be, as John A. Hobson, Emily Greene Balch, Mary Parker Follett, and David Mitrany all believed, an alternative solution to the problems that generated late nineteenth-century imperialism. It was a way to respond to lateral pressure without further harming working people in the industrialized world and without further marginalizing the people of Africa, Asia, and Latin America.

As early as 1851 a complete elaboration of the functionalist argument appeared in the work of a liberal internationalist system-builder. John Wright, who described himself as an Anglo-Irish promoter of railroad development in Illinois, called his tract: *Christianity and Commerce, the Natural Results of the Geographical Progression of the Railways or A Treatise on the Advantage of the Universal Extension of Railways in our Colonies and Other Countries, and the Probability of Increased National Intercommunication Leading to the Early Restoration of the Land of Promise to the Jews.*

Wright proposed an agreement among the statesmen and scientists visiting London's Great Industrial Exhibition to establish a universal rail network. The resulting global system of railways would provide the infrastructure for a global market in industrial goods, and in the raw materials needed to produce them.

Britain's then-current policy of promoting free trade would finally be able to assure the greatest possible prosperity not only for Britain, but also for the whole world. Anticipating twentieth-century arguments about development, Wright promised Africa, India, East Asia and Latin America that the plan, "cannot fail to soon place all alike on an equality with the advanced kingdoms of the world, and in many instances, render their sources of wealth superior" (Wright 1851: 12).

Finally, of course, Wright promised to usher in the millennium of peace, even in the unstable Arab provinces, where a new prosperous state based on freedom of religion and freedom of emigration would replace Ottoman rule and thus, in that sense, restore "the Land of Promise to the Jews."

Wright told those who would dismiss him as a utopian that the promise:

> of producing such mighty results and at the same time uniting the commerce of East and West in one common bond of union may at first appear speculative, even impossible. But when we reflect how the United States, less than two centuries ago a mere penal settlement of divers European nations, has acquired a degree of power and

importance, bidding fair to surpass that of Greece or Rome . . . in less than four score years since the Declaration of Independence . . . should we hesitate?

(Wright 1851: 13).

Perhaps not, but as Abraham Lincoln, that more celebrated promoter of Illinois' railways (and likely a student of the same rhetoric book), discovered, even America's exceptional history would not prove that integration was simple under the functionalist's, or any other's logic. Wright certainly failed to anticipate the American Civil War let alone the great-power wars that would punctuate the evolution toward a liberal world order.

It is perhaps even more tragically ironic, given the subsequent history of imperialism, decolonization, and development, that Wright, an Irishman, would, in 1851, so completely embrace the British policy of laissez-faire. *Christianity and Commerce* appeared immediately after the worst year of the Great Hunger that reduced Ireland's population by two-thirds, one-half of that by immigration, the other by starvation, the most devastating famine ever to hit any nation in Europe. When crop failures began, in 1845, Britain's Tory government:

> [Q]uickly ordered supplies of American corn shipped to Ireland . . . Public works projects were devised to give employment to men, women, and children . . . More dramatically, [Prime Minister] Peel proposed a genuinely radical and politically courageous reform. For years, British farmers (and, more to the point British landowners) had enjoyed government-sanctioned protections in the form of high taxes on imported grains. The so-called Corn Laws were a linchpin of Britain's agricultural economy and indeed its social structure, for the land-owning aristocracy profited immensely from protection against foreign competition . . . those landed aristocrats also happened to be the core of Peel's party. The prime minister, however, decided that the Corn Laws would have to go, that the emergency in Ireland demanded nothing less.

(Golway 1997: 8)

Peel paid the political price. His party lost the elections, and the Whigs, the long-time advocates of removal of the Corn Laws, came to power.

For the Irish, nothing could have been worse. The liberal fundamentalists of the new government saw the failure of the Irish potato crops as a godsend, a way to demonstrate the validity of their absolute reliance on the market. They closed down the public works projects and ended public distribution of grain. The Irish starved, but liberals proved their point. As London's administrator "closed up the food depots he argued that it was the 'only way to prevent people from becoming habitually dependent on government'" (Golway 1997: 11).

Functionalists since John Wright have rarely equaled his enthusiasm, especially if they reflected on the nineteenth-century famines and the origins of the American Civil War and the subsequent battles involving industrial powers (for example, Wilson 1898). Yet, late nineteenth-century function- alists believed that the evidence for their views was ever increasing. Even during the First World War—the cataclysm so often used as evidence for more pessimistic views—British promoters of the functionalist vision on the democratic left, Hobson (1915) and Woolf (1916), worked to recon- cile this vision with contemporary, more legalist, proposals for a league of peace. Later, of course, Mitrany offered his views as an alternative to what he considered a fruitless search for ideal constitutional principles for inter- national peace, as embodied in the League and UN Charters (Mitrany 1933, 1943, 1948; Joyce 1945).

After the Second World War, when European statesmen actually attempted to follow the functionalist logic, a more nuanced neofunction- alism appeared. National governments would not simply transfer powers, bit by bit, to supranational authorities in a fit of absence of mind; instead, government leaders have to be placed in situations where their own inter- ests in retaining power lead them to transfer state functions increasingly to the regional level. The scientists and professional administrators, on whom functionalists have always relied, will have to be politically sophis- ticated and they will still need farsighted actions by high-level politicians at critical junctures (Haas 1964: 47–50).

Yet, even while neofunctionalists see some conflict as inherent in the process of greater international functional integration, they still do not see all the sources of conflict that critics of classical liberal political economy recognize. Some are especially important in relation to decolonization and development. First, as the critics of the industrial system have long recog- nized, the revolutionary productivity of its "new economy of force and knowledge," to use Hobson's language (1912: 74), always comes at the expense of dignity of some members of society. Moreover, as Choucri and North argue, it has always come at the expense of the environment. Finally, despite the useful myths that sometimes engage those of us who are social scientists, men and women are motivated by specific, concrete aspirations, including, for some, the desire to maintain traditional social relations threat- ened by industrialism. Despite the compensation offered by economic growth, people may fight when technology threatens to transform their lives, as Karl Polanyi (1957) forcefully argued (and see Chapter 2).

At times, international institutions have helped break the link between lateral pressure and these sources of conflict. Nevertheless, the history of industry and international organization confirms E. E. Schattschneider's (1975: 60) dictum, "What happens in politics *depends on the way in which people are divided* into factions, parties, groups, classes, etc." When an insti- tution provides an outlet for engagement in one conflict rather than others, the displacement of the conflicts not pursued may be more important to the resulting social order than is the resolution of the one conflict that the parties play out. Throughout the Cold War, the world organizations diminished conflict within the system of Western industrialized nations and their less-industrialized dependencies. However, in the last generation, as the UN system has become subject to a tighter version of the liberal economic logic at the base of the functionalist vision, it has become less effective.

How world organizations became involved in "development"

Governments gave the League of Nations some responsibilities for the less industrialized world simply to serve the interests of those in the already industrialized nations. League members often discussed access to the raw materials, and the League reports on the topic abounded (Greaves 1931; Kopp 1941). The reports argued that the South's importance was likely to *increase* over time as industrial states needed more and more raw materials that could only be found in the colonies. The International Labor Organization (ILO) had its greatest success in the interwar years within what we would now call "newly industrializing countries," including Japan. The ILO helped raise labor standards in Japan, and, thus, helped forge a coalition between, on the one hand, labor and business groups in the industrialized world—who wanted the newly industrializing states to abandon their "more competitive" labor practices—with the labor and nationalist movements in the periphery, on the other hand. In Japan, the advocates of adhering to global labor standards included those who wished to ease the burden of factory workers, the "mothers of the country's soldiers" (Perigord 1926: 177; Yoshiro 1968: 74–75).

The League's most significant involvement with the less industrialized world came through the system of mandates, whose norms were extended in the early years of the United Nations to become a generalized regime for universal decolonization. Robert H. Jackson (1990) argues that liberal internationalism, from Adam Smith onward, has entailed the norm of decolonization. Liberal arguments in favor of continued colonization always rely on some argument about a specific, temporary infirmity of the people in question, some reason why they are not, at this time, ready for self-rule. Thus, for example, at the time of the Irish Hunger, the "moral evil of the selfish, perverse, and turbulent character of the people" explained why they should be subjects of liberal fundamentalist rule from London (Golway 1997: 12). Some scholars (including Greaves 1931: 169) even argue that the League's idea of mandates—which justified colonies only as long as natives were incapable of self-government in the increasingly complex, industrial world—became a world political program only due to the strength of the democratic left within the imperial powers.

Nevertheless, it is equally true, as one of the intellectual leaders of the anticolonial movement in Africa and the Caribbean, C. L. R. James, argues that even in colonies where decolonization appeared to be the non-violent transfer of authority from Europeans to a Europeanized native elite, mass movements forced the hands of the colonial governments. Moreover, they, at least initially, provided the native elite with its legitimacy (James 1977). What the League and UN systems did was to allow coherent alliances between these various anti-imperialist forces to form (recall Chapter 2).

The postwar anti-colonial movements put decolonization on the agenda of the international agencies with the support of the Roosevelt and Truman administrations, as James Mayall (Mayall 1990: 116) concludes:

> It was American liberalism . . . which set the stage on which the drama of anti-colonial nationalism was enacted . . . in 1945 the Americans regarded the British Empire as a major obstacle to their plans for an open, non-discriminatory world order. . . . In the early postwar years, before the Cold War changed their priorities, they also lent their support at the United Nations to Third World states in their campaign to speed up the process of decolonization, and to extend the principle of international accountability from the trusteeship territories to the remaining colonial possessions of the European powers.

Although the Cold War increased American sympathy for the colonial powers, the competition between the United States and the Soviet Union assured that the aspirations of the anti-colonial movements would remain central to all the UN agencies.

The organizations' impact

The UN system provided a variety of supports to nationalist movements demanding an end to colonialism. The international agencies became forums in which the nationalists could speak and demand independence. Secretariats supported the production and wide dissemination of reports that promoted the presumption that colonialism was a holdover of a less progressive past. The United Nations increasingly demanded and received the right to investigate the readiness of non-self-governing territories for self-government. In one later case, Namibia, the United Nations even defined itself as the granter of independence, in direct opposition to the colonial power. To those schooled in the great power politics, these forms of inter-national support may seem incidental. Nevertheless, successful nationalist leaders of the postwar era almost all argue that they were critical.[2]

This broad, transnational, anti-colonial coalition, which had appeared by the early 1950s, also became a social force promoting "development," the system of designing projects, transferring funds and experts, building roads, schools, hospitals, etc., and then evaluating the results.[3] Notwithstanding John Wright's prediction, international functional cooperation has not made most African, Asian, and Latin American nations, "on an equality with the advanced kingdoms of the world." Yet, Third World governments and development professionals operating aid bureaucracies (especially those operating in the field) tend to agree about the positive impact of this project. As A. F. Robertson concludes in his ethnographic study of the entire system (from donors, to intergovernmental intermediaries, to recipients), the insiders' justifications sound populist, and people involved in those activities recognize their justifications to be contradictory (Robertson 1984). "Development," a professionalized, hierarchical, top-down process, whose centers of power lie literally half a world away from its clients, is designed to give "the people" what they want: longer lives, better health, more chances for their children.

From this perspective of development as a populist project, the international institutions have been somewhat successful. As a result, in some of the many states created in the second half of the twentieth century, development activities helped incorporate the masses into the, often disappointing, political systems that they or their parents had fought to create.

Populist development has done this in two ways. One involves successful appeals to interests. Third World governments *have* provided resources to lengthen lives, improve health, and improve the chances of the next generation—all of which have helped increase the state's legitimacy. Perhaps more significantly, the project of development has appealed to Third World aspirations. "Development" turns the popular masses into a cadre fulfilling an historical project, John Maynard Keynes's project and John Wright's project, the project of making all people "secure of the comforts and necessities of the body" (Keynes 1971: 21; see Chapter 2 above) and all nations "on an equality with the advanced kingdoms of the world."

In shaping aspirations toward the project of material prosperity and equality with the "advanced" states, Third World governments and their allies have succeeded in emphasizing particular lines of political conflict while obscuring others. As Mayall (1990: 103–105) argues, the development system helped Americans stabilize the liberal world under American leadership, overcoming the imperial trading blocs and raw materials problems of the interwar period. As Jackson (1990: 112–118) argues, for the governments of many of the post-colonial "quasi-states," the overseas transfers provided by development projects have become essential for stability, and certainly for their legitimacy. Thus, the roles played by postwar world organizations in decolonization and development should be thought of as part of a transnational political system regulating conflict in the vast international economic region that was formed among the industrialized states with market economies and their Third World dependencies.

The 1970s' crises of international institutions and of populist development

Of course, only in a few parts of the world, only in some of the newly industrializing countries, perhaps only in South Korea and Taiwan, were all the aspirations for populist development achieved in this epoch after the Second World War. In other parts of the Third World, for many years, these aspirations still remained reasonable and politically important because governments with the development ideology remained in power and they remained capable of serving the less demanding "populist" welfare interests of their citizens. By serving those interests, Third World governments kept anti-modernist forces in check. The conflicts over raw materials essential to the industrial states, the conflicts that had so worried the League of Nations, were held in check as well, at least until the oil crisis of 1973 to 1974.

The oil crisis not only called into question the stability of the postwar resources regimes, it transformed the entire system of institutions involved with development. The crisis began when a group of governments, mostly of states brought into existence under the League and UN decolonization regimes, linked some of their non-development-related aspirations to their relatively new, sovereign control over resources. Arab OPEC countries deployed the "oil weapon" in their October War with Israel. In the wake of the resulting rapid rise in world prices, much of the Third World plunged into a 30-year-long depression that has cast serious doubt on the reasonableness of any development aspirations. In a number of Third World states, the combined debt and aid crises of the 1980s ended the system of small net transfers from the First World. That led to Third World budget cuts that challenged government stability and populist legitimacy. This was especially true in oil-rich countries that had not planned for the plunging oil prices of the 1980s.

One of the most significant achievements of Western statecraft in the 1980s was the Reagan administration's success at breaking the commodity power of the Arab oil producers (Augelli and Murphy 1988: 154–178). Similarly, the major achievement of the First Gulf War was to further break any link between non-development-related aspirations and the control of oil. These events reversed factors that had undermined the power of international development institutions to manage the inherent conflict between Western industrialized nations and their less industrialized dependencies. OPEC no longer had the oil weapon and high oil prices no longer impeded Third World growth.

Yet, the economic crisis and the crisis of international institutions remain, undermining the populist legitimacy of the governments of Third World "quasi-states." This, too, was largely a matter of statecraft. In the 1980s, the Reagan administration sharply reduced US direct contributions to most Third World governments, all but eliminated new US contributions to the main bodies of the UN system, and even sharply reduced the rate of new US support to the Bretton Woods institutions. Moreover, the Reagan administration broke off discussions with the Third World about any paths to development other than laissez-faire liberalism and it put the international institutions on notice that the United States would undermine those institutions of international civil society supporting a much broader agenda (Augelli and Murphy 1988: 185–189).

The UN agencies, in turn, increasingly adopted an analysis of Third World economic problems that focused on Third World *domestic policies* as impediments to prosperity, the so-called "Washington Consensus" (see Chapter 8); in the view of many of the international agencies in the 1980s, Third World governments became the problem rather than the solution.[4] Many Western bilateral donors supported this analysis and American policy in general, by joining in programs coordinating the increasingly limited aid available to most Third World states through "policy dialogue." Such "dialogue" communicated preferences for laissez-faire policies, and for the abolition of populist welfare-oriented government spending to Third World governments just as forcefully as they were through the "structural adjustment" programs of the Bretton Woods agencies. In effect, the Reagan administration initiated what has become the standard practice of using the entire flow of assistance to Third World countries as a single pool of incentives to adopt liberal fundamentalist economic policies (Augelli 1986). The shift has been the twentieth-century equivalent of Britain's policy about-face toward Ireland in 1846 from welfare-oriented Tory *noblesse oblige* to market-obsessed Whig laissez-faire.

Future historians will have to assess whether the effects have been the same. Certainly, we know that inequality grew at an unprecedented rate in the 1980s and early 1990s (see Chapter 10), many regions stagnated, and, in many parts of the world (including Africa and the former Soviet Union), the twentieth-century trend of ever-increasing life expectancy reversed, in some cases, quite sharply. However, it would be hard to attribute a specific proportion of these outcomes to the undermining of the populist project of "development."

For a generation, the forces trying to reassert that project have been weak. The few continuing development activities oriented toward a social-democratic perspective and supported by the Nordic countries, the Netherlands, Canada, and the UN have not had a similar impact on liberal fundamentalist development policies, largely because they have not been backed by as many resources. It is true that the UNDP's orientation toward "human development" began at the same time as the Reagan and Thatcher revolutions, and that UNICEF's reorientation toward seeing development as a matter of human rights is a recent development (Oestreich 1998). Nevertheless, the funds committed to those programs have never neared the level of the support "coordinated" to neoliberal ends through "policy dialogue." In fact, due to the power of an anti-internationalist, liberal fundamentalist Congress, even the Clinton administration did little to reverse the rejection of populist development that began with Reagan.

Consider just the issue of providing support to the UN system. As one part of its overall program, the Reagan administration backed efforts by Republican members of Congress to encourage administrative reform in the

UN by withholding a certain percentage of US dues to various inter-governmental agencies until they complied with American requests. Ironically, the initial proposal came from the moderate Senator from Kansas, Nancy Kassebaum, and a widely respected internationalist who was called as "Africa's greatest friend in the Republican Party." She made the proposal, in large part, to assure a higher proportion of UN spending took place in the field. Other Republicans much less sympathetic to the UN quickly hijacked the idea. For almost twenty years Congress with-held an ever greater proportion of UN dues, despite increasing UN compliance with ever more restrictive American conditions. Table 6.1 tells the story as it applies to the regular budget of the UN, only one part of the sharply reduced US commitment to the old populist project of development.

Reagan and every president since has promised to pay the US's immediate arrears as well as the accumulated debt. In the US's initial attempt to gain international support for the post-September 11 "War on Terrorism," George W. Bush convinced Congress to repay a significant part of the debt. George H. W. Bush (who left office in January 1992) had a small effect on the trend. The Reagan and Clinton administrations place the blame for non-payment on Congress, whose lower house must initiate all spending measures and whose upper house must approve any ambassadorial appointment and any treaty by a two-thirds majority. It would be more accurate to say that neither Reagan nor Clinton chose to expend political capital to persuade conservative members of Congress to allow the US to meet its financial obligations.

There is a sad irony in the shift in US policy after the tragedy of the Al Qaeda attacks. The failure of the older populist project of development helped create the political space into which Islamists have moved in the era of neoliberal fundamentalism. The resentment of the hijackers had been fueled by the post-1970s failures of the Egyptian and Saudi regimes, by the era of stagnant oil prices and rising populations, the dismantling of the Arab welfare state, and the failure of the Third World alliance. Tariq Ali (2003) sees the recent decades of neoliberalism triumphant as of a piece with the Cold War era Western policy of backing the development states of

Table 6.1 Arrears to regular UN budget, 1982–2002

Year	US arrears (million $US)	Total arrears (million $US)	US arrears as percentage of total
1982	3.4	147.9	2.3
1987	252.8	353.4	71.5
1992	239.5	500.6	47.8
1997	373.2	473.6	78.8
2002	446.0	1111.0	40.1

Source: Global Policy Forum 2002 http://globalpolicy.igc.org/finance/tables/

vicious anti-Soviet dictators; in the Middle East, he sees both as matters of imperial policy aimed at securing the key natural resource of the Automobile and Jet Age. Perhaps, but the earlier policy was less contradict-ory, and for many of the citizens of the dictatorial dependencies, the promise of "development" made it more benign.

Nevertheless, while undercutting the populist legitimacy of many Third World governments, global institutions and the Western powers have continued to support the development of civil society in the Third World. The delegitimation of populist, development-oriented states in the 1980s and into the 1990s often accompanied the creation or reintroduction of pluralist political systems in which parties really compete for popular support. For those of us with an interest in Africa, the connection between the two phenomena has been especially close. It was hard to watch the recent wave of democratization without getting a sense that some outgoing parties left with some relief; "democratization" often looked like "giving up." In most states where shifts to liberal democracy have taken place in recent years, what had originally been populist, development- and welfare-oriented governments have had to make way for new governments with a laissez-faire development orientation. In many countries, especially those where protracted, internationalized conflicts preceded democratization (in Central America and the Caribbean, Southern Africa, East Timor) the UN played a key role in the transition, providing aid in running elections, observing them, and certifying their fairness (Joyner 1999).

New development issues for international institutions

It is, yet, unclear whether this further opening of civil society within the Third World will continue. If it does, then the range of political alterna-tives in most Third World states will continue to include advocates of laissez-faire as well as anti-modernist parties that reject the liberal-functionalist vision of an expanding world of peace and prosperity through industrial capitalism. What is especially unclear at this point is whether international institutions will develop the same openness to different world-views as may become apparent in the Third World. Will it be possible for less industrialized states with anti-modernist orientations to find the same degree of support within international institutions enjoyed by less industrialized states with the approved, laissez-faire orientation?

If we think back to Choucri and North's "master variables," we can find the three areas where a further development of international civil society might occur. The first involves issues of *population*, where a general interest of the industrialized countries in regulating migrants from the Third World may mean that international support for family planning and migration policies can be separated from the ideology of Third World recipient governments. The second concerns *resources*, where the issue of equal access by all industrial powers, debated since the League, still provides a basis for First World support of the Third World, despite the "defeat" of OPEC. If, for example, the recent establishment of direct US administration of oil-rich Iraq means restricted European access to Gulf oil, we might begin to see that industrial center becoming as generous a supporter of Third World alternatives to liberal fundamentalism as the Soviet Union was throughout the Cold War. Finally, there is the *technology* "bads" of pollution, where North–South cooperation is usually essential to build effective international regimes.

Yet, "development," per se, the ever-expanding populist project for the legitimation of Third World governments supported by the industrial powers, may go the way of decolonization. Analysts a generation hence may look on it as just another historically significant, but temporary, issue of global governance, a way of establishing manageable political cleavages among those with more and those with less power over the master variables.

7 What the Third World wanted

The meaning of the NIEO

Briefly, in the 1970s, Third World oil producers controlled one of the "master variables" of world politics, which encouraged all Third World governments to gain greater control over their own development by pressing for reforms in the world economic organizations. The reformed institutions would, they believed, usher in a "New International Economic Order." In Chapter 4, I argued the Third World has been marginalized in current debates about global governance due to unsympathetic elite interpretations of these events in the 1970s. The last chapter outlined the thirty-year crisis in the system for resolving the inherent differences between the privileged industrialized world and its more populous peripheries. The NIEO would have provided an alternative to that long crisis, one rooted in the same critical liberal tradition that informed the postwar Free World Order. The thinking behind the NIEO, the "NIEO ideology," was relatively conventional, and it responded to real problems, something that most policy analysts in the US never understood. This misunderstanding convinced successive US administrations to avoid serious discussion of the NIEO proposals, which doomed negotiations that may have led to something preferable to the past generation of North–South conflict.

The conventional wisdom in the North about the South's NIEO proposals

Those in the North who thought the most about the NIEO proposals tended first to react to them with judgments rather than explanations. Those few who sympathized with proposals for the NIEO spent little time trying to understand why Third World officials supported the project. The views of the unsympathetic are doubly interesting because they reflect judgment that most American policy-makers shared.[1] Different groups developed separate "state-centered Realist" and "liberal fundamentalist" versions of this conventional wisdom. Both versions assumed that policy makers rationally seek to increase their wealth and power. Rather than being a disinterested affirmation of a particular ethic, Third World promulgation of the NIEO was an example of a traditional alliance among nations seizing opportunities for material and political advantages offered by the postwar international system and especially by the existence of the United Nations. More significantly, both versions held that Third World governments chose their economic analyses and moral principles in order to blame their own inability to solve crucial domestic economic problems upon the international system. They did not choose their analysis because good evidence and argument could be given to demonstrate that the global economic structure was biased against poorer nations, but because choosing to say so deflected internal or external criticism of failing development policies. Some liberals proposed an explanation of the "actual" fundamental conflict between the unsympathetic United States and Third World countries: the unpopularity of most Third World governments explained their economic incompetence. The fundamental difference between the United States and the Third World was that Americans pursued effective, rational international economic policies that serve the interests of all people around the world equally, but that Southern governments have only the particular economic interests of a local elite in mind.

Many conclusions based on the conventional wisdom could have been investigated at length, but few were. Robert Tucker, in *Inequality of Nations* (1977), for example, based his conclusions on the NIEO texts presented in the United Nations in the early 1970s and he used nineteenth- and twentieth-century classics of Western international law and politics to clarify the deeper meaning of those documents that appeared contradictory or ambiguous on the surface. Tucker could have checked his interpretation with some simple research to verify that (1) the themes that he identified from the NIEO texts were the ones that actually formed the core of the Third World's position, and that (2) Third World officials knew and accepted the classic Realist lessons.

Daniel Patrick Moynihan (1975, 1978), the combative US ambassador to the UN, made the different argument that most Third World officials had encountered Fabian ideas during their schooling. Moynihan believed that we can remove ideological masks by demonstrating the ideologues' unwillingness to accept all the implications of the theories they espouse. His goal as ambassador was to demonstrate the undemocratic and inegalitarian propensities of those officials who appeared to proclaim social democratic and egalitarian ideals. He demanded justifications for any Third World policies that conflicted with what he believed were the South's true interests and he encouraged the United States government to make concessions to meet the Third World part way in order to encourage shifts in the Third World position, which he expected would reveal baser interests.

Moynihan's experiments were indecisive. His colleagues pointed out that few of them had been exposed to, let alone advocated, Fabian principles and they said that the few American concessions were beside the point since they heralded no significant shift in US policy. Moynihan's only effect was to disprove the hypothesis that the Third World position represented wholehearted advocacy of social democratic principles, something of little surprise to social democrats.[2]

Other Northern critics argued that it would not be politically wise to test their own, more complex, understandings of Third World motivations. After a frustrating attempt to work with colleagues at the UN Conference on Trade and Development (UNCTAD), University of Chicago economist, Harry Johnson (1977) decided that they, and all other supporters of the NIEO, were simply incompetent. Johnson believed that self-interest assured that UNCTAD staffers and African, Asian, and Latin American officials would never admit their misunderstanding of "economic realities."

Martin Bronfenbrenner, a Chicago-trained economist who prided himself in rooting out student radicals and marshaling the field of economics to isolate any departments that supported them, (1976) went further. He noted the irrationality of some Third World proposals from the standpoint of his own, fundamentalist, version of liberal trade theory and pointed to themes and language in the NIEO proposals similar to those the Nazis had used to justify their policies. He, therefore, equated the NIEO proposals with fascism and the tactics of their advocates with those employed by the Mafia. The South's views were clear, and that there was no need for further debate: the North must simply support more-reasonable alternatives to the Southern demands in the hope that the South's mercenary interests could be satisfied short of bringing down the liberal economic system.

Stephen D. Krasner (1981) offered a less alarming picture. Yet, for political reasons, his analysis was less susceptible to verification than that of the economists. They argued that it would be pointless to engage in the political action needed to expose the malign interests that the NIEO ideology masked. Krasner believed it would be harmful.

Krasner began with the usual assumption that leaders act rationally in seeking wealth and power, but he put those assumptions in a particularly state-centered Realist form. For example, he assumed that while foreign aid might facilitate economic development, leaders always prefer to rely on domestic resources. He argued that the modal Third World government, given its lack of political modernization and its peripheral position in the international system, benefited from supporting the NIEO. The typical African, Asian, or Latin American government is unable to organize the *domestic* resources necessary for development. However, because it has so little power, and thus can gain little help through traditional bilateral bargaining, a Third World government will try to gain the resources from other states through international organizations that give weak states an inflated impact on decisions. To organize their joint action within international organizations, Krasner argued, Third World governments adopted dependency theorists' ideas about international exploitation. These ideas further benefited the weak states by providing justifications for their failed attempts to pursue development using their own resources.

Krasner easily illustrated the internal weakness of the average Third World state and its relative international weakness. (However, he was not able to explain why the leadership of the Third World came from the strongest states—domestically and internationally—in each Third World region.) The fact that the politics of the NIEO had gone on in international organizations was incontrovertible. Moreover, at least a few Third World leaders themselves made claims similar to Krasner's about how much governments had learned from dependency theories. Nevertheless, the more important parts of Krasner's argument, particularly his assumptions about the objective motivations of governments and about the preference any government should have about ways to solve economic problems, were harder to prove. Even so, Northern states could have tested those assumptions during the NIEO debate itself. In particular, the assumption that one irreducible underlying cause of Third World support for the NIEO program was a desire for greater power could have been verified by a unified Northern effort to satisfy the South's specific demands to see if the hypothesized power-lust reappeared in the guise of new demands once the old were met.

Krasner recommended against such experiments. He argued against even small concessions if they would mean that the Third World would gain additional influence in those international organizations crucial to the liberal economic regimes that were under stress in the 1970s. A state-centered Realist theory tells us that international regimes are the most stable when they accurately reflect the power structure underlying them. Institutions that give too much influence to the less powerful would be dangerously illegitimate (Krasner 1974, 1980). Consequently, a Northern policy-maker who accepted Krasner's theory would ignore NIEO proposals and refuse to make any concessions.

Thus, the conceptions many in the United States had of how Third World leaders came to adopt and support the NIEO made resolution of the 1970s North–South conflict impossible. Some of the most trusted social scientists and policy-makers drew conclusions about the NIEO ideology, that were peculiarly inadequate. While those conclusions were testable, no Northern policy-maker who trusted their authors would want to test them.

Alternative assumptions

What if we begin with the alternative, Gramscian or Institutionalist, assumption that learning and ideology have important, relatively autonomous roles in politics? Rather than making the overly simple assumption that national governments always seek to increase their wealth and power, what happens if we assume that policy-makers pursue a variety of different goals given to them by the *specific* ideology that they hold at the time? That ideology both defines problems and suggests lines of action. Officials may amend their views when they find that a previously preferred way of acting does not serve to achieve a desired goal, and when another interpretation, consistent with most of their ideals, is available for them to adopt. In that sense, political leaders are rational and they do learn; but they learn without having prior commitments either to Realist theories of international politics or to liberal fundamentalist views of economic policy, the prior commitments that the Northern conventional wisdom about the NIEO assumed.

In addition, the ideologies governing behavior may change when officials confront fundamentally new problems not accounted for in their currently held beliefs. In that situation, they choose to believe the available interpretation most consistent with their goals. Operational ideologies also may change when officials see new opportunities to achieve their goals due to (say) the weakening of their opponents. In these instances, policymakers will adopt an available political analysis that promises the ability to exploit the new opportunity. Again, officials adopt a set of ideas and act on those ideas, not on the "interest" that led them to adopt new ideas. Indeed, they only know that "interest," and are thus able to change the way they pursue it, when they have adopted certain beliefs as their own. It is these beliefs that motivate their action.

This claim also helps explain the existence and stability of international regimes, and it does so in the traditional, functionalist, way, the way that Mitrany or Follett would explain them. Stable regimes are not matters of balancing power; they are the result of successful collective learning and shared understandings of policy problems. International regimes exist to solve specific problems, to provide a specific collective good, something that all who contribute to the regime benefit from and recognize as important. Regimes reflect a consensus among those who contribute to them. Building regimes is synonymous with building such a consensus. Other things being equal, regimes remain stable as long as they provide that collective good. We cannot avoid unstable regimes just by assuring each government gets just as much out of the international institution as they put in. We avoid unstable international regimes maintaining the underlying consensus and by maintaining consensus when the regime encounters unanticipated problems (Scott 1977). As most democratic theorists, including Follett, would suggest, one way to assure that most of the problems a regime could generate have been anticipated would be to consult as many people as possible, including all those that will be affected by the regime (Tinbergen 1976: 82, and see Chapter 5). Other things being equal, we should try to include all the states affected by a regime in any discussions about their reform.

The core of the NIEO ideology

Seen in this light, the story about what Third World governments want to achieve through their embrace of the NIEO ideology logically begins in the 1940s. Even though Asian, Latin American, and African states agreed with many of the principles underlying the "new economic order," the Free World Order, then being framed, its framers did not take all of the Third World's concerns into account. In the interwar years and throughout the Second World War, most of the governments of Latin America and the semi-autonomous local governments in Asia and Africa pursued development plans supported by a whole range of trade and currency restrictions (Gardner 1964: 109–132, 195–216; Bell 1956: 260–263). Consequently, during the War and at its end, what would later be Third World governments preferred creating postwar international economic institutions that would allow national regulation of international economic relations while assuring those national regulations conflicted with each other as little as possible.[3] In the early 1940s, this vision of the postwar institutions was the dominant view around the world. Representatives of the neutral government of Argentina and the Congress Party in India could find what Fred Block (1977) calls "national capitalist" spokesmen from Britain and Australia agreeing that international institutions should approve of national regulation of the economy and should only serve to make the regulations that different governments desired, compatible. In addition, of course, Soviet officials, representing an economy that required regulation, sang the same tune. However, that tune was not pleasing to the most powerful people in the most powerful country. The most significant American policy-makers imagined postwar international economic institutions as progressively abolishing national restrictions on the world economy rather than merely regulating them (Gardner 1964: 195).

The American vision became the blueprint for the Free World institutions. Socialist states whose economies required regulation never became active members. States that had been wealthy before the War went along because the United States, under the influence of critical liberal internationalists gave the previously rich market states the opportunity to reconstruct their economies. Such, at least, was the position the *Economist* took in the name of Europe after the Marshall Plan was developed (July 17, 1948: 90) and after having ridiculed the United States throughout the months between the end of the War and the development of the Plan (*Economist* October 26, 1945: 652; November 22, 1947: 828). Latin America and the independent and colonial areas in Asia and Africa accepted the system, while unconvinced of its value for them. Nevertheless, with no alternative for managing the global money, finance, and trade problems that they, as much as the Europeans or North Americans, wanted managed globally, they accepted the American view.

A new problem then confronted Asian, African, and Latin American policy-makers in the late 1940s, the problem that led to the adoption of the ideas that became the core of the NIEO ideology. How should they argue for those restrictions upon strictly liberal international exchange that they might want to continue to use as part of their development plans? The ideological milieu of the 1940s provided two possible justifications.

First, a "scientific" principle that such restrictions were acceptable if econ-omists could show them to be an efficient way to achieve specific goals such as national industrial development. Keynes and many other critical liberals appealed to this principle when they supported the "national capi-talist" vision of postwar regimes (Block 1977: 7–8). Keynes's last major speech, given at the first World Bank–IMF governors' meeting, exempli-fies the argument (Horsefield 1969: 123). Alternatively, there was a justification based upon the rights of sovereign states and their duties toward one another. These ideas were new; they had been developed during international discussions about the creation of the United Nations and the operation of the wartime "United and Associated Nations," the anti-fascist alliance.

However, unlike appeals to economic science, appeals to the rights and duties of states did not demand the most economically rational policies possible. A state's policies had only to be the ones that could achieve some set of goals that governments were said to have the sovereign right to formulate for themselves. Moreover, supporting those goals was the *duty* of other members of the "United Nations." Officials of the United Nations Relief and Rehabilitation Administration (UNRRA) presented the most significant version of the economic rights and duties of states. They argued that each state had the duty to aid the economic development of every other state, that this aid should be given no matter what political and economic disagreements a country might have with another country's economic ideology or economic policies. It was, for example, the duty of a capitalist state to aid the economic development of socialist states. Moreover, the material extent of this obligation was directly proportional to the material differences in life from one country to another; every state had duties to aid all materially less advantaged states. In fact, UNRRA Director, and former mayor of New York, Fiorello La Guardia, made a memorable, impassioned defense of these principles at one of the first meetings of the postwar United Nations (UNGA 1946: 51).[4]

In the late 1940s, Latin American, Asian, and African officials chose the principle of states' economic rights and duties because it not only justi-fied deviations from liberal policies, it also justified claims for foreign assistance similar to that given to the previously wealthy war-torn nations through UNRRA and the Marshall Plan (Brown 1950: 136; *Economist* May 8, 1948: 782). Throughout the 1940s, representatives from what would become the Third World argued for international economic regimes that would regulate rather than abolish national interventions *and* for aid similar to what the United Nations had given to Europe. Major speeches included those by Argentina (UNGA 1946: 8), Brazil (UNGA 1946: 89) (including a speech by later UNCTAD official and member of the innovative Pearson Commission, Roberto de Oliveira Campos [UNGA 1948: 168–169]), India (UNGA 1947: 46), and Lebanon, by George Hakim proposing the first version of the Special UN Fund for Economic Development, a still-born institution that, nonetheless, triggered the World Bank's first low-interest loans to the Third World (UNGA 1949: 9). Delegates justified both claims by citing UN statements defining states' rights and duties and by citing the UNRRA precedent. Latin American officials, in particular, argued that it was only fair that richer countries aid them because they had contributed to European reconstruction through UNRRA in response to US appeals based on the economic rights and duties of states.

Significantly, as this list of nations suggests and Wilcox affirms (1949: 42), in the 1940s the larger and wealthier states from each region led the Third World. This began the pattern that contradicts Krasner's thesis that relative weakness explained the adoption of NIEO ideas. Later, a diverse group of ideologically committed governments would be active, joining but not displacing the larger and wealthier states (Hart 1982: Chapter 4).

By 1950, these leading Asian and Latin American governments had formed the core of the NIEO because proposed liberal international economic regimes threatened their pre-war goal of achieving industrial development using as wide a range of policy tools as possible. At the same time, Third World governments had available to them a particularly attractive justification for the policies that they wanted to pursue, in part because supporters of the liberal order had treated that justification as a legitimate one when they created UNRRA. More significantly, that justification suggested that other states had moral obligations to aid the industrial development plans that Third World states advocated. Delegates from Africa, Asia, and Latin America reiterated these ideas at every international meeting on economic matters. Around this principle grew the entire NIEO.

Analysis of the world economy: response to unanticipated problems

Most studies of the NIEO highlight Raul Prebisch, his observations about terms of trade shifting against products produced in the Third World, and his ideas about the structures of the global economy impeding Third World industrial development. Third World officials invoked Prebisch's analysis for more than 30 years. It was the first major addition to the simple precepts that formed the core of the NIEO ideology.

Prebisch wrote his major work (1950) in the late 1940s. Yet, delegates from Brazil (UNGA 1950: 138) and Egypt (UNGA 1951: 19) introduced his signature argument in General Assembly debates concerned with something Prebisch had never considered—the impact that the formation and later depletion of Korean War-era strategic stockpiles of raw materials on Third World economies. Those policies were, nevertheless, examples of Prebisch's preoccupation: policies of states at the core of the world economy creating unanticipated hardships for the periphery.

By the early 1960s, the Third World's unanticipated trade problems included its shrinking share of world trade, a trend opposite to what wartime economists had predicted (Pincus 1967: 126–127). Third World governments felt cheated out of the trade-induced growth that the rich nations enjoyed just as they had felt cheated out of the growth in the 1950s that more balanced interventions the raw materials' markets would have encouraged.

Prebisch explained the declining Third World trade share, but his was not the only available explanation. The "cultural constraints on development" (lack of "modernization") cited by Northern development experts (for example, Rostow 1953: 12) also clarified the problem, but those ideas were not consistent with the right of any state to choose an economic development plan compatible with its culture.

More significantly, Third World leaders now had an alternative *global* explanation of the source of their problems, and liberal internationalist supporters of the postwar order offered compatible explanations of the declining trade share. The GATT's 1958 report on the problem, written by Gottfried Haberler, directly blamed the developed market economies (Friedeberg 1969: 53–56). Northern trade policies, like those associated with strategic stockpiling, created tariff and non-tariff barriers to Third World goods.

Why then did the Prebisch thesis rather than the "Haberler thesis" become the center of Third World policy analysis? Both explained that key issue in the same way: it was the result of the North's greater influence over international economic relations. A new manifestation of an old pattern, said Prebisch. A violation of recently achieved liberalizations that should benefit all, said Haberler. Third World officials found Prebisch's ideas preferable to Haberler's because Prebisch's were compatible with the core of the NIEO ideology, the preference for trade regulation and the principle of states' economic rights. Haberler assumed there was only one way to develop: by adopting liberal policies wholesale. Supporters of Haberler's view could argue, as many still do, that the core of the Third World's new ideology was irrational and that an increasingly liberal world is better for everyone than a system of internationally regulated national regulations. NIEO supporters would counter that the case has never been proved: the system the Third World wanted had never been tried, and the Free World Order was only a partial liberalism, a system that liberal economists have always recognized as discriminatory against the South due to the concentration of power in the North.[5]

The Group of 77 and the "democratization" of international relations

Prebisch's analysis of the world economy had become the official position of the Third World alliance by the first UN Conference on Trade and Development in 1964. There, the South proposed a set of trade principles that Northern governments rejected (Moss and Winton 1976: 43–51).

Prebisch's theory explained that result: people in the center can influence most global economic decisions; people in the periphery cannot.

Accepting Prebisch's thesis meant searching for new Third World means to influence economic relations. It meant creating producers' alliances and it meant actively and self-consciously pursuing Third World unity not only through the regional economic development schemes Prebisch's followers then supported (Cardoso 1977), but also through further development of the alliance's shared views. A speech by Alfonso Patino of Colombia in 1963 is typical:

> Against blind respect for those [market] forces and against anachronistic trade restrictions imposed by the strongest against the weakest ranges the vigorous new ideology which inspired the convening of the [UNCTAD] conference. That ideology . . . will constitute a new phase in the age-old struggle for the liberation of peoples and respect for human dignity.
>
> (UNGA 1963: 27)

In short, accepting Prebisch's ideas meant looking for ways to change institutions that structured and governed international trade by shifting the power over those institutions to the South.

By the late 1960s, the South had articulated its desire to gain more power over international institutions in a political analysis, a view of how international economic regimes can and should be changed. Third World governments argued for the "democratization" of international relations, meaning by that two different things. First, as Indonesian (UNGA 1968: 2) and Tanzanian (UNGA 1969: 30) delegates argued, international institutions should be used to "energize" public opinion in developed countries to support Third World goals. Second, beginning with the Cairo Declaration of 1964 (Moss and Winton 1976: 94), Third World governments argued for making binding international decisions "democratically," that is, "on the basis of a one-nation, one-vote" (Gosovic 1972: 57).

The tension between the two principles reflects the fact that the desire for "democratization" stemmed from a Third World desire for greater control over international economic relations and not from prior principles about the best form of decision making. The state-centered Realist version of the Northern conventional wisdom correctly identifies this "structural power interest," but misidentifies its source. It was not the result of an inherent interest that states have in gaining power over others, an interest that per-haps would best be masked by more pleasant ideas like "democratization." The conscious Third World desire for greater power over international economic decisions came as a part of the analysis adopted to understand and cope with a real, practical problem. Even when Third World officials argued that the organization should try to influence Northern public opinion, very few Southern representatives invoked "popular sovereignty" as a justification (or mask). Most only said that they believed that, in the North, public opinion actually influenced decisions, and that they wanted the majority of the states in the United Nations to have indirect influence over those decisions. Third World governments justified the one-nation, one-vote and UNCTAD conciliation decision-making procedures based on the equal rights and duties of states, the principles at the core of their ideology.

Reiterating the foundation in response to an unanticipated opportunity

The experience of the early years of the Third World's attempts to gain greater power over the world economy hardly suggested that the alliance gathered under the new ideology would achieve its goal. By the late 1960s, the group had begun to fragment. It reunited in the early 1970s, seizing opportunities created by the 1971 breakdown of the Bretton Woods system of fixed exchange rates linked to an American guaranteed price for gold. In doing so, the South made the final significant addition to its ideology. This was the notion that Northern states owe something to the South in compensation for colonialism.

The more radical African governments, including Guinea (UNGA 1961: 49) and Ghana (UNGA 1960: 35) in the Nkrumah era, had long held this view. However, if restitution defined the duties of wealthy states, then some wealthy states had little duty to aid the poor; it would be hard to identify a significant level of colonialism or neocolonialism practiced by (say) Norway, Finland, or Poland. In fact, the governments the most enamored of the restitution principle were Eastern European socialist states who would, as a result, have been relieved of any duties (MacPhee 1979; Moss and Winton 1976: 204–207, 310–314). By 1970, the debate over restitution helped split the South into a radical and a moderate camp. The radicals were mostly African and Asian, nonaligned, and recently independent. The moderates were Latin American, aligned with the West, and had been independent longer (Moss and Winton 1976: 194–205, 856–867).

The 1975 "Charter of Economic Rights and Duties of States" (Moss and Winton 1976: 902–906) resolved the issue. Third World governments agreed, as they had in the 1940s, that the equal rights and duties of states made it incumbent upon all states to aid the economic development of every other state along the path chosen by its government. Nevertheless, in the 1970s debate over the NIEO, all Southern states began to tell former colonizers and neocolonialists that a principle of restitution required them to repair the broken postwar international economic institutions in ways that would favor the Third World.

This manipulation of justifications and the resulting reunification of the Third World behind its original principles was not the result of direct bargaining and exchanges of concessions. Certainly some individuals played important roles, including the Mexican delegate who appears in UN records as the first to raise the idea that certain Northern policies made it incumbent upon the North to negotiate a new order (UNGA 1971: 79) and certainly Mexico's president, who put the "Charter" itself on the world's agenda. Nonetheless, those individuals only could act given the political opportunities created by the first signs of the breakdown of the Free World Order, and they acted by articulating a new grounds for consensus, not by suggesting new bargains.

The postwar international economic institutions began to fail, as Block (1977) illustrates, due to unanticipated problems affecting the wealthy market states, problems severe enough that the United States trade restrictions began to pressure other wealthy states to bear some of the burden maintaining the international monetary regime. The American actions, in August 1971, reenergized the Third World alliance in that autumn's General Assembly session. Radical and moderate Third World governments united to claim American compensation for the adverse effects of the new economic policy, compensation that would take the form of negotiating new regimes rooted in the Third World ideology (UNGA 1972: 27–98).

Simultaneously, individual oil producers and, later, OPEC as a whole, seized on the industrial West's growing oil dependence. With the Arab OPEC embargo on sales to the US and the Netherlands throughout the October 1973 war with Israel, oil prices soared. With the unity of the Third World already reaffirmed, the massive oil price hikes of 1973 and 1974 were met with enthusiasm across the South.

This shocked Northern policy-makers who had predicted most Third World states would condemn the oil producers. After all, Third World states were those most likely to experience economic and political turmoil in the wake of the energy crisis (Singh 1977: 6–9). Instead, the Group of 77 used the opportunity presented by the crisis to present its entire package of proposals for a New Order.

Alternative explanations of Third World demands and the discipline of International Relations

What did the Third World want? From the 1940s through the 1980s, African, Asian, and Latin American governments wanted more power over international economic regimes. They wanted regimes that coordinated, rather than abolished, economic interventions at the national level. They wanted all of the advantages of trade-induced growth that they could get, and that mostly meant that they wanted the North to reduce barriers to Southern industrial exports.

In the early 1980s, Northern analysts who had reached similar conclusions about the sincerity and relative moderation of the Group of 77's proposal suggested sensible North–South compromises. In a 1981 book sponsored by the Council on Foreign Relations, Miriam Camps and

Catherine Gwin argued that the hope for a world without national restrictions on trade, migration, and finance was far too optimistic. Thus, even those committed to liberalism, had to accept the greater realism of the South's position and focus on how best to coordinate national interventions (Gwin 1977; Camps and Gwin 1981). The World Bank's Paul Streeten (1981) made a similar case. The Bank's president, Robert S. McNamara, convinced retired German Chancellor Willy Brandt, a Social Democrat, to form an independent commission that eventually delivered a report, largely written by Britain's Tory former Prime Minister Edward Heath, advocating much the same set of reforms supported by the Council on Foreign Relations (Brandt Commission 1980).

Radical scholars, including *Dependentistas*, lambasted the reforms proposed by Northern liberal internationalists (see Shoup and Minter's 1977: 264–272 discussion of Camps's work for the Council; and Frank 1981), and they blasted the NIEO proposals, which they saw as essentially the same. On that point, the radicals were correct. The ideology that informed the NIEO was reformist, not revolutionary. It grew on the same roots—Moynihan called them "Fabian," more accurately, they were "Keynesian"—as the ideology that informed the postwar international order in the first place.

Yet, in the 1970s and 1980s, the American supporters of the postwar order who recognized the kindred spirit of the NIEO proposals were few. The hardships that followed the oil crisis, and the South's "irrational" enthusiasm for the OPEC policies that started the crisis, reinforced American beliefs about the South's irresponsibility, incompetence, and lack of good faith.

Why were American policy-makers, so off the mark? A significant part of the blame falls on the intellectual institutions in the United States that contributed to the "liberal forgetting" about the origins of the postwar world order and the long history of the Third World's disagreement with those views. Moynihan came to the United Nations as a man of great intelligence and vision, a policy scholar in his own right, but someone who had to rely on the views of the scholarly community that knew more about the Third World than he did. Yet, the first experts he and other American policy-makers relied on, economists including Johnson and Bronfenbrenner, were convinced by their own deductive science that the ideas about development that grew out of Prebisch's policy experience were absurd and not worth discussing. In contrast, British Keynesians of the same generation, including Paul Streeten at the World Bank or Robert Cassen (the principal author of the Brandt Commission reports), had experienced the "national capitalist" arguments about the need for an internationally regulated system of national regulation of trade made by Keynes in the 1940s. They had interacted with Third World development economists and policy-makers for decades. They knew that, for their authors, the NIEO proposals were not a mask for thievery and fascism.

Experts in International Relations provided no better guidance. Hundreds of articles and books on the NIEO appeared in the 1970s and early 1980s, most of which made arguments like Tucker's or Krasner's. Vanishingly few of the studies involve reading the primary documents of the North–South debates over governing the world economy from the beginning, or talking at length with the Third World principals about the history of their proposals and what they hoped to achieve. There were many reasons for this. By the 1970s, both historical research and in-depth interviewing had gone out of fashion. "Science" seemed to be better served—that is, cumulative results could be achieved faster—by making vast amounts of content-analyzable data from public sources or by following the lead of the economists and creating deductive theory. In part, the problem was the tendency of prestigious American International Relations scholars to flock to policy relevant topics—which, as long as OPEC was boosting oil prices, the NIEO seemed to be. Within that group of scholars, empathetic, first-hand knowledge of Africa, developing Asia, or Latin America (except as an extension of US foreign policy) was rare. Additionally, of course, there was the cumulative impact of the leading explanations themselves. Most, like Krasner's, advised policy-makers to avoid the kind of direct engagement with the Third World that could have led to a more benign interpretation of the NIEO.

Data-focused, "scientific" International Relations actually might have made more headway than the ill-informed commentary of prestigious scholars did. Ole Holsti's (1962) paradigmatic study had demonstrated that John Foster Dulles's rigid worldview made him incapable of ever seeing the Soviet Union as benign. Similar studies of American policy-makers might have demonstrated the consequence of similarly rigid views about the Third World in the 1970s. Unfortunately, most of those who shared Holsti's research program ignored the new field of International Political Economy (see Murphy and Nelson 2001; Holsti 1976). Moreover, even when the brilliant and wide-ranging James N. Rosenau *did* begin to study the NIEO, the assumptions about Third World motivations that he shared with other American scholars got in the way. Rosenau (1981) wrote that it would be much easier to understand the NIEO if we had chronicles of all the various deals struck between different Third World representatives as they put together their coalition. As Rosenau pointed out, it is hard to find evidence of such bargaining. Unfortunately, that is because little bargaining took place; the foundation of shared ideas meant there was little need for inter-alliance bargaining in the heyday of the NIEO, moreover, the process of decision-making within Third World groupings over a generation was something different.

Douglas Smyth (1977) notes that the South's policy analysis tended to lump together many sets of proposals that only one regional group of Southern nations originally wanted, and that only a few states had an "objective" interest in supporting. This was not a result of bargaining.

It was a consequence of the oldest of the South's principles, which said that any government's view of what it needed for its national economic development should be given international consideration.[6] Policy proposals made at regional meetings invariably became items in the Group's proposal. Moral principles advocated at regional meetings did not. New moral principles, new foundational arguments, became matters of intense discussion and consensus making.[7]

Instead of coming from bargaining and exchanged concessions based on conflicting interests, Third World agreement appears to have come about through debate and learning. Perhaps we should not be surprised. Clifford Geertz (1964) and Goran Therborn (1980), who work from very different traditions of social theory, argue that when we search for the deeper meaning of developing operational ideologies we should not be guided by some theory of deep structures or objective interests and strategic bargaining. Rather, we should look to the worldviews our subjects already know and follow. If existing worldviews prove an insufficient guide, we should assume newly adopted ideas reflect an attempt to understand and cope with real problems, we should assume a basic human interest in cooperative problem solving. This is the "objective interest" that democratic theorist Jürgen Habermas agues all interpretive social scientists assume as part of their conviction that their empathy can give them insight (Habermas 1971: 309, 314).

Very distinguished interpretivist social scientists outside of International Relations came to conclusions about the meaning of the Third World ideology similar to those presented here. Ironically, perhaps, those scholars included a Russian historical anthropologist (Erasov 1972) and a Croatian historian of economics (Pertot 1972). Not surprisingly, few American scholars and policy-makers knew about them or consulted them. The 1970s may have been the era of détente as well as of the NIEO, but few of us could overcome the scholarly prejudices engrained by the Cold War.

It is more surprising that so few Americans learned from their Keynesian colleagues associated with Brandt Commission and the World Bank, where Paul Streeten worked alongside one of the NIEO's most persuasive promoters, Mahbub ul Haq, who later spearheaded the effort to define "human development." This was a missed opportunity, a chance to mend the liberal world order. No similar opportunity has appeared since.

8 Freezing the North–South bloc after the East–West thaw

The missed opportunity of the NIEO preceded the decade in which US Republicans worked to break the back of the Third World oil cartel and to undermine the international institutions that had provided the political space in which the Third World alliance had developed (see Augelli and Murphy 1988). The Reagan and Thatcher era began a generation of liberal fundamentalism triumphant, a period of what Susan Strange (1986) called "Casino Capitalism," similar to the 1920s or the early Gilded Age.

Analysts rarely lionize Reagan for his victory over the Third World; his administration's role in the collapse of the Soviet system overshadows the other accomplishment of its statecraft. The disintegration of the industrial model that provided the major alternative to liberal internationalism had the effect of strengthening the particular subspecies of liberalism that was triumphant at that moment. Neoliberalism, "the Washington Consensus," became hegemonic.

In 1989, economist John Williamson (1990) coined the term, when he argued that all the powerful agencies influencing the transformation of post-Soviet and Third World economies—the US government, the IMF, the World Bank, and most of the other aid-providing nations whose funds were subject to "policy coordination"—agreed on ten prescriptions for every "developing" economy. Development would come with: (1) balanced budgets, achieved by (2) cutting support for infant industries and redistributive social policy and (3) tax reform; (4) financial, (5) monetary, and (6) trade liberalization; (7) welcoming foreign investment; (8) denationalizing state enterprises and (9) "ensuring [of] secure property rights" (taking away the state's power to nationalize again); and (10) wholesale deregulation.

Certainly, the sometimes-desperate search for policy alternatives in the states newly liberated from Soviet socialism, and Reagan's prestige there, gave credence to the liberal fundamentalism that guided the government in Washington. Moreover, the neoliberal policies were self-reinforcing. Once an old-style populist development state gave up one policy tool, under the pressure of international donors, other tools began to look like costly burdens. Once a government had denationalized, it made sense to cut the support for infant industries that was now just going into private hands, and to welcome foreign investment needed to replace sectors decimated by the policy shifts.

The opening of the Berlin Wall and the fall of the Soviet Union were, undoubtedly, victories for human freedom, examples of the transformative strength of largely nonviolent struggle. Yet, few social transformations are purely good or purely evil.

In their February 1990 forecast for the new decade the editors of the venerable Third World news magazine *West Africa* (no. 3780 February 5: 163) insisted:

> One legacy of the ending of superpower conflict would thus seem to be that the agenda for the next decade will much more be one of North–South than of East–West. With the possible fusion of the First and Second Worlds, the Third World now moves to center stage.

The editors supported their claim with three bits of evidence from the recent news: Willy Brandt's decision to try to restart negotiations on reforming international monetary and financial institutions, the announcement of the broad reform agenda that a reinvigorated United Nations would take up in 1990, and, the creation of a new Third World leadership group to coordinate action within all international organizations and conferences. The Group of 15 was meant to be a club of nonaligned states centered on those governing the bulk of the Third World's population yet balanced to represent the diversity of opinion within the much larger group.

The same issue of *West Africa* (p. 196) also reported a quite different view. A controversial historian of pan-Africanism, Tony Martin, pressed to comment on events in Europe by those attending his Du Bois Memorial Lectures in Accra, stated that the disintegration of the Communist bloc would mean a further consolidation of white racism as United States and Western Europe aided Eastern Europe's development. North–South relations would not be at the center of the world agenda of the 1990s. Africans could only make strides if they put autonomy and unity at the center of their own agendas.

In the same month, Africans heard a third assessment: Pope John Paul II arrived in Cape Verde at the beginning of a tour of Sahelian nations to highlight Africa's needs at a time when the privileged nations of the world were all too focused on the needs of the more-advantaged people of Eastern Europe (*West Africa*, no. 3780 February 5: 199). The Pope's message was that North and South had choices to make: Northerners need not limit their generosity to others like themselves. A positive transformation of North–South relations could be made in the 1990s.

Of the three, Martin's assessment proved the most prescient. Even the evidence that led the editors of *West Africa* to their rosier scenario really should have pointed toward a bleaker view of the prospects of North–South relations in the 1990s. The changes in international institutions at the end of the Cold War, after more than a decade of crisis, pointed to the consolidation of North–South relations that were less generous and less conducive to real development than those that existed before the crisis.

Still, there was also something to be learned from John Paul's speech, and not just from its text, but also from its context. His words and their setting share a single message. The text emphasized the opportunities inherent in crisis, the possibilities for choice. The context of the Pope's speech provides a clue to what reasonable choices might still exist. At a moment when many were consigning socialism to history's rubbish bin, Poland's most-celebrated anticommunist chose to make his commentary on the liberation of Eastern Europe as the guest of an incontrovertibly successful, Marxist-oriented, democratic socialist: Aristedes Maria Pereira, president of a nation whose transformation since its independence in 1975 had been profound.

One of Europe's first colonies, as well as one of its last, Cape Verde suffered 500 years of grinding exploitation and periodic devastation by drought and famine. Its history epitomizes all of the hypocritical horrors of Europe's five centuries of world supremacy; what was sinful and hidden at home in Europe became "necessary" and commonplace in the colony. (Pereira, for example, himself was one of the many children of a Catholic priest, a connection that the otherwise chummy Pope failed to note.)

This fractured society could still nurture the political movement organized by Pereira's comrade-in-arms, Amilcar Cabral, who defeated the Portuguese colonial army in Guinea-Bissau. The defeated army returned to Portugal to overthrow Europe's last fascist state and, as a consequence, to end European colonialism in Africa.

From 1975 until 1990, Cape Verdeans had fifteen years to undo five centuries' damage. By 1990, citizens had replanted forests on land that colonialism made a moonscape. Famine had become a memory, even though rains had failed in at least half the years since independence. Life expectancy had reached North American levels. Given Cape Verde's unusual success in dealing with Africa's four-fold crises of the 1980s (debt, drought, environmental degradation, and political decay), the leaders of the "most seriously affected" states turned to Pereira as their leader and representative in international forums, even though his country remained the most remote (ideologically as well as physically) from the rest (Davidson 1989; Murphy 1987).

Those Third World governments that make the kind of choices that Cape Verde's has made will continue to find some small opportunities for transformation even after the warming of East–West relations. These include opportunities in the yet incomplete reconstruction of North–South international institutions (as emphasized by *West Africa's* editors), as well as the greater opportunities available to those Third World governments that pursue Martin's preferred strategy of unity and autonomy.

I reach these conclusions using a framework centered on Gramsci's concept of a "historic bloc" to help understand both the changes in East–West relations in the 1990s and the crisis in North–South relations that predated the end of the Cold War.

The North–South historic bloc

Most of us who study the Third World have come to employ frameworks that posit a unitary world economy, whether it is the structural economics of "core" and "periphery" pioneered by Raul Prebisch, the various political economies and sociologies of "dependency," the self-styled "revolutionary internationalist" theory advanced by Nigel Harris (1987) and Michael Kidron (1968), or the world-systems theory of Immanuel Wallerstein. These frameworks have special appeal, and remain significant, particularly because progressive Third World intellectuals developed them as a means of making sense of their own experience. As an Argentine government economist, Raul Prebisch experimented with neoclassical orthodoxy and then Keynesianism before coming to his own synthesis (Cardoso 1977; Prebisch 1984). Similarly, as an agronomist for the colonial government, Amilcar Cabral, to whom Wallerstein acknowledges a special debt, started with a simple comparative approach, treating countries as separate social formations, before he came to see the capitalist world-system as a single class-riven society.

The unusual capacity of some of those frameworks to anticipate and make sense of the end of the Cold War strengthened the case for their general adoption. Nearly a quarter-century ago, at the beginning of the "Second Cold War" (marked by the Soviet intervention in Afghanistan and the start of the Carter–Reagan United States' military buildup), Wallerstein (1980) pooh-poohed the widespread notion that the East–West conflict would remain the fundamental divide in world politics. He argued, instead, that the struggle for supremacy among Europe, Japan, and the United States would soon come to the fore. That conclusion seemed strange when it first appeared, in the month that Americans elected Reagan president. Now, after the second Iraq War, it looks plausible if not prophetic. Even more prophetic was the work of world-system's sociologist Christopher Chase-Dunn (1982) and his colleagues on "socialist states" in the capitalist world-system. They argued that what was different about the Soviet Union and its Eastern European satellites was not their attempts to create fundamentally new, post-capitalist social formations, but their relative position within the singular modern social formation of world capitalism. These states occupied a semi-peripheral position, which gave them opportunities for autonomous development that the peripheral states of the Third World did not have. Nevertheless, if the opportunity for moving from semi-periphery to core status were to arise, Eastern European societies might be pushed back into the main world market and "socialism," in retrospect, might be seen as "the transitional system between capitalism and capitalism."

Yet, despite the prescience of some world-systems thinkers, their framework is not sufficient to understand the effect of changes in East–West relations on North–South relations. After all, from 1945 until (at least) 1990 the East–West division meant something more than a division between a large, relatively autonomous economic region and the rest of world society. It represented a division between two complex, international social systems with autonomous economic bases as well as separate political and ideological superstructures. In contrast, the North–South division, remained, for the most part, a division *within* a single complex social system, a system defined by a single interdependent economy and by a host of superstructures, international institutions linking the South to the North, from the UN Trusteeship Council, to the World Bank, to UNCTAD.

Antonio Gramsci's concept of an "historic bloc" helps capture these distinctions. In the postwar period, that is, until well into the 1990s, the Soviet Union, its Eastern European satellites, and its dependent Third World peripheries can be thought of as constituting one "historic bloc." The wealthy capitalist OECD states along with most of the dependent Third World constituted another. Since the early 1950s, China incorporated a third massive social system of this kind. In addition, since at the late 1950s, when it freed itself from significant external financial obligations, India constituted a fourth.

Gramsci's concept proves useful because he developed it, in large part, to help understand another situation in which the territorial and social boundaries of societies were shifting and the boundaries of juridical states did not necessarily correspond to the most meaningful boundaries between social systems. His concern was the history of Italian state building from the early Renaissance through the Italian imperialism of his own day (Augelli and Murphy 1993; Murphy 1998b). Any conceptual framework that makes it difficult to see that the boundaries of social systems are not, themselves, contestable and often contested, would not have served Gramsci's purposes. Similarly, in an era when one group of national societies appears to be attempting to rejoin the capitalist core, and when observers as divergent as Tony Martin and John Paul II see the further marginalization of another group of national societies, we also need a broader framework.

A historic bloc is, "the dialectical unity of base and superstructure, theory and practice, of intellectuals and masses, and not, as it is sometimes mistakenly asserted, simply an alliance of social forces" (Forgacs 1988: 424). It is the set of social relations in which in all aspects of a particular mode of production—including contradictions—can develop fully. Gramsci developed the concept by pointing to a series of ways in which social life is like a *blocco*. It is an *alliance* of social forces. In that sense, the postwar "North–South bloc" could be identified as being the alliance among three groups: the "Atlantic" or "Trilateral" ruling class (Pijl 1984) some of the subordinate classes within the OECD states (Augelli and Murphy 1988: 140), and the rising governing class, the "organizational bourgeoisie," in dependent Third World states, a class made up of those who occupy positions at the top of both public and private hierarchies (Markovitz 1977, 1987).

However, a historic bloc is always much more than just an alliance. It is like an English "block," something that only can be understood when we look at all its faces—economic, political, and cultural/ideological. It is also like an architectural "block," a building. To be functional, the whole "structure of the superstructure," the building above ground, has to have a coherent form, including coercive structures of the "state proper" (like the walls of a building) and enabling structures, political and social space, "civil society" (like a building's rooms and halls).

Others have found different ways to describe the social unities that Gramsci calls "historic blocs." David M. Gordon and his colleagues (Gordon 1980; Gordon *et al.* 1982) call the historical superstructures "social structures of accumulation." Alain Lipietz (1987, 1988) and other Regulation School theorists write of the unity of an "industrial paradigm" and "macroeconomic structure" as a "regime of accumulation." The Regulation School investigates regimes of accumulation along with their superstructures, which they call modes of regulation, "the totality of institutional forms and implicit norms that assure the consistency of behaviors and expectations within the framework of the regime" (Lipietz 1987: 83). Together, a regime of accumulation and mode of regulation constitute a historic bloc within which a characteristic "mode of development" becomes possible, "founded on an industrial paradigm, stabilizing itself in a regime of accumulation, and guaranteed by a mode of regulation" (Lipietz 1987: 83).

Both groups of scholars concentrated their attention on the Northern part of the historic bloc in which capitalism developed from the end of the Second World War through the 1970s. They emphasize the "Fordism" operating across lead sectors within the OECD, the system where both profits and markets for goods were reciprocally assured by high wages and all economies of scale in manufacturing, thus establishing economies of mass-consumption and capital-intensive mass-production. They highlight the role of the welfare state in helping maintain that system, as well as the role played by postwar intergovernmental economic institutions, the International Monetary Fund (IMF) and the regular cooperation among treasury ministries and central banks organized through the Bank for International Settlement, in shielding First World states from short-term fiscal pressures that could make Keynesian policies untenable.

The North–South links in the same historic bloc—the economic as well as superstructural connections linked the First World to the dependent Third World—are as easy to summarize. In the postwar world, the South was the place where an industrial regime of high wages, economies of scale in manufacturing, mass-consumption, and capital-intensive mass-production was *not* encouraged. Quite the contrary, the institutions of global governance and the regular patterns of cooperative "bilateral" relations (bilateral aid, bilateral investment incentive programs) encouraged Third World economies to remain directed toward the ends identified by the classic writings on imperialism. Third World economies maintained low-wage sectors providing primary commodities used in the industrial economies of the North. Until the mid-1970s, Northern investment in Third World manufacturing did little to transform local economies fundamentally, let alone to transform the traditional relations between core and periphery. In fact, arguably, the postwar years proved John A. Hobson's (1965[1902]) turn-of-the-century argument: in the postwar, Fordist, West— in a world where wages in the core were high—the importance of the periphery as an outlet for Northern investment capital, declined.

Certainly, the direct control of the North over the South, which Hobson argued was designed to serve that investment, had diminished. For those willing to accept *ex post facto* functionalist explanations for social institutions, the fact that the periphery may have become *increasingly* peripheral to the reproduction of core capitalism in the postwar period would be sufficient explanation for the most striking consequence of North–South relations in the postwar period: decolonization. Direct coercive political control of the South by the North was no longer necessary.

Of course, the actual history of decolonization is more complex. Three elements stand out. First is the mid-century emergence of mass movements for local autonomy throughout the colonial world. Second is the role of formal international institutions encouraging decolonization, which the United Nations inherited from the League of Nations, a role that members constantly strengthened as the percentage of newly independent states within the United Nations grew (see Chapter 6). Third is the role of the competition between the two new postwar superpowers, both less involved with overseas empires than the Belgians, British, Dutch, or French had been before the war, and both with their own reasons for wanting to appear the champion of self-determination.

Soviet-American competition continued after decolonization. However, unlike the Soviet Union, the US government stood at the center of the development system and greatly influenced every postwar global intergovernmental organization when "development" became the most important item on the organization's agenda.

The typical, self-interested Northern justification of the development system converges with the typical, self-interested Southern justification, if we consider the system a non-coercive superstructure, a part of the North–South bloc that helps cement the alliance between the subordinate Third World organizational bourgeoisie and dominant ruling class in the North. Even by strengthening the Third World state and by providing "populist" benefits, "development" helps maintain the position of the most privileged groups within Third World societies, groups who are often organically linked to the state and, thus to its success, in a way that the most privileged groups in the North are not.

If the development system can be considered a key non-coercive super-structure of the North–South bloc—encompassing some of the most significant institutions of North–South civil society—then overt and covert military intervention by the North (most frequently by the United States, but also by France and, more recently, by the United Nations) might be considered the key coercive institution of North–South "political society." Again, if we look backward, it appears as if intervention "functionally" served to stop Third World regimes from attempting autonomous development outside the North–South bloc, whether or not such an attempt involved choosing to ally with an alternative power center (especially the Soviet Union). However, the actual logic by which that pattern emerged was, again, a bit less direct than a retrospective rational reconstruction might suggest.

Once again, both national governments and social movements were the key actors on the world stage, even though formal intergovernmental organizations provided more than just a setting. Throughout the Cold War, the United States and the Soviet Union (not to mention France, Britain, and China) took opposing sides in a host of locally emerging protracted social conflicts in the Third World. The immediate divisions reflected everything from a desire to demonstrate resolve in a nuclear world where direct military confrontation was unthinkable, to an honest desire to aid local supporters of "international socialism" or the values of the "Free World."

Of course, the postwar world was one in which there were international institutions designed to manage and reduce violent confrontations between sovereign states: the Security Council, UN peacekeeping, and the International Court of Justice. Throughout the Cold War, those institutions worked well only when the states in violent conflict were both allies of the same superpower (Zacher 1979). The international institutions helped manage the violent conflicts between the less-developed allies of the United States, for example, between Greece and Turkey in Cyprus and between Egypt and Israel after Sadat changed superpower partners. The international institutions did not stop superpower violence against members of their own blocs. Nor did they stop the boundary wars between the blocs.

Crises in the North–South bloc

Gramsci's ultimate purpose in developing his concept of a historic bloc was to emphasize that only within such a coherent ensemble of coercive and enabling institutions, linked to a particular base of technologies and relations of production, could the "normal" development of society occur; only in such an ensemble can the inner logic of capitalism identified by

Marx unfold. Such blocs become the framework for history, a framework within which people's normal lives occur, like the Parisian apartment block George Perec uses to frame the many stories in his novel of the late industrial age, *Life: A User's Manual*.

In the postwar North–South historic bloc, a kind of normal life went on, at least in the North. Capitalist development and capital accumulation continued, especially in the separate Northern nation-states, each like a separate luxury apartment linked to others by "enabling" institutions (the GATT, IMF, OECD, and European Community) which were as significant to "normal" life as halls, stairs, elevators, dumbwaiters, and garbage-chutes are to those who live in any block of expensive flats.

Normal life continued in the servants' apartments of the Third World as well. C. L. R. James's (1977: 28) oil-crisis era assessment was accurate; "Colonialism is alive and will continue to be alive until another *positive doctrine* takes its place." Still, decolonization meant that the servants could buy their flats. Some (Singapore, Hong Kong, South Korea, Taiwan) were able to fix them up quite well, although Nigel Harris (1987) argues that this was only because local capitalists there had an unusually clear understanding of the few opportunities offered by the expansionary logic of Fordist capitalism and their societies were small enough that integration into the "global manufacturing system" could bring general prosperity. However, even those living in states without these advantages, those living in the humbler units of the Third World saw the material quality of their life improve until sometime in the 1970s.

The same cannot be said for the 1980s and 1990s, especially in Africa and much of Latin America. When commentators on Africa call the pre-AIDS problems of the 1980s "the crisis," they had in mind a complex of social problems of the base (ecological degradation, famine) and superstructures (debt, political decay) that reflect a crisis of the North–South historic bloc. When a society is in crisis, when a historic bloc is crumbling or partially deserted (like a house in a city under siege) or when it no longer can support the dynamic life within in (like a flat that a family has outgrown) patterns of normal life cannot return until the bloc is rebuilt, reclaimed, or other structures found.

Those who argue that there has been a crisis in world capitalism since the oil-price-hike induced recession tend to concentrate on contradictions within the industrial regime or the fiscal crises of governments in the First World. Those problems first appeared in the early 1970s and were made acute by the "cascading monetarism" of the early 1980s as state after state in the industrial world had to cut back on government expenditures in order to stem the outflow capital attracted by high US interest rates (Lipietz 1989). Yet, as Samir Amin (1987: 28) argues, because the "normal" development of capitalism has not been bounded within individual nation-states or even within the whole of the "advanced" capitalist world, "any crisis of the capitalist system will be a crisis of the international division of labor and thus, especially, a North–South crisis." Moreover, it will not be "merely" an economic crisis, but rather a crisis of the entire social order linking North and South. The African and Latin American crises and the crisis of Fordism are one and the same.

The connections become particularly evident when we consider the concurrent crises in the institutions of global governance that link North and South. The postwar system of intergovernmental organizations has been in a state of ongoing crisis and decay for thirty years, at least since the unilateral US decision to end the IMF's fixed exchange rate regime in 1971, a decision designed to support a national (rather than multilateral) attack on the "stagflation" that first became acute in the Nixon administration.

The consequences of that decision have been manifold. In the North, the most significant result has been the institutionalization of a floating exchange rate system that does not provide the same multilateral support for expansive government economic policies, and, hence, for the welfare state, as the old regime did. In the South, the most important consequence has been the resulting shift in the agenda of the IMF itself. No longer needed as protector of the fixed-exchange rate system, the IMF's dominant role has become enforcer of "sound" government policies in the Third World, a main promoter of the Washington Consensus.

While the IMF's role in North–South relations has increased since 1971—and, especially, since the beginning, in the 1980s, of the recurring Third World debt crises—the 1971 decision otherwise contributed to the spiraling decay of the North–South aspects of the postwar international organization system. Fears about the stability of the dollar contributed to OPEC's unprecedented unity in the 1970s, and, thus, to the petroleum alliance's ability to raise and maintain oil prices. OPEC's power, and its willingness to use that power to promote the Third World's proposals for reforming international economic organizations, shaped the agenda of the United Nations system in the 1970s. The Third World's call for a New International Economic Order—based on global Keynesian rather than neoliberal ideas—not only offered a new vision of North–South relations, it helped undermine the institutions of the old order simply because of opposition it engendered in the North (recall Chapter 7).

Ronald Reagan came into office in 1981 the sworn enemy of the Third World alliance and of the entire United Nations system. He inherited a strong weapon to use against OPEC: the high interest rates engineered by the Federal Reserve System at the end of the Carter administration, a policy designed to "squeeze" inflation out of the stagnant economy. That meant engineering a sharp recession in the United States economy, which, given the defensive macroeconomic policies that other industrial states had to follow in a world of floating exchange rates, meant a worldwide recession, one significant enough to cause a great deal of energy "conservation" as Northern factories closed and production fell. At the same time, the policy contributed to the Third World debt crisis, and to the willingness of debt-ridden Third World oil producers to break OPEC pricing and production norms (see Augelli and Murphy 1988, Chapter 6).

Reagan's first, surprising, targets in the United Nations system were the institutions that Third World partisans had long claimed were the strongest institutions of neocolonialism, the IMF and the World Bank. Ultimately the administration relented after exhaustive interagency studies proved that those agencies, on balance, worked to force laissez-faire policies on the Third World (US Department of Treasury 1982; National Advisory Council 1983). Nevertheless, the US policy of non-support for other international organizations involved in North–South relations continued. From 1985 onward, the United States, which previously provided about a quarter of the UN system's finances, stopped paying much of its assessment (recall Chapter 6), plunging the central organs of the United Nations (which support peacekeeping operations) as well as the Specialized Agencies (with their "development" programs) into a financial crisis at the moment that the human costs of Third World debt and IMF–World Bank "structural adjustment" policies were becoming the most acute (Helleiner 1987; especially Loxley 1987).

Reconstruction ahead

By ending the Third World challenge to postwar North–South relations and by privileging institutions that encourage market discipline on Third World development policies, the Reagan administration began to confront the challenge of reconstructing the North–South historic bloc. To construct a historic bloc, a social movement (a party, faction, government, or so forth) must figure out how to piece together not only an alliance of social groups, but also the ideas that will motivate that alliance, the political institutions that will both dominate its opponents and help keep the bloc together, and the institutions of production, distribution, and consumption which will mediate the relations of the dominant and the dominated with their physical environment—the economic institutions on which the social order will rest.

Breaking the power of OPEC helped reestablish, at least temporarily, the North–South energy system on which postwar prosperity in the industrial countries relied. Transforming the system of intergovernmental organizations involved with development not only represented a triumph of the particularly laissez-faire, liberal fundamentalist ideology that Reagan represented, it provided a fairly low-cost way to dominate opponents in the reemerging North–South order by transforming their interest. The policies imposed upon debtor countries diminished the capacity of members of the Third World organizational bourgeoisie to rely upon positions in *public* hierarchies for their power, at the same time as the policies imposed upon debtor countries further privileged positions at the top of hierarchies in the *private* economies of the Third World.

Still, the puzzle was far from solved. The position of the dependent Third World in new bloc remains subordinate, more subordinate than in the postwar North–South bloc. Responses to the thaw in East–West relations point in that direction, at the same time that they suggest that the most likely outcome will be a unitary world capitalist order, still centered on the OECD, but with the dominant US, Japanese, and European centers playing slightly different roles. Eastern Europe will be integrated back in to this order. China and India will struggle to be included in the first truly global industrial order.

One immediate, short-term consequence of the East–West thaw was a strengthening of the role of the United Nations in dealing with violent protracted social conflicts that spill across Third World boundaries. Superficially, in the early 1990s, it appeared that the system envisioned at Yalta, with the two superpowers presiding over a system of relatively universal international conflict management, had finally emerged. The United Nations took on new peacemaking, peacekeeping, and peace-sustaining roles in Afghanistan, throughout Africa, in Central America, the Iran–Iraq War, and in Southeast Asia, including the unprecedented role as guarantor of elections in many long-independent states.

However, looked at more closely, these innovations did not involve a return to the sort of cooperative policing of the world by the wartime victors envisioned in the UN Charter. It would be more accurate to argue that the UN's expanded role in conflict management was a continuation of the postwar pattern of successful multilateral intervention in conflicts between or within states that are dependencies of *one* of the dominant superpowers. Now, however, *only* one of the superpowers is relevant. The UN's new successes have been cases where the Soviet Union or its military allies have withdrawn from conflicts, or else cases where both parties in the conflict have come to rely upon the United States. Kosovo, where Russia opposed intervention, was a US operation, similar to its Cold War interventions, but with no active superpower support for the US's opponents. The second Iraq War has been similar. There has been no sign of an increased effectiveness of the United Nations in managing conflicts where the powers are, themselves, directly responsible for the violence, that is to say, where the one remaining superpower is responsible for the violence.

The coercive institutions may play a more significant role in maintaining the North–South order because improving East–West relations weakened the cooperative institutions of the North–South bloc. The threat that Third World states will join the Soviet camp no longer serves to buttress the development system. Development funds have dried up. Even more significantly, to the extent that development assistance actually can bring other regions into the world of mass production and mass consumption market economies, Eastern Europe, has become the focus of that effort. West

Germany's incorporation of the East involved the largest international economic transfers, the largest "aid effort," since the Marshall Plan. The expansion of the European Union eastward will bring equally massive and long-term transfers from wealthier white states to slightly poorer white states. Meanwhile, aid from white to black and brown, aid from North to South, will continue to shrink.

What, then, was the basis for the hope expressed in 1990 by *West Africa's* editors and evidenced by Willy Brandt's return to North–South issues as well as by the formation of the Group of 15? The debt crises had become endemic and the structural adjustment policies urged upon Third World debtors had most often failed, on their own terms, leaving states in greater balance of payments difficulties. Moreover, even the intellectual leaders of the Reagan revolution had come to recognize that their attack on UN economic institutions had undermined their ability to regulate economic relations among industrialized states, especially when it came to regulations necessary for the new, "Information Age," industrial sectors. The authors of a right-wing collection on international regulation (introduced by Reagan's UN ambassador, Jeanne J. Kirkpatrick) argue that international regulation through the UN system is probably essential; what matters is who designs it. The important thing, they say, is to minimize the Third World's role (Adelman 1988).

It was conceivable throughout the Clinton-era 1990s that Northern governments could be convinced to let the international economic institutions adopt policies of "adjustment with a human face" in order to protect the IMF and World Bank's deeper purpose, maintaining international freedom for capital. "Adjustment with a human face" simply means that debtor governments would be given greater credit, greater opportunity for surviving a debt crisis without gutting the state, in exchange for maintaining those programs that support "human resource development"—health care, primary education, sanitation—basic material needs (Jolly *et al.* 1992). Some consider social programs of this kind the most important development policies for the least developed states, those with great poverty, great dependence, and no absolute advantages in the world trade system. Nevertheless, only in a limited number of Third World states, including democratic socialist Cape Verde, do governments make such commitments in the first place after two decades of neoliberal prescriptions from the major donors.

If movements like Cape Verde's revolutionary party governed larger states in the Third World, the possibilities might be more dramatic. Perhaps they *will* prove to be more dramatic in a world that includes Lula's Brazil and the ANC-governed South Africa.

To explain, let me go back for a moment to the different ways that world-system's theory and this chapter's interpretation of the postwar historic blocs treat the Soviet Union and its sphere. The world-system's theorists emphasize *the choices that were open* to the dominant social forces in the Soviet Union in this century due to its "semiperipheral" location in the world economy (with characteristics of both the core and the periphery) governments had choices not available to those in the Third World. Given the size of the Soviet economy, one reasonable choice at the end of the Second World War was separation from the rest of the world economy. The Soviet economy was large enough that economies of scale could be achieved in most of the new industries that state planners envisioned. The Soviets should have been able to make tractors and trucks, automobiles and airplanes just as efficiently as anyone else because demand for each of those items within the Soviet economic space itself should have been enough to pay for all the fixed costs of the most-efficient (usually meaning, the largest) production system. Other, smaller, semiperipheral states did not have that option. In most, as in South Korea or Taiwan, the governing parties rationally chose to try to fight their way into the core. In those countries, local demand alone would never be enough to allow the most efficient production systems in the newer industries. An "open" orientation, at least, an industrial strategy aimed at competition with the core, was sensible.

In thinking about historic blocs, Gramscians emphasize the *choices actually made* by leading social forces. The Soviet choice, for example, was not a foregone conclusion until, perhaps, 1946. Throughout the Second World War, until the last stage of negotiations over the International Monetary Fund and the World Bank, Soviet officials worked with the British and Americans to create postwar economic institutions that would have created a truly global "interrelated trading area" to use Rostow's (1948) term, in which the technical division of labor could have involved many commodity chains crossing East–West lines. The early discussions on creating the postwar civil aviation regime, on forming the WHO and its links to questions about transportation, and even the talks on forming the International Trade Organization involved a Soviet Union that has not yet determined its postwar orientation. Similarly, the British flirted with the plausible option of maintaining autonomy, a project that united apologists of empire on the right with those on the left like the young Labour MP who used a pseudonym to condemn "The Bretton Woods Plan for World Domination by the USA" (see Murphy 1994: 170–177).

Today, other large semiperipheral states may have options similar to those the Soviet Union faced in 1945. Of course, they cannot develop efficiencies in the newest industries without being part of a global market. After all, the business plans for Microsoft's largely successful attempt to have Windows machines dominate the internet or of Boeing and Airbus for the next generation of jets are based on a truly global market, but the industries of the postwar Automobile Age could be maintained within smaller national or region economic spaces. A large degree of autonomy still is an option open to Brazil, India, China, and some regional blocs within the Third World.

Yet, of course, today, all three major states, including Lula's Brazil, have fully embraced the global economy, and much of the liberal funda-mentalist vision that has dominated policy debates for twenty years. This brings us back to the image of Aristedes Pereira and the Pope in tiny Cape Verde back in 1990. Fourteen years later, Pereira's party is still in power, holding the barest of margins against its opposition, ironically, another party that has been a member of the old democratic socialist Second International. Both parties embrace the global market. Both try, under the most difficult situation of dependency—a tiny country with no natural resources, no rain, and no industry—to maintain some degree of human dignity by maintaining a public realm that satisfies human needs. Moreover, despite the acrimony of their political division, both parties have been successful. Cape Verde, at the time of the oil crisis, one of the poorest and most devastated of Europe's colonies, now has a Human Development Index score that is among the very highest on the continent. As the North–South bloc forms anew, there remain sites of deep social transformation, places that let us at least imagine a truly post-colonial world.

9 Global governance
Poorly done and poorly understood

We live in a world of polities of unprecedented size. The billion-plus nations of India and China dwarf any earlier centralized states and their governments rule populations as large as all humanity just 150 years ago. The population of the informal US Empire—extending west to east from its military protectorates in Korea and Central Europe, north to the pole, and south to its dependencies in Latin America, Africa, and Asia—is greater still. In a world of such large, incontestably real political organizations, we might wonder why so many people spend so much time investigating an even larger, but more dubious, world polity or system of global governance.

The best arguments for paying attention to global governance are ethical and moral. This chapter outlines some of those arguments and then explores the ways different analysts explain the nature and origin of the global polity and the different answers they give to the moral questions raised. The most persuasive analysts emphasize that "what world government we actually have" avoids attacking state sovereignty, favors piecemeal responses to crises, and has emerged at a time when creative intellectual leadership was not matched by courageous political leadership. Consequently, for some time to come global governance and its politics will provide an insufficient answer to the moral questions that compel us to look at what world government there is. Global governance is likely to remain inefficient, incapable of shifting resources from the world's wealthy to the world's poor, pro-market, and relatively insensitive to the concerns of labor and the Third World. Despite its promise, it will remain an institutional framework for marginalization.

Democracy, globalization, and the insufficiency of contemporary governance

The historically minded tell us that something akin to "global" governance has been emerging ever since the European conquests of the fifteenth century. By 1900, the world was divided into colonies and zones of interest of the European powers, the United States, and Japan, and a weak system of inter-imperial institutions—the gold standard, the balance of power, European international law, and the first global international organizations—regulated the whole. The moral controversies surrounding that system energized scholarly observers at the time; consider John A. Hobson's *Imperialism*. Today's controversies differ. The era of formal empire has passed and the twentieth century was, if nothing else, the century of democratization—at least *within* most countries. Not surprisingly, it is as a problem of democracy and democratic theory that questions of global governance now emerge most dramatically.

Western political theorists including Noberto Bobbio, Jürgen Habermas, and, most notably, David Held (1995, 1997), has argued that the contemporary growth of unregulated transnational economic activity undermines the democratic gains won over the last century. To restore and further the democratic project they advocate both the deepening of domestic democratic processes and the extension of democratic forms beyond the nation-state. They champion international institutions both ruled by the people and powerful enough to regulate the global markets in labor, money, goods, and ideas that have expanded so rapidly in recent decades.

A second important strand of moral argument for strengthened global-level governance is less concerned with globalization's undermining of substantive democracy and more concerned with the consequences of an unregulated world. Analysts linked to the United Nations Development Programme (UNDP), the originator the needs-oriented Human Development Index, and to the Brookings Institution, have explored the limited provision of "global public goods," understood primarily as goods that are unlikely to be provided by unregulated markets (Kaul *et al.* 1999, Mendez 1992; Reinicke 1998). Many of the UNDP's arguments appeal strongly even to the most fundamentalist believers in liberal economics. It is hard, for example, to argue against the global monitoring of infectious diseases that could devastate any vulnerable population. Other UNDP claims are more contentious; many of the world's privileged would deny that distributive justice, peace in far away lands, or the protection of the cultural property of the poor constitute "public" goods. Some even find the UNDP's recent embrace of the theory of "global public goods" a bit disingenuous. After all, the UN agency is in the business of promoting one of the least widely accepted of such "goods"—redistributive development assistance from the world's wealthy to the world's poor—and advocates of development assistance have reason enough to argue for the insufficiency of current efforts without embracing the liberal economic rhetoric of public goods. Even the most solidaristically inspired aid provided by social democratic governments has been shrinking over the past decade. Increasingly, the fixed amount of Northern aid to the South covers only the immediate demands of the growing number of humanitarian crises, and maybe contributes to servicing the debt incurred for earlier assistance. Over the past decade, the aid system that had grown since the last years of the Second World War began to atrophy, leaving a governance deficit that contributes to the widening gap between the world's wealthy and the world's poor (Thérien and Lloyd 2000).

Today, almost half of the world's population lives on less than $2 per day. Utilitarian ethicist Peter Singer (1999) reminds us that the average US or EU citizen could raise at least a dozen of these people out of their destitution simply by reducing personal consumption by 20 percent and giving the money to Oxfam or UNICEF. Moreover, the ethical norms to which that US or EU citizen is likely to subscribe would, according to Singer, demand that these citizens do this and probably much more to aid the world's disadvantaged. If the world's privileged were morally consistent, we might expect that the budgets of UNICEF, the UNDP, and the rest of the global development agencies to dwarf those of the Disney Corporation, the Pentagon, or the Common Agricultural Policy. They do not.

Of course, the role of global institutions extends well beyond their service as potential conduits of the charity of the rich. Some analysts argue that the most powerful of the public institutions of global governance—the International Monetary Fund (IMF), the World Trade Organization (WTO), and even the World Bank—through their promotion of unregulated economic globalization, have contributed to the growing numbers of the destitute as well as to the growing privilege of the world's rich. Consider the evaluation of the impact of globalization and the market-promoting practices of the IMF and World Bank on the poor undertaken by the Department of Social Medicine at the Harvard Medical School (Kim *et al.* 2000).

There are even more troubling, and more widely accepted, instances of the moral insufficiency of contemporary global governance. In the 100 days from April to July of 1994 between 500,000 and 800,000 people, including at least three-quarters of the entire Tutsi population of Rwanda were systematically slaughtered, despite a widely ratified UN Genocide Convention and ample early warning provided to the UN Secretariat and the Security Council by its own officers in the field. Analyses of the etiology of the genocide blame not only the Secretariat, the Security Council and its permanent members, but also the entire international aid community, public and private, which for 20 years nurtured a deeply aid-dependent regime that increasingly incited ethnic hatred and violence (Uvin 1998; International Panel 2000; Barnett 2001).

The consequences of the failure to avert the genocide have mounted from year to year. The Tutsi military government that seized power to stop the slaughter went on to trigger a cascade of wars across Central Africa that eventually involved, "some one-fifth of African governments and armies from across the continent . . . as well as perhaps a dozen or more armed groups," according to the Organization of African Unity's Panel of Eminent Personalities to Investigate the 1994 Genocide in Rwanda and the Surrounding Events. They go on to say:

The alliances between and among these groups, with their varied and conflicting interests, has been bewildering. The situation is further endlessly complicated by . . . enormous mineral resources—an irresistible lure for governments, rogue gangs and powerful corporations alike—and by the continuing problem of arms proliferation sponsored by governments throughout the world as well as a multitude of unscrupulous private hustlers.

(International Panel 2000: pars. ES57–58)

Preventing genocide and the avoidable cascading violence of regional war, finding ways efficiently to provide essential international goods that markets will never provide, and challenging globalization's sudden reversal of the twentieth-century's democratic gains, are some of the most compelling reasons for trying to understand the nebulous global polity and the governance it provides.

Ideas, regimes, global public agencies, private authorities, and social movements

When Robert W. Cox (1996a, 2002: 33–34) begins to describe the global governance of the 1990s, he calls it the *nébuleuse*, the cloud of ideological influences that has fostered the realignment of elite thinking to the needs of the world market. Neoliberalism—Thatcherism, Reaganism, or its updated, kinder, "Third Way" grand strategies for economic globalization—certainly is one prominent face of contemporary global governance (cf. Murphy 1999). Cox and the many analysts who have been influenced by his work emphasize that ideological face, the institutions promoting that ideology, and the elite social forces that have been the best served by it. Other analysts focus on an even wider array of faces that the putative global polity presents.

If there is a global polity, then certainly its dominant ideology is liberalism, both economic and political. Since the end of the Cold War, governments almost everywhere have embraced the market. With the one major exception of China, most governments now turn to liberal democratic principles for their legitimation, even, of course, when the large gaps remain between their principles and their practice. Nonetheless, liberal principles are far from the only norms that have power at the global level. Much of the recent scholarship on international relations focuses on the international *regimes*, the norms, rules, and decision-making procedures that states (and sometimes other powerful actors) have created to govern international life within specific realms. At the centre of most regimes lies international law, customary law for some of the oldest and most durable of regimes, and treaty law-conventions reached through multilateral negotiations—for the myriad newer regimes. In the last generation, the number of international environmental regimes has grown from a handful to hundreds. International regimes affecting virtually every major industry now exist, and they grow in complexity from year to year (Young 1994; Braithwaite and Drahos 2000). Moreover, a host of post-Second World War and post-Cold War regimes exist that effectively limit the sovereignty of many states—everything from the IMF and the World Bank's requirements for financial probity to the Western European and American conventions that demand democratic governments within the region.

Most of us who teach global governance have experienced the skeptical or pitying looks of undergraduates when they hear us speak about the *nébuleuse* of neo-liberal ideas linking elites who manage the world economy or the welter of multilateral regimes that we claim share in the governance of global society. To our students these analytical constructs have much less of the solid reality of "the Pentagon," "the Treasury," or any of the other governing institutions that they hear about daily on television and in the newspaper.

Unfortunately, because they do hear about them on the daily news, our students, and other relatively well-informed citizens, are likely to invest the world organizations—the WTO, the UN and its constituent parts—with a bit too much reality, forgetting that they too, at bottom, constitute agreements among their state members. Certainly, some global institutions are increasingly powerful and secretariats can develop as much autonomy from their state members as the managers of large firms can have from their shareholders and corporate boards. Moreover, because global organizations create most of the multilateral forums where regimes negotiated, because they help identify the common interests that become the bases for new regimes, and because these states often give secretariats the responsibility for monitoring compliance, international organizations do provide one of the best sites for beginning an investigation of global governance. Nonetheless, they usually remain the creatures of the most powerful of their state members.

In the early 1970s Robert Cox *et al.* (1973) organized a classic set of case-studies that reveal the real, but limited and specific autonomous powers of the major world organizations—the IMF, World Heath Organization (WHO), International Labor Organization (ILO), and so on. A generation later, Bob Reinalda and Bertjan Verbeek led a European Consortium for Political Research project to update the results. Their conclusion, "Globalization and regional integration are not associated with a clear cut growth in the autonomy of international organizations" (Reinalda and Verbeek 1998: 5). Some organizations have gained; some have lost. Many of those that have gained—organizations promoting the conservation of the environment, the protection of political rights, and the opening of markets, as well as the losers—notably, the ILO—correlate with the issue areas in which the number of regimes have exploded in recent decades, as well as with the post-Cold War elite consensus identified by Cox and others.

What really is new about global governance in the last decade is neither a shift in power from states to global intergovernmental organizations nor the kind of explosion of international conventions in which a change in quantity (the number of new regimes) has meant a change in quality (the locus or nature of global power). Yet, there has been a fundamentally new development: global-level "private" authorities that regulate both states and much of transnational economic and social life. These include:

- private bond-rating agencies that impose particular policies on governments at all levels (Sinclair 1994);
- tight global oligopolies in reinsurance, accounting, high-level consulting that provide similar regulatory pressure;
- global and regional cartels in industries as diverse as mining and electrical products, and
- the peculiar combination of oligopolistic regulation, *ad hoc* private regulation, and non-regulation that governs global telecommunications and the internet.

Some analysts add the increasing authority of:

- internationally integrated mafias; and
- a narrow group of economists who define the norms of that profession and thereby regulate the treasury ministries, the most powerful of the intergovernmental agencies, and the private institutions of financial regulation that want to adhere to economic orthodoxy (Strange 1996; Cutler *et al.* 1999; Hall and Biersteker 2003).

Private global regulations include environmental and labor standards adopted by companies that then have private accounting or consulting firms to monitor product and workplace compliance. Arguably, these regulations are more significant than some current intergovernmental regimes that have the same purpose (see Chapter 11 and Braithwaite and Drahos 2000: 237, 280).

John Braithwaite and Peter Drahos's (2000) massive empirical study of the range of regulatory regimes that currently impinge on global businesses makes the further point that much of the impetus for contemporary public international regulation comes from transnational interest groups, including associations of progressive firms attempting to impose the same costs for environmental and social standards on their competitors, and, of course, traditional consumer groups, labor groups, environmentalists, and so forth. Much of the scholarship on global governance details the roles played by transnational social movements in the development of international regimes in both promoting and responding to the recent wave of globalization (Keck and Sikkink 1998; Smith *et al.* 1997; Waterman 1998; O'Brien *et al.* 2000; Berkovitz 1999; Meyer and Prügl 1999). Analysts point to a long history of such involvement. Social movements have been among the most prominent inventors of regimes and integration schemes ever since Friedrich List organized German businessmen to champion the early nineteenth-century customs union. Moreover, as Braithwaite and Drahos (2000, Chapter 25) emphasize, in periods like ours, when new lead industries emerge and when the scale of businesses of all kinds is growing, relatively egalitarian social movements—women's movements, democracy movements, consumer movements—find unusual opportunities to contribute to the creation of relatively progressive regulation of the new, more global, economy.

Our own period also is characterized by non-governmental organizations (NGOs) playing a further essential role in international governance. Increasingly, as a consequence of liberal fundamentalist marketization, the services once provided by public intergovernmental organizations are now contracted to private, non-governmental, often "social movement"-style, organizations. Today, more often than most of us realize, it is NGOs that run the refugee camps, provide disaster relief, design and carry out development projects, monitor and attempt to contain the international spread of disease, and try to clean up an ever more polluted environment. Moreover, most of them do so primarily with public funds from major donor governments and intergovernmental organizations, officially enamored of the efficiency of NGOs and the "empowerment" that they foster, but also, many analysts suspect, because NGOs provide these necessary international public services on the cheap (Weiss and Gordenker 1996; Weiss 1998). The shift to the public funding of private NGO relief and development efforts is part of what has allowed donor aid budgets to remain stagnant or even fall throughout the post-Cold War era, even though the number of humanitarian emergencies and the numbers of those in absolute poverty have grown.

The global polity, "global governance," then, is all these things: a worldwide management strata sharing neoliberal ideology, a growing network of both public and private regimes that extends across the world's largest regions, the system of global intergovernmental organizations, some of which are relatively autonomous and powerful, and transnational organizations both carrying out some of the traditional service functions of global public agencies and also working to create regimes and new systems of international integration.

How we ended up with the world polity we have

Conventional wisdom tells us that we often get the government we deserve. Political science tries to find additional explanations. Different schools have different pieces of the overall puzzle as to why we have what we have. Unfortunately, so far, few have attempted to put those pieces together to give us the complete picture.

James N. Rosenau, one of the most distinguished students of international politics and someone who has triggered the recent renaissance of scholarship on the global polity (Rosenau and Czempiel 1992), emphasizes the role of private transnational associations, linking the strong evidence of the growing empowerment of such groups to the material attributes of contemporary globalization. A world in which transformations in telecommunications have lowered the costs of political education and created opportunities for more and more subgroups to work with one another is a world of increasingly skilful citizens able to act both above and below the levels of traditional national politics (Rosenau 1992, 1995, 1997). Rosenau both captures and explains the unusual global political turbulence of the last decade, the "fragmengration" or "glocalization" of politics as new social alliances find new political opportunities in spaces above and below existing states. He is less clear why so much of this creative movement in world politics seems to have added up to the supremacy of the neoliberal agenda both within and across states.

Sociologists of the Stanford University-centered World Polity School have paid more attention to this development, arguing that the social institution of cross-border citizen to citizen cooperation—international NGOs and transnational social movements—is an expression of liberal norms, a coevolving social construction based on those norms (Boli and Thomas 1999. Xiaowei Luo (2000) has even argued that if one looks at the evolution of technology-focused organizations, we can see a transformation of the global liberal culture away from a free-market fundamentalism characteristic of the nineteenth century toward a "social development" style liberalism similar to that underlying the UNDP's broad calls for the improved provision of global public goods. Luo objects to the view that there have been oscillations between the liberal fundamentalism associated with the temporary dominance of mobile financial capital and the critical liberal internationalism of the periods of relative peace and prosperity. From that perspective, it would be incorrect to characterize today's global polity as one dominated by a relatively fundamentalist version of neoliberalism.

Other social constructivists, for example, political scientists Martha Finnemore (1996) and John Ruggie (1998) would probably disagree. Yet, they would share the Stanford School's fundamentally rich understanding of global institutions as dialogical phenomena, as states of affairs created by international actors in their interaction. What becomes central, for the constructivists, is the understanding that state leaders have of the way in which their commitments to each other constrain or enable their own action. In the world of socially constructed international institutions, persuasive communication matters. State leaders, global businessmen, nongovernmental activists, even the occasional International Relations scholar, influence each other's understanding of their own "interests" and of the moral and social world in which they live. Liberal norms, for example, exert power not due to their inherent validity or rightness, but because they are regularly enacted within certain realms, because some international actors have become convinced of their rightness and validity.

Perhaps because political scientists like Ruggie and Finnemore are drawn to focus on entire networks of social communication in which state interests become identified and defined, they are apt to see a range of significant actors within the world polity. Perhaps even more than Rosenau, these scholars recognize that, despite the real diffusion of power above and below the state (and to private agencies at all levels), powerful states remain the most significant sites of consolidated power over people and territory in the contemporary world.

As Cox would argue, it is in the most powerful of state agencies (the Treasuries) and in the most powerful clubs of states (the WTO, IMF, and World Bank) that neoliberalism is triumphant. Certainly it matters that global norms have an impact on and help to construct national interests, just as it matters that some intergovernmental agencies and private institutions are increasingly powerful, but we are not going to be able to explain the nature of global governance without understanding the ways in which powerful states construct and pursue their grand strategies.

Finnemore's and Ruggie's kind of historically rich social constructivist analysis has not been the one most frequently applied to the problem of state-to-state cooperation in recent years in the United States (and, to a lesser extent, in the former West Germany) where a great deal has been learned from rationalist studies of regime formation. Robert O. Keohane's (1984) *After Hegemony: Cooperation and Discord in the World Political Economy* influenced much of this analysis. One of Keohane's central insights is that even when states share potential interests they often need to form intergovernmental institutions to serve them; intergovernmental regimes are, most often, an active form of cooperation that allow states to pursue non-zero-sum games. Based on this insight, analysts have been keen to employ a variety of rationalist models from liberal political economy and strategic game theory in order to explore questions about the relationship between domestic politics and international cooperation, the likelihood of regimes forming to govern different problems, the potential role of knowledge and knowledge elites in promoting particular cooperative solutions, and the lessons that can be learned from the history of regime formation looked at through a rationalist lens (Hasenclever *et al.* 1997; Milner 1997; Young 1999)

Analysts from the Third World are quick to point out the limits to all of the explanations so far mentioned. As South African Peter Vale (1995) argues, the intricacies of state-to-state cooperation are of little relevance to the vast majority of Africans, Eastern Europeans, and others whose states have broken down and for whom the arrival of global liberalism and the increased influence of multilateral institutions has meant only the intensification of "market-driven poverty." The moral issues raised by the contemporary problems of global governance, Vale stresses, simply cannot be understood within conceptual frameworks that focus on states and ignore the fundamental conflicts between the privileged and the world's marginalized people. Significantly, one realist scholar working within the rationalist framework has argued that even some of the most widely touted regimes formed among the most privileged nations—NAFTA and the European Monetary System—amounted to coercive impositions upon Canada's Liberals and on Southern European governments of the Center and Left (Gruber 2000). The Dean of Realist International Political Economy in the United States, Princeton's Robert Gilpin (2000), is blunter, arguing that if there is anything that looks like liberal global governance it is an expression of the power and preferences of the United States.

Yet, it is certainly not just that. Susan Strange devoted much of the last years of her life demonstrating that the US and Western European governments shared the responsibility for giving up state power to the global market through a series of "rational," short-term self-interested decisions with consequences recognized as disastrous by at least some political leaders on both sides of the Atlantic (Strange 1996). Moreover, the social forces that have continued to back the neoliberal agenda are truly transnational, which implies that to understand contemporary global governance we need to develop a class analysis that transcends national boundaries. Kees van der Pijl (1998), Bill Robinson (Robinson and Harris 2000), and a number of other scholars who John M. Hobson (2000: 128–133) inelegantly calls "orthodox neo-Marxists" has begun to develop such an analysis. Yet, I doubt that any of us (for Hobson includes me in this group) would argue that we have it quite right. Arguably, Karl Deutsch's (1957) empirical work on the evolution of transnational elites during periods of international integration is more sophisticated than anything developed in recent years. Certainly, if there is an emergent global, non-state specific capitalist class, it is evolving along with American power and the institutions of global governance. The global polity is not simply a superstructure responding to the interests of an already differentiated global ruling class. Global governance is more a site, one of many sites, in which struggles over wealth, power, and knowledge are taking place.

It may be more accurate, or at least less controversial, to argue that contemporary global governance remains a predictable institutional response not to the interests of a fully formed class, but to the overall logic of industrial capitalism. "Economic globalization," understood as industrial capitalism's pressure towards larger and larger market areas, necessarily means that at some points the real economies will escape the boundaries of states, as the global economy has today. Contemporary observers are bound to see such moments as representing "triumphs of the market" over the state, but, no doubt, at the same time there will be simultaneous pressure to establish new institutions of governance at a "higher," more inclusive level, at least at the level at which new markets have developed. Historians of intergovernmental organization and international integration note that for the last two centuries at least, the ideology most often used to justify new, powerful, and autonomous international institutions has been a kind of "scientism," the argument that there are socially beneficial, technical tasks that should be handed over to "experts" to be done for us, the argument of many functionalists, and certainly the argument of the nineteenth-century critical liberal "experts in government," the fathers of global governance (see Chapter 3). Not surprisingly, Martin Hewson and Timothy J. Sinclair (1999) argue, almost all of the partial explanations we have for global governance implicate one or more of (1) the unfolding of professional expertise, (2) marketization, and (3) the material infrastructure—the communication and transportation networks—that make globalization possible.

What is to be done?

This brings us right back to questions of democratic theory: must globalization inevitably be accompanied by the anti-democratic government of "expertise" or by the non-government of marketization at ever more inclusive levels? Are, as Ian R. Douglas (1999) argues, "globalization" and "governance" simply two inseparable aspects of the modern project of elite control? Is it possible to marshal the egalitarian forces that Rosenau correctly sees as being empowered by the technologies of globalization to create a democratic system of global governance that would both prevent repetition of the tragedies of the post-Cold War decade and provide essential goods that global markets will not provide?

Much of the recent analysis of these questions has focused on the system of global intergovernmental organizations, on impediments to the transformation of the UN family of agencies and the newer, non-UN, WTO. A recurrent theme in the pages of the international public policy journal *Global Governance* is the ubiquitous impediment of US foreign policy. Throughout the 1990s, the US gave rhetorical support to a variety of innovations in global governance from expanded humanitarian operations, to the vast agenda of the Beijing women's conference, to the creation of the International Criminal Court. Yet, perhaps more often than not, US action has not matched its words, preventing Security Council action in Rwanda, refusing to adhere to the land mines' ban and Criminal Court agreements that it had originally championed, and failing, year after year, to pay its UN dues. Moreover, as long-time senior UN staffer Erskine Childers argues, the Bush and Clinton administrations were the 1990's most consistent and powerful advocates of marketization and a system of global governance promoting "market democracy," a phrase that earns Childers's (1997: 272) acid comment:

> If I may ask in an Irish way, what in the name of God is "market democracy"? Thirty years ago the phrase would have been strongly

challenged as the intellectual rubbish that it is—or the insidiously undemocratic trickery that it also is.

Less combatively, Childers's colleague John Washburn (at one time, the senior international civil servant holding a US passport) advises that people concerned with strengthening and democratizing global governance ignore the US and let the UN "look after itself." He carefully explains why US political culture and institutions assure that the country will remain an inconsistent leader and, largely, an obstruction to ethical global governance (Washburn 1996), an argument similar to the one presented in Chapter 6 about the institutional impediments to the US negotiating toward the NIEO.

Arguably, the International Criminal Court Treaty and the Ottawa Convention on Landmines are successful demonstrations of Washburn's preferred strategy. Both are significant extensions of international humanitarian law promoted by the political leadership of close US allies and non-governmental movements with deep ties inside the US, but achieved over the opposition of the US government. There is also reason to believe that both innovations can have most of their desired effects even without US adherence (Thakur and Maley; 1999, Benedetti and Washburn 1999). The strategies used to achieve both treaties suggest that it is possible, in some fields, to nullify the impact of the United States's separation of powers and history of isolation that gives its legislators the power and desire to block democratic extensions of global governance.

Unfortunately, few of the conventions needed to establish a more powerful and more democratic form of global governance can be designed that cleverly. Where significant corporate interests are likely to be implicated, where real attempts are being made to control lucrative global markets—as, for example, in the most far reaching of the environmental regimes proposed at the 1992 Rio Conference—the "indispensability and indefensibility" of US policy, as some analysts have called it, is likely to remain (Agrawala and Andresen 1999).

Many rationalist analysts—whether neorealist or neoliberal—would leave it at that. If the strengthening and democratization of global governance are not in US interests, then there is no particular point in pursuing such goals until the relative power of the US sharply declines or US interests change. If the most powerful economic interests oppose such developments, it is difficult to imagine how they can be pursued successfully.

Constructivists recognize that interests are never given; they are historically embedded, enacted social structures, subject to rethinking and enacting differently. Not surprisingly, much of John G. Ruggie's work as Assistant UN Secretary General supported Kofi Annan's (1998) effort to convince American and global corporate leaders to change how they understand their interests relative to the UN's agenda. Towards that end, the Secretariat sponsored a superb study by the University of British Columbia's Mark Zacher, to, in Ruggie's (1999) words:

> Provide business leaders and government officials as well as the public at large with a comprehensive account of the important roles played by the United Nations in facilitating order and openness in the global economy.

The far-from-radical Zacher, who has produced a series of exhaustively researched studies explaining the origin and impact of international institutions governing almost every dimension of global governance, from security, to trade, to telecommunications, to health, was in an unusually strong position to conclude that without what world government we have, "it would truly be 'a jungle out there' for firms . . . that cared to venture beyond their own national borders" (Zacher 1999: 5).

In this context, Braithwaite and Drahos's analysis is especially significant. They begin with the reasonable assumption that transformations of global business regulation will take place in the next decade. This has happened every time there has been a leap in the scale of the world's leading industries, that is, at every industrial divide since the Industrial Revolution. The beginning of the Information Age in the 2000s is no different from the beginning of the Automobile and Jet Age in the 1950s, or the Second Industrial Revolution of the 1890s, or the Railway Age of the 1840s. The nature 0f that new regulation that will emerge is not preordained. Based both on the longer history of international regulation and on a close reading of changes that are more recent, Braithwaite and Drahos end their study with a set of strategies for "recapturing the sovereignty of the people" over global business. This is to be done, they argue, by, on the one hand, assuring that social and environmental standards are ratcheted up, rather than down, as business becomes more global and by promoting greater, rather than less, real competition (Braithwaite and Drahos 2000: 607–629).

Significantly, many of the strategies they advocate have, in fact, been those employed over the last twenty years by international women's movements and by movements pressing for global support for democratization and human rights—the two groups of egalitarian social movements that have been the most successful over the last two decades (see Chapter 4 and Murphy 2001b, 2002). Recall, for example, what Braithwaite and Drahos call "model mongering," meaning the constant, experimental promotion of an ever-growing array of possible solutions to globalization problems faced by business and governments. Consider small-scale gender-based lending, reproductive freedom, primary education for women, and other elements of a quarter-century-old Women in Development agenda. All have been successfully mongered to a host of institutions whose primary concerns are not gender equity, but who have become convinced that these program will reduce poverty, minimize costs of development assistance, placate an increasingly powerful Northern women's constituency, expand consumer markets, and help clean up the environment.

Braithwaite and Drahos's strategies do not provide answers to all of the moral questions raised by today's inadequate global governance. They rely on the piecemeal, haphazard formation of global regulation. They assume no change in the institution of national sovereignty. They are based on a realistic understanding of global power in that they rely on countervailing powers and can only be employed by groups whose welfare is in some way of interest to those they call, "the global lawmakers . . . the men who run the largest corporations, the US and the EC" (Braithwaite and Drahos 2000: 642). It would be naive to assume that every victim of the market will be of interest to these men. Yet, it is significant that this exemplary attempt to understand one part of global governance suggests some realistic hope for its improvement.

10 Political consequences of the new inequality

Before turning to further discussion of the techniques that might be used to reform global governance, this chapter considers the newer patterns of marginalization and empowerment that mark the current industrial era. I focus on the political agenda that, as a consequence, may link the interests of Braithwaite and Drahos's "global lawmakers" with those of some of the victims of the market. I note that, within countries, formal democracy is flourishing. Almost everywhere, state power is waning, gender inequality has diminished, and, according to most experts, income inequality across the world's households has risen. The consequences of these new patterns include: (1) more frequent protracted social conflicts, (2) a newly politicized sphere of international public health, (3) a new global gender politics, (4) the new global politics of the super-rich, and (5) the new politics and ethics of the world's privileged. Moreover, the responsibilities of the intellectual communities that study world affairs have grown, in part, because popular media present a decreasingly coherent picture of each of these patterns; and that incoherence, itself, may help sustain global inequalities.

I first presented these arguments as my presidential address to members of the International Studies Association (ISA). I framed them as a list of things that "every citizen should know" about world affairs and argued ISA members would welcome a professional obligation to understand these issues and teach about them. The ISA may be unique among the peak social science associations in its continued commitment to the progressive ideals of the social movements that institutionalized the modern social sciences a little more than a century ago. Many presidents of the ISA have been committed social activists, as well as distinguished scholars. Many have been part of that tradition of critical liberal internationalist intellectual leaders who have both learned from and informed activist communities concerned with creating a more peaceful and prosperous world. Consider Bruce Russett's signal contribution to the Catholic bishops' deliberations on nuclear deterrence, Herbert Kelman's facilitation of each stage of dialogue between Israel and the Arab world, and J. David Singer's life of peace activism. Others have worked for social transformation within the

Academy. Consider Peg Hermann's quiet efforts to build cultures of toler-
ance within psychology, political science, and International Relations and
Robert O. Keohane's work to make American International Relations and
political science welcoming to women. Others have been activists within
their own communities. One of those, Fred Sondermann of Colorado
College, was also the last ISA president from an undergraduate college.
Fred was a family friend, an active citizen in my hometown, and someone
who influenced my choice of career.

There is an older connection between the teaching of International
Relations at my college, Wellesley, and his. It is part of the long history
of activist scholars working on international institutions.

In 1893, three visiting faculty members at Colorado College made a
famous trip up Pikes Peak: Katharine Lee Bates, of Wellesley College,
Woodrow Wilson, of Princeton, and William T. Stead, editor of the *Review
of Reviews* and the man E. H. Carr (1939: 76) called "the most popular
and brilliant" international affairs writer of the day. Their conversation
kept returning to their one mutual interest, the role of international "federalism" in promoting peace and prosperity. Wilson was completing his study
of the creation of the American national system (1898). Stead (1899),
inspired by his visit with Bates to Chicago's Columbian Exposition, was
beginning to imagine a continental system of liberal economics and politics across Europe. Yet, the most famous outcome of the long day's
discussion was a poem by the one of the three who was, at the time, the
most famous, Bates's "America the Beautiful."

Bates's role as a liberal internationalist intellectual leader is part of the
lore of Wellesley College. She hired Emily Greene Balch, the pioneering
International Relations scholar who received the 1946 Nobel Peace Prize
for her work promoting the continuation of the League's economic and
social institutions after the Second World War. The poet also started the
distinguished collection on "international federalism" in Wellesley's library
used by Keohane when he wrote his 1984 classic, *After Hegemony*, and by
Charles P. Kindleberger (1973) while working on his paradigmatic *The
World in Depression*.[1]

On the surface, little can be seen of that commitment in Bates's famous
Pikes Peak poem. Nonetheless, it is there in her vision of the United States
as a work in progress and a place that will have global responsibilities
(compare Sherr 2001). For example, staring down at the endless line of
hopper cars filled with gold ore winding from Cripple Creek down to the
towering belching chimneys of Colorado Springs's constantly burning,
hellish smelters, she wrote:

> America, America
> May God thy gold refine
> Till all success be nobleness
> And every gain divine!

In 1962, Fred Sondermann shared Bates's hope that Americans would use its incomparable riches and power both consciously and justly. Many students of International Relations will recall his argument because professors still assign Sondermann's 1977 essay, "The Concept of the National Interest" (Sondermann 1977). When he became president of the ISA, he was concerned with responsibilities of undergraduate teachers to let students know that they are able to *shape* the national interest; it is not something that shapes them.

It was a very different world then, a Cold War, bipolar world of three billion people. Decolonization was really only just beginning. Racial and income inequalities within the US were under attack even while Americans enjoyed an unprecedented military and economic supremacy even over our allies in Western Europe and Japan. Yet, most Americans—even those of us with our *5 Dollars A Day* guidebooks and stories to tell about wartime ruins that remained in Europe and Japan—had yet to assimilate the meaning of our dominance.

Today, as we International Relations professors always tell our students, the Cold War is long over and we live in a uni- or multi-polar "globalized" world. We have come to assume that our students understand both the relative military and economic superiority of the United States and the relatively equal levels of economic privilege that exist throughout the industrial centers of what was once called the "Free World." Sometimes we also mention to our students that we live in a human world that is twice as large, twice as populated, as it was in the early 1960s. Less rarely, we tell our students anything about the outcomes of the greatest twentieth-century global movement against inequality—the movement for decolonization—or about the shifting and growing inequality that has marked human life over the last generation.

That is my purpose here. Over the last thirty years:

- Formal political inequality has diminished. (Limited democracy has flourished.)
- Public-sphere gender inequality has diminished and continues to diminish. (Women almost everywhere have gained increasingly equal legal rights, political opportunities, job opportunities, and wages.)
- The impact of the reduction of formal political inequality has been lessened due to diminished power of the nation-state relative to the markets and to local, international, and transnational political forces. (Democratization does not mean as much as it once might have because the nation-state is less important than it once was.)
- Income inequality has risen. The bimodal distribution of income across the globe is becoming even more distinct. (The rich have gotten much richer while the poor have grown in number and many are staying just as poor.)

Why should all citizens know about these trends? Why do International Relations professionals have an interest in making that knowledge available?

The recent triumph of formal democracy will affect the conditions for international peace, one of the perennial questions of International Relations. Moreover, the commitment to substantive democratization has been the central element in each of the waves of scientific progress within our field. The social commitment of International Relations scholars has remained in the forefront in large part because scholars who have been part of the democratic enterprise have, in fact, learned more about the operation of world politics, whether they were the early twentieth-century critical internationalists like Balch and John A. Hobson, the interwar realists like E. H. Carr, or the Cold War-era pioneers of scientific studies of peace and war like Russett and Singer (Murphy 2001a).

Sources of information about the current wave of democratization are myriad, but one of the very best starting places for faculty and our students is the empirical work done by Mike Ward and his colleagues at the universities of Colorado and Washington (O'Loughlin *et al.* 1998; Gleditsch and Ward 2000), much of it first presented at meetings of the ISA.

Citizens need to understand the trend toward gender equality, the second positive element of the new global pattern, because it represents a trend of substantive democratization that is both less precedented and more likely to be sustained than the rise of liberal-democratic national governments. Gender equality in the public sphere—that is, in the worlds of paid work and of law and politics—should not be confused with gender equality per se. The double burden of "productive" work for wages on top of socially reproductive work remains. This is especially true even for women in societies where wage and participation gaps have narrowed the most. Nonetheless, the trend of women throughout the world gaining increasingly equal legal rights, political opportunities, job opportunities, and wages is of world historical significance. Perhaps even more significant, as recent work by World Bank documents, is the fact that the rates of change in those variables are fastest in the regions of the world where the gaps were the greatest (Tzannatos 1999).

International Relations scholars have not studied these trends as actively as have researchers within organizations like the World Bank, UNDP, UNIFEM (UN Development Fund for Women), and the UN Research Institute on Social Development, although ISA meetings increasingly attract scholars, such as Isabella Bakker (1994) and Diane Elson (Grown *et al.* 2000), who have long been associated with these issues and these institutions. As the field strengthens its own research programs in this area, International Relations scholars will do well to look to them and to other feminist economists such as my Wellesley colleague, Julie Matthaei (2001).

The third and fourth elements of the new inequality should be more troubling to a field in which scientific progress and a commitment to substantive democratization have gone hand in hand. Many of us, including

Susan Strange (1996) in *The Retreat of the State*, have been struck by the tragic irony that, in so many places, democratization has taken place at a time when the state is too weak to provide the majority with the economic transformation for which they struggled. The mid-twentieth-century apartheid state made it possible for Afrikaners to rise to equality with South Africa's anglophone ruling class. The new, downsized South African democratic state of this century cannot do the same for its black majority. International Studies Association members have developed an especially rich understanding of this irony, although scholars who have felt they are on the periphery of the field have done much of this work. They include not only scholars from outside the United States such as Susan Strange and the late Claude Ake (1995), but also comparativists from North America.

The final element of the new inequality is the most troubling. When Fred Sondermann spoke to the ISA membership over 40 years ago, we lived in a world of rich and poor, a world with a bimodal income distribution. At the top were mostly people in the nations of the ISA's membership, the US and Canada, industrialized nations that had been spared the destruction of the Second World War. At the bottom were India and Pakistan, China, and much of Southeast Asia, many of them less than 15 years from real independence, and the many still-colonized nations of Africa.

Forty years ago, most expert observers expected the world's income distribution to shift from what they considered a socially unstable bimodal form to the unimodal distribution that characterizes most domestic societies. The incomes of the poor of South Asia, China, and Africa would grow to blend into those of the growing incomes of the world's industrializing nations in Latin America, Southern Europe, and the Middle East. In turn, they would grow to blend with the incomes of Western Europe and Japan, which would have joined the United States. Instead, as a World Bank study by Branko Milanovic (1999) based on household surveys, demonstrates, rural and urban areas in South Asia and Africa and rural areas in China have remained stagnant, albeit to different degrees, as their populations grew. At the same time, especially in the most recent decades, the bulk of the world's economic growth was accumulated by individuals within the wealthy OECD states, places where domestic income inequality has grown sharply as well. The bimodal distribution of world income has remained.

Milanovic estimates that world income inequality in the 1980s and early 1990s grew much more rapidly than domestic income inequality grew in the US and the UK, a period when the ratio of the average line-worker's salary to the average CEO's salary grew tenfold. Income inequality across the world's households may have grown during the lives of today's average 20-year-old undergraduate as much as it did in the 200 years before she was born.

Milanovic's conclusions, and similar ones reached by other agencies of the UN family (Cornia 1999, summarizes UNDP and WIDER (World Institute for Development Economics Research) studies that confirm the World Bank study) and by many independent scholars, remain controversial. If one starts with country-by-country data, conservative estimates of income distribution changes within countries, and optimistic estimates of changes within China, it is possible to conclude that global income inequality has declined slightly in the last five to ten years (Melchior *et al.* 2000; Dowrick and Akmal 2003). With this different approach, the global pattern depends on whether one uses purchasing power parity measures (which are better if one is concerned with issues of material well-being or relative poverty) or standard figures that reflect the market exchange rate of currencies (which are better if one is concerned with issues of capital accumulation or relative power).

No matter how one measures it, a significant difference certainly remains between the world's most extremely privileged few whose control of resources and of the labor of others continues to grow and the large numbers who remain in absolute poverty. Yet, it may be unclear why this sort of inequality should be something that all citizens should think about.

To explain, let me go back to that connection between the goals of the field of International Relations and the project of substantive democratization. In our "globalized" world of weakened states, many—perhaps most—substantive collective decisions have been delegated to the market. Increasingly unequal incomes mean increasingly unequal market power. In a world in which we let the market do much of our collective business, increasingly unequal market power means less and less democracy.

Beyond that simple correlation between one part of the new inequality and the substantive goals of International Relations schools, I want to suggest five other ways in which the new inequality is likely to affect the lives of all citizens. These are the five political consequences outlined before:

- the new politics of protracted social conflict;
- the new global health politics;
- the new global gender politics;
- the new politics of super-empowered individuals;
- the new politics of those who are merely greatly empowered.

Near the end of his report, Milanovic (1999: 51) asks how the world's income inequality can possibly continue. He speculates, "Such a high inequality is sustainable precisely because the world is not unified, and rich people do not mingle, meet, or even know about the existence of the poor other than in the most abstract way." The five political consequences discussed here all involve indirect, although not abstract, ways in which the increasing numbers of the world's poor and their increasing relative poverty do affect the world's rich, including most International Relations professionals, most of our students, and most of the readers of this book.

International Studies Association members have been at the forefront of the scholarly work that identifies and explains the first: the politics of protracted social conflict. Ted Gurr (2000), Albrecht Schnabel and Ramesh Thakur (2001), and others have demonstrated the direct connections among persistent patterns of inequality—especially when they fall across lines of group identity, as they usually do—and regimes of economic hardship in the long-standing violent conflicts that have torn apart Africa, the former communist states, and other parts of the world. The first point is simply that we have an obligation to make our students aware that, in all likelihood, their lives will be marked by greater, not fewer, tragedies like those they remember in Somalia, Rwanda, and Kosovo, as Immanuel Wallerstein (1999) has consistently and persuasively argued in recent years.

As most International Relations professors in the US know, one of the ironies of the post-Cold War, "globalized" era is that the window provided onto the worlds of protracted social conflict by the American news media has shrunk. Today, even more than when Fred Sondermann presided over the ISA, readers of American dailies are likely to be given only momentary glimpses of the battle in Western and Central Africa—when, for example, Bill Clinton sends a personal videotape to the combatants to ask them to make peace or George W. Bush makes a whirlwind trip to the continent—only to have the small window for "African" stories blocked out the next day by the even more horrific—and never explained—typhoons and floods covering Mozambique or oil-related coup in economically desperate São Tome. As the Rockefeller Brothers Fund (2000) "Global Interdependence Initiative" argues:

> The public does not know whom or what to blame for the global problems about which it is concerned, nor does it know whom to hold accountable for their resolution; these limitations in public understanding are reflections of the episodic, crisis-driven nature of media coverage of international affairs – the world as "global mayhem." More of this kind of attention to global issues should not necessarily be sought or welcomed by advocates for international causes, since the only action that can result from global mayhem is charity for victims ("fixing the person"), not systemic efforts to prevent problems and promote well being (fixing the condition).

The decreasingly coherent picture of the world of protracted social conflict available to our students may help create the ignorance of our world's growing inequality that makes that inequality "sustainable," in the way Milanovic suggests. It also gives International Relations analysts a special responsibility to provide the public with the larger historical context and the explanations that can make these random stories coherent.

All of us will be affected by the new inequality by much more than the random glimpses of the seemingly bizarre worlds of protracted social conflict that will be offered to them by CNN or *The New York Times*. Some aspects of the new global health politics are more likely to be encountered more directly and with more immediate salience. These are health problems of the world's poor that have penetrated enclaves of the world's rich. Drug-resistant tuberculosis from a newly impoverished Siberia rapidly moves to every continent and the disease becomes nearly as great a killer at the end of the twentieth century as it was at the beginning. Cholera moves from Andean barrios to suburbs of Boston. New strains of AIDS are following the routes of the international sex trade to the homes of its wealthiest consumers. There is a new international politics that surrounds these new disease patterns, a politics that links the world's rich and the world's poor (see, especially, Berlinguer *et al.* 1999; and Farmer 2003).

This is not the only aspect of the new global health politics. There is also the reaction that is building to the wealthy world's increasing attempts to externalize the costs of its own health problems. The first stage in the World Health Organization's tobacco-free initiative involves Gro Bruntland's use of the organization's treaty-proposing power to force developed countries to consider things like a global ban on the promotion of cigarettes to children and women (WHO 2001). In theory, the treaty could end the practice of making agreements with tobacco companies to compensate some of their rich-country victims, while at the same time using the leverage provided by free-trade agreements to open foreign markets to the same practices that domestic agreements preclude.

International Studies Association members have only recently been at the forefront of research into the new global health politics, but the world of members who cross the fields of international public health and International Relations, such as Kelly Lee and Richard Dodgson (2000), promises to open up an entirely new field.

Dodgson (1999) has done much of his research on the politics of the International Women's Health Movement, the social movement at the center of many of the global conferences of the 1990s and a shaper of much of the current global development agenda (also see Higer 1997). The new global health politics and the new global gender politics are linked. Most of our students will not experience that linkage directly, nor will they necessarily directly understand the link between growing income inequality and the empowerment of women that is part of the base of the new global gender politics. We need to let them understand that connection.

The pattern that is familiar in North America is also typical in other parts of the world. Poorer women have entered the world of paid work to maintain household incomes of families pressured by technological and market forces that drive down workingmen's wages. At the same time, in the most privileged parts of the world, as Matthaei (2001) argues, wealthier women have rebelled in support of an elite feminism that helped articulate the political agenda for legal and wage equality, an agenda with worldwide effects. Matthaei paints a wonderfully hopeful picture of the convergence and further development of these trends in the industrialized world. Gender roles, across all social classes, become less rigid. The possibilities for more effective egalitarian politics across other lines of difference grow.

The scenario cannot necessarily be extended to the rest of the world. When the undergraduates of 2004 become middle-aged, the gender politics of Pakistan or Brazil will not be the gender politics of the US today. The global gender politics of 2030 will differ because a transnational women's movement with egalitarian principles already exists, albeit one now led by Western cadres. The relative empowerment of women in the less-privileged world is likely to make that movement even more committed to global equality than it is today. The international women's movement will likely become an even more important vehicle for, in Milanovic's words, "rich people . . . to mingle, meet, or even know about the existence of the poor."

There is a rich tradition of scholarship by International Studies Association members that allows us to make and to test such predictions. It includes the path-breaking studies compiled by Robin Teske and Mary Ann Tétreault (2000) and Margaret Keck and Kathryn Sikkink's (1998) *Activists beyond Borders,* winner of both the ISA's Chad Alger Prize and the Graymeyer Peace Prize.

A cartoon in the first Sunday paper of 2000 could serve as the transition to the fourth of the political consequences of the new inequality. The two protagonists in "Stone Soup," feminists from the privileged part of the world, who have become empowered after being forced into wage employment, discuss their hopes for the new millennium. They revolve around the amassed market power of what the *Times* foreign correspondent Tom Friedman (1999) has dubbed, "Super-empowered individuals."

The first woman in the comic says, "I wish Bill Gates would just buy Afghanistan and free all the women there." Her bemused friend responds, "And I was just wishing you could be more optimistic." To which the first responds, "*I am!* It could happen!!"

In one sense, it was possible. If Gates had spent twice a relatively liberal estimate of the gross domestic product of Afghanistan in 1998, it would only be about a quarter of what he earned that year. In retrospect, given both the tragedies of September 11, 2001 and the continuing turmoil in the country, it may have been a bargain.

Friedman's point, made equally strongly by the 1998 UNDP *Human Development Report,* is that individuals with Gates's level of market power are relatively new. J. D. Rockefeller may have been able to buy and sell a few countries, but they were many fewer than Gates could, and they were mostly colonies in those days anyway. The new global politics of super-empowered individuals centers around the opportunity costs of the decisions that people like Bill Gates make about what to do with their wealth. By granting a billion dollars over ten years to the United Nations,

Ted Turner can thwart the well-planned effort of democratically elected, isolationist Republican strategists to create a permanent rift between the United States and the world organization. Similarly, by deciding to fund the development and distribution of vaccines for a host of the most destructive infectious diseases, the Gates Foundation accomplished with the stroke of a pen something that activists within the WHO had been struggling to achieve for decades. At the same time, the Gates Foundation may have reinforced a wide but dangerously mistaken belief that international public goods are likely to be sufficiently supplied by private charity alone.

There is significant work by ISA members that can teach this last lesson (Kaul *et al.* 1999). On the other hand, ISA members have been slow in investigating the *empirical* phenomena of the role that the super-wealthy have played in world politics. Somewhat inadvertently, I came across evidence of that role in my own work on the history of international institutions and industrial change (Murphy 1994 and Chapter 11). I found that nineteenth-century European aristocrats and twentieth-century Western plutocrats played essential roles as sponsors and benefactors of international agencies in their early years. They also kept the most essential global institutions alive during the previous era in which they were in crisis (the League's economic agencies during the Depression and the Second World War). Very few scholars, perhaps only Kees van der Pijl (1998), recognized the implications of that finding when it was first published, although some activists within the international NGO world did.

In the near future, we may see more research on the international power of the super-rich. One thing that bodes well is the agenda of the Social Science Research Council president, sociologist Craig Calhoun (2000), who is calling for much greater attention not only to the role of transnational social movements (see the point above) but also to the historical and ongoing role of major philanthropies. Those organizations serve as the relevant vehicles of much of the super-power of the men and women in whose hands the world's wealth is increasingly concentrated.

Let me be clear, I am not arguing that citizens should learn about the super-rich either because they are worthy of emulation, or of disdain, or because attempts to shift the preferences of the super-empowered are likely to provide rewarding avenues for democratic political action. The point is, rather, that given the increasing concentration of the world's market power, all of us need to expect that the preferences of the super-rich will have an increasing impact on world politics.

Nonetheless, it is important for students of International Relations to understand that the shape of the world's income distribution will place ethical and political demands upon them that will be similar to the somewhat uninteresting dilemmas faced by the super-empowered. As mentioned in the last chapter, the utilitarian ethicist Peter Singer (1999) reminds us that the average American college graduate, without significantly reducing her quality of life (as measured by the UNDP Human Development Index), could provide the income to raise scores of people out of absolute poverty or bring the incomes of at least a few impoverished people up to the point at which a high level of human development—long life, good health and education, the material conditions for self-actualization—is possible. Singer would have us think about the opportunity costs of every consumption decision we make that sacrifices the basic needs of the world's least-advantaged for our own ephemeral pleasures.

Undergraduate teachers of introductory world politics, as the only people most of the attentive public will ever hear talk about any social issues from a truly global perspective, may have a special obligation to make this argument. Frankly, though, I am not sure I want to be forever reminding my students of the dozens or the hundreds of the world's poor who will always be traveling with them. Nonetheless, I do want my students to understand the structural violence, and the possible consequences of that structural violence, existing in a world in which some of us are so relatively rich and others are so relatively poor.

Peter Uvin's (1998) disturbing analysis of the aid system and the Rwanda genocide pictures the worst of what can happen. For more than a decade, with the very best intentions, almost the entire range of bilateral, inter-governmental, and nongovernmental aid agencies ignored all the early warning signs of genocide identified by decades of scholarship, some of it done by past ISA presidents. Funds that were pittances to Northern donors—private and public—became, in the Central African context, vast treasuries maintaining a grossly unequal society and financing training in ethnic hatred. There is every reason to believe that the pattern Uvin describes in Rwanda will be repeated throughout the lives of today's undergraduates. They need to understand it.

International Relations scholars have done less than we could to make explicit the pathways through which gross global inequalities lead to the separation of power and responsibility. No single research paradigm provides a sure guide. Robert H. Jackson's (1990) philosophically conservative, historical, and legal analysis of the construction of quasi-states is revealing, perhaps just as revealing as Hartmut Elsenhans's (1991) critical political economy of global development (with which I am much more sympathetic), or Charles Tilly's (1998) more analytical, trans-historical sociology of the micro-mechanisms of durable inequality. However, one thing that all these frameworks have in common is a willingness to treat national boundaries as categories that naturalize and support the exploitation and the hoarding of advantages that become the inequalities of a larger system. All of these frameworks allow us to see states and their creatures—including international institutions—as potential instruments of marginalization.

Fred Sondermann always emphasized that American International Relations analysts and our students—the people with whom we share the responsibility for preserving and extending our community's knowledge of world affairs—are able to become conscious of, to shape, and to transform those naturalized boundaries that keep us from knowing or caring about people in other lands. He believed that, with modesty and compassion, this group that makes up the largest, least visible, and least celebrate group of internationalist intellectual leaders can shape the national interest. Today we need that modesty and compassion even more desperately because Americans, and citizens of all countries, are forced by circumstances to think of the interests not only of their nation, but of a larger, perhaps even a global, world. Perhaps only concepts at that global level, the level of the "global" interest or of human needs will serve as a guide to the new world politics that has appeared in the wake of the new inequality.

11 Leadership and global governance for the Information Age

Today's new patterns of inequality grow out of the current era of globalization. In 1997, an article in *Forbes* made the case that the growing inequality was a trivial, if sad, consequence of a pattern that actually served the global interest. The article asked who was to blame for the rich getting richer:

> The rat is Richard Cobden . . . [the] 19th-century British liberal who dedicated his life, with missionary energy, to freer trade. He's the chap who started a chain of circumstances that has made the whole world richer, but some people richer than others.
>
> (Lee and Foster 1997)

The new patterns of income inequality owe as much to dialectic of liberal internationalism as democratization and narrowing gender gaps do. Yet, inequality is not an inherent consequence of the triumph of liberalism. In past industrial eras, on each of the prior steps toward a truly global industrial economy, public institutions have mitigated some of the inequality that capitalism generates.

A new industrial era has arrived, yet we do not have such institutions. At least, it is unclear whether the current set of institutions will successfully manage the inherent conflicts between the promoters of capitalist industrialism and industrial workers and people in the Third World. Braithwaite and Drahos's (2000: 642) "global lawmakers" still hold organized labor and the Third World responsible for the crises that ended the decades of halcyon growth after the Second World War. Yet, history tells us that even in the fields of labor and development—and also in the environmental field, where the institutions of the Information Age also remain underdeveloped—the right combination of intellectual and political leadership may still result in effective international governance.

Environmental issues may prove the most tractable of the three. Intellectual leadership can come from scientists and those policy analysts who are heir to the critical tradition of liberal internationalism. If the world economy were booming, one kind of political leadership, sponsorship, might come from states whose industrial policies make them "first movers" in environmental affairs. Potential benefactors of experimental international environmental agreements, a second essential type of leader, will be harder to find. Nevertheless, governments of first-mover states may be able to devise means for handling the redistributive issues associated with international pollution. Simultaneously, they and other governments will have to find new means of managing the even more intractable conflicts between capital and labor and between the more- and less-industrialized regions of the world. However, those who the "global lawmakers" are least likely to see as reliable allies have few incentives to focus their intellectual and political effort on international institutions. Better, immediate and more compliant, political targets exist for workers and for the South.

The context of current debates about reforming global governance

I have argued that there have been a series of stepwise changes in paradigmatic scale of capitalist industrial economies at the core of the world system. Industrial societies grew from the regional/national economies of the Industrial Revolution to the intercontinental market that linked the Western capitalist countries and the dependent Third World in the golden years of the 1950s and 1960s. Each transition to a more encompassing industrial order was initially marked by a period of relatively slow economic growth, rapid marketization, and fundamentalist versions of liberalism. Up to now, a second, more significant, phase has always followed, one marked by the increasing role of a more socially oriented liberalism. We are at the beginning of a new industrial era, what some call "the Information Age." We know that the core of the global economy in this era will be larger than the core of the Western industrial economy in the mid-twentieth century. The new core will include South Korea, Taiwan, parts of Southeast Asia, and those parts of the former Soviet system that are being the most quickly integrated into the European Union. It will include other regions as well, but probably not all the states that are now trying to enter the core: China, India, the whole of Eastern Europe, Turkey, Latin America, and even many Arab states.

Some of the Information Age international institutions are in place. Intelsat and the mid-1960s agreements on integrated shipping helped create the infrastructure for the new era (Murphy 1994: 195, 236). The World Trade Organization along with its new regimes for dealing with intellectual property and trade in services help define the market area in which goods of the lead industries of early twentieth century will be traded (Wilkinson 2000; Sell 2003).

In the past, new industrial eras also meant new international regimes for labor and for the less-industrialized world. Those regimes reflected, in part, the political victory of egalitarian social movements whose motivating ideologies have been quite a bit more radical than liberal internationalism. Nonetheless, this is consistent with core liberal propositions that go back to Adam Smith and Immanuel Kant. Recall that Smith and Kant reliance upon divided, "republican," government. Both Smith and Kant expected that any putatively "republican" state captured solely by the interests of profit-takers would not be able to sustain an open, highly productive economy. Instead, an economy based on cartels, monopolization, corruption, and cozy scams linking capitalists and the state would take hold, as it had in company-run colonies of Smith's day. This is, of course, similar to the way Susan Strange (1996) characterized the contemporary world economy even before the California electricity crisis, the Enron scandals, or Halliburton's "surprisingly" successful bid to restart Iraq's oil industry. Powerful egalitarian social movements help restore the "divided government," the republican polities, that allow a liberal economy to be a source of prosperity.

Arguably, the recent partial successes of democratic movements and the support given to such movements by the United Nations, may let us anticipate the international institutions that will balance conflicts with the Third World throughout the Information Age (Augelli and Murphy 1995; Boutros-Ghali 1995). In the Automobile Age, the global lawmakers did not offer the Third World "real" development, that is, the opportunity to create industrial economies that could compete with the OECD. However, Africans, Asians, and Latin Americans did receive decolonization and, until the Reagan and Thatcher years, they gained the form of populist "development" that improved material conditions. In the Information Age, real development—becoming like the core—is still out of the question, but the world's ruling circles have offered many Third World societies support for liberal democracy. That may not be enough, especially given how ephemeral democracy has proven to be in the parts of African regions embroiled in protracted social conflicts as well as in Pakistan, Indonesia and other states where Western security interests have rekindled collaboration with "safe," but anti-democratic military elites.[1]

International institutions to deal with the labor conflicts created by a globalizing world economy also remain underdeveloped, as do regimes to deal with environmental problems. Environmental issues are relatively new to *global* public policy. While Thomas Malthus may have worried about the potential for human overpopulation and Alexander von Humbolt may have promoted the scientific study of the whole earth in the early nineteenth-century, it took until 1945, when biologist Julian Huxley, became UNESCO's first Executive Director, for environmental issues to become a regular topic of intergovernmental conferences (Haas 1992: 9–25). Yet, when they did neither analysts nor policy-makers saw them as fundamentally new. Governments found it easy to include these new issues under the "meta-regime" that has been in place since the middle of the nineteenth century.

The environment and kindred problems

To understand that meta-regime, it is useful to contrast domestic and inter-national public policy problems. Policy-makers concerned with environ-mental, labor, or development issues confined within a single country can focus on convincing legitimate authorities to legislate wise policies and then enforce them using appropriate, coercive sanctions and economic induce-ments. Domestic governments may also use less-expensive cooperative instruments such as, in the environmental issue area: (1) monitoring prior pro-environment agreements made among citizens and firms, (2) helping different groups recognize their own interests in preserving the environ-ment, and (3) working with the same groups to design new agreements that serve their interests. These are often the *only* instruments available to intergovernmental policy-makers.

The problem is not that the international community lacks coercive authorities. Even where such authorities exist, their actions are likely to be illegitimate. A preponderant military power can force other states to do its bidding. So can an intergovernmental financial organization, at least rela-tive to severely dependent states that need the organization's approval to keep afloat. In either case, analysts might argue that the sovereignty of the target states is "merely juridical." Nevertheless, even the "merely juridical" sovereignty of the many entities that Robert H. Jackson (1990) calls "quasi-states" assures that they will view such international coercive authority as illegitimate. This lack of legitimacy makes today's international coercive authorities a poor foundation for long-term international public policy.

Advocates of international coercive authority, including today's advo-cates of American unilateralism or Empire, are apt to point out that the number of "quasi-states," those that are potentially subject to such authority, is large. If we use the operational definitions implied by Jackson, we would begin with all those states whose governments can be and regu-larly have been removed or kept in power by the military forces of an external patron. We would add countries whose governments depend on foreign assistance (say, those where aid is at least 25 percent of central government revenue) or on taxes collected on international transactions (say, those who receive more than 25 percent of their revenue from taxes on trade). Of the World Bank's "low income" countries, only China and India would always escape classification as "quasi-states." A few higher income countries throughout the Caribbean and Central America as well as Bolivia, Peru, Egypt, Israel, Jordan, Syria, most of the states of the former Yugoslavia, and some of the states of the former Soviet Union, at times, have fit under the same operational definition. All their govern-ments are potential targets of foreign commands that they could not refuse without imperiling their existence.

Yet, relative to environmental and labor policy, it is significant that even this rather liberally defined group of states that might be subject to international coercive authority excludes the newly industrializing countries (large and small) and Brazil, the most significant of the rainforest countries, as well as the huge manufacturing states, India and China. In fact, none of the countries Alice Amsden (2001) includes among "The Rest," the late industrializing economies that currently challenge "the West" are subject to international coercive authority, which is why it cannot be relied upon to cope with international environmental or labor problems.

Despite the lack of legitimate coercive authority at the international level, governments have created effective and legitimate intergovernmental regulatory organizations. Recall, that typically those organizations conduct research and hold meetings for discovering and promoting common interests among potentially antagonistic social forces. When governments formally agree with one another to pursue some form of intergovernmental regulation (which usually means pledging that private interests within their societies will be compelled to act in certain ways) states often give intergovernmental organizations the task of monitoring adherence to the agreements. Occasionally, the intergovernmental bodies may demand that member states impose sanctions against a member who has violated an agreement. More frequently, governments deputize an international executive to provide specific services to some or all members, for example, the technical assistance to treasury ministries and central banks provided by the IMF.

Before 1945, before the development of an international environmental agenda, this limited repertoire of managerial means had helped regulate conflicts between labor and capital and between the First and the Third Worlds for almost a century. These conflicts resemble the postwar international environmental problems of resource depletion and pollution in at least five ways:

1   They grow out of the industrial system.
2   In each case, decisions about long-term investments in industry have a great deal of influence over the degree anyone can manage the problem.
3   As a consequence, in each case one productive aim of governmental and intergovernmental regulatory efforts is to shape long-term investment decisions toward more benign ends (for example, safer factories for workers, the export of leading-edge technologies to the less-industrialized world).
4   The investors who first move toward these more benign ends become major allies in the larger regulatory effort because they have an interest in imposing similar investment costs on competitors, as long as that does not mean that the first-movers lose the advantages conferred on them by their early investment.
5   Once in place, regimes regulating each of these problems may require little enforcement. The stickiness of long-term investments makes the

actions required by the regimes a matter of habit, at least until replacement investments need to be made.

Relative to water pollution, for example, the key large investment decisions are among different designs and locations of sewage and garbage disposal systems, industrial plants and refineries, ships and tankers, fertilizers and crop systems. Even the most significant of these decisions can be shaped by the governmental and intergovernmental regulatory environment simply because wise firms (whether public or private) take projections about the regulatory environment into account. Shell Oil, for example, has a 50-year planning horizon.

A decade ago, in one of Shell's planning exercises, strategists concluded that the company's decisions should be made so that it could thrive in two, equally probable, future worlds:

> In one . . . regional conflicts plague the world, environmental problems are attacked piecemeal, and low prices shape energy use. In the other, sustainable development takes hold. International cooperation blossoms to combat environmental damage and global warming. Governments discourage fossil fuel use and promote renewable energy.
>
> (Smith 1993: 74)

Critics complain that Shell's own decisions to explore, refine, and transport fossil fuels will have a major effect on which of these two scenarios becomes a reality. Nonetheless, it is fruitful for environmentalists to push for public policies that could convince Shell that their second, more benign world will be the one in which they will have to act. The relevant variables identified by the planners are, after all, familiar matters of government action or intergovernmental cooperation: combating environmental damage and global warming, discouraging fossil fuel use and promoting renewable energy. If governments instituted policies toward those ends, Shell would not only respond with its own investments that would help make the goal a reality, the firm would have reason to advocate that all other firms be held to the same, or stricter, environmental standards. This interest is characteristic of all the companies that have become "first movers" on environmental issues, the firms that have been the first to make massive investments in technologies that may reduce environmental damage.

Policy innovations suggested by the Business Council on Sustainable Development (BCSD) exemplify this process. The BCSD brings together the leaders of a host of the world's largest firms, from Shell to the Dow Chemical Company, to Nippon Steel, to India's giant TATA, to Volkswagen. These companies have all learned from experience that it can pay to be an environmental first-mover. Generalizing from their individual experiences, they convinced the International Organization for

Standardization (ISO) to establish a Strategic Advisory Group on the Environment (which, like most ISO groups, essentially represents key companies) to prepare international standards for the "eco-efficiency" of industrial products and services. The aim is to assure that products have at life-cycle analyses and environmental audits (Schmidheiny 1992: 95; Clapp 1998).

The self-interest of the BCSD firms is transparent, but it is enlightened. They believe that in a global market of Green consumers and of governments increasingly influenced by the environmental concerns of their publics, ISO standards labeling the environmental desirability of every product and service will benefit environmental first movers over all their competitors. Alice Tepper-Marlin's project to create a similar set of international private labor standards, SA8000 (see Chapter 4) follows the same model, as does Secretary General Kofi Annan's pet project, the Global Compact, which has private firms signing on to the core labor, environmental, and human rights standards established by the United Nations. The Compact does not establish a monitoring regime, but it does create a complex process by which companies each year report exemplary "best practices" and a host of nongovernmental organizations evaluate those reports and help compile what will be, essentially, a continuously updated process handbook of the practices of first movers companies in each of these fields (Ruggie 2001; Hughes and Wilkinson 2001).

The Global Compact and standards that play to the preferences of Green consumers represent only one of many ways that the self-interest of firms that have acted as first movers can be enlisted to extend the impact of cooperative international institutions involved in environmental or labor regulation. Perhaps most significantly, the first large investors in progressive labor or environmental practices have every interest in becoming the eyes and ears of the regulators, thus strengthening the typically inadequate monitoring systems established through intergovernmental agreement. Moreover, the longer history of international industrial regulation suggests that once the investment costs associated with a new regulation have been absorbed, the need for monitoring and for taking sanctions against violators diminishes. Conforming to the regulations becomes a matter of habit; after all, the major decisions, for example, the decisions to make large investments in the cleaner of the available technologies, have to be made very rarely. Even if a period of economic stagnation gives firms temporary incentives to cut costs by cutting corners, the older habit of investment in conformity with "high cost" regulations is likely to return along with the prosperity that would make a new round of big investments possible.

In this light, it is instructive to compare the debates over "international labor legislation" that took place in Western Europe and the United States from the 1870s through the 1930s to current debates about global and regional environmental legislation. At the turn of the twentieth century, many of the most prominent economists from all parts of the political spectrum insisted that it would be impossible for the goals of contemporary labor reformers to be achieved short of revolution. They argued that a single state, like Germany, might reduce hours of work or provide social security for a time, but that the logic of market would assure that German firms would soon lose out to cheaper competitors. Yet, by 1933, at the height of the Depression, James T. Shotwell could write that most of labor's original goals for the International Labor Organization (ILO) had been achieved (1934: 189, 214).

He was not being disingenuous or ironic. Laws then on the books in most industrialized countries mandated the eight-hour day, limited child labor, allowed unions to form, and required reasonable wages, weekly days of rest, equal treatment for foreign workers, equal pay for equal work, and government safety inspections of work places.

In the 1930s, such rules were enforced by interventionist states supported by an ILO that actually had greater power to monitor international adherence to labor standards than it does today. By the booming 1960s, adherence to such standards was more a matter of habit, part of the regularly calculated costs of doing business throughout most of Western Europe, the US, Canada, Australia, New Zealand, and Japan. Today's regulatory experiments, the Global Compact and the models on which it is based, equally aim to make adherence to the highest labor and environmental standards a matter of habit for companies in the Information Age.

Intellectual leadership

As Peter M. Haas (1990, 1997) and his colleagues point out, natural scientists have played a key role in the formation of all international environmental regimes. The scientists sometimes convince governments directly. In other cases, the pressure of social movements activated by or, at least, willing to use, the scientists' results has been critical. Economists, lawyers, and diplomats—people who, the scientists often complain, oversimplify, ignore interaction effects, and refuse to recognize the pervasive uncertainty associated with all predictions in the environmental sciences—do the intellectual work of designing new regimes (see, for example, Molina 1993).

Similar cooperation between different types of intellectual leaders, and similar tensions, characterized the first stage in the formation of international regulatory institutions since their beginning. However, the differences between the different types of intellectual leaders have always proved less significant than the values that they share (Murphy 1994: 64–67).

Sponsors

Intellectual leaders always face an uphill battle. Governments, like all habit-driven actors, resist pressure to do new things, even if they are in their own interest. The problem comes in getting the attention of state leaders, in getting them to sit down, focus on, and discuss the various proposals in order to recognize those interests. No matter what the issue, some governments have always been reluctant to discuss the creation of new functional regimes. Nevertheless, for more than a century and a half, there have been persuasive sponsors available to call such meetings. The nineteenth-century conference system relied on the *noblesse oblige* of Europe's princes. When Baron Pierre de Coubertin created the modern Olympics in 1900, he was simply following the fashion of Europe's most powerful aristocrats. Acting in their personal capacity, Europe's crowned heads called the conferences that created the first generation of international organizations, from the International Telegraph Union, to the original global trade organization, to the UN Food and Agriculture Organization's predecessor, to the ILO, to Interpol, to the precursor of UNESCO, sponsored by Napoleon III, the Kings of Belgium, Italy, and Germany, the Prince of Monaco, and Queen Victoria's Prince Albert respectively (Murphy 1994: 77–79).

In the first quarter of the twentieth century, a kind of "democratic *noblesse oblige*" replaced the aristocratic version. Half a dozen major conferences sponsored by Woodrow Wilson's immediate predecessors and by the presidents of France and Switzerland anticipated Wilson's promotion of the League of Nation. All three countries, even the isolationist US continued to play similar roles through 1929, always justifying the effort involved by referring to the responsibilities for fostering international cooperation given to those progressive states that already enjoyed republican constitutions. During the Second World War, the major allies, the countries considered for permanent memberships on the Security Council—Brazil, China, France, Great Britain, the Soviet Union, and the US—split the task of hosting the international conferences needed to create the global institutions of the postwar era (Murphy 1994: 181–186).

Beginning in the late 1940s, international organizations themselves became the characteristic sponsors of international conferences. Since the 1972 Stockholm conference on the environment a combination of sponsorship linking an interested international organization and a state concerned with promoting a particular agenda, has been typical. Even today, when the main international coercive authority, the United States tends to oppose extensions of the mandate of global governance, it has not been particularly difficult to find national and intergovernmental sponsors for the meetings that led to everything from the Landmine Convention to the International Criminal Court. The recent history of the Global Compact may even be revealing a new pattern of sponsorship involving secretariats (in this case, the United Nations ILO, UN Environmental Program, and UN Industrial Development Organization), and private universities working alongside some of the firms first involved in the process.

Benefactors

It is one thing to pick up the bills for a big global meeting. It is quite another to underwrite an experimental international regime. Yet, bene-factors willing to pay for the costs of international cooperation over many years have been essential to institutionalization of many international regimes in the past. The first generation of international organizations relied on their aristocratic sponsors to pay for the secretariat that carried out research, monitored prior international agreements, and prepared peri-odic international conferences. The presence of such a benefactor was often what convinced habit-bound governments to experiment. After all, if Napoleon III was willing to pick up most of the bill for the Telegraph Union, the Kaiser was willing to pay for the Labor Office, or if Italy's Victor Emmanuel III was willing to the underwrite the work of the International Institute of Agriculture, no one would object. In fact, in these cases, significant institutionalization only took place after political or economic crises destroyed the capacity of the original benefactor to under-write the institution. When the noble benefactor disappeared, member governments had to put up or shut up.

Since the Second World War, the initial costs of new international orga-nizations have continued to be borne by their sponsors. Older international organizations have provided staff, space, and operating funds for months or even years. Thus, for example, the UN Relief and Rehabilitation Organization provided much of the initial support for UNICEF, the UN secretariat underwrote much of the early work on population, and the World Bank provided the initial funding for hybrids like the International Fund for Agricultural Development. In many cases, the US was the key benefactor, especially when large transfers of funds were needed, as with the IMF and World Bank. In the 1980s, when American students of inter-national cooperation worried about "the decline of US hegemony," one of the legitimate concerns stemmed from the fact that the government's accumulated debt made it no longer in a position to act as such a major benefactor of international cooperation. Even with the end of the Cold War and the rise of the US to a position of global military supremacy, that situation has not changed.

Perversely, given the capacity of the potential benefactors of late twentieth-century international institutions, the various international commissions on North–South relations since the 1980s, beginning with the Brandt Commission (1980, 1983) and including the Commission on Global Governance (1995) proposed new international agreements that would have required something on the order of a two- to fivefold increase in aid. The 1992 Rio Conference on the environment and development made a similar unrealistic call for new redistributive funding as part of its proposed "Global Compact," a massive program of aid to the Third World designed to encourage more responsible industrial policies (Murphy 1992; Sell 1996).

In that context, Kofi Annan's rhetorical shift of the Rio Conference's language makes sense. In the 1990s, the best governments could hope for in international environmental cooperation was to agree on the relatively cost-free kind of eco-labeling promoted by the BCSD. When UNEP trade talks began to focus on such measures, officials delightedly discovered the agenda was one on which, "there was so much agreement between industrialized and developing countries." The meeting became one of the few recent international environmental forums that "did not degenerate into North–South conflict" (UNEP 1994). Annan's Global Compact extends the model further. UN agencies become sponsors and benefactors of agreements among first-mover firms that see economic or social good in ratcheting up environmental and labor standards. Similarly, in 2003, Annan began sponsoring and encouraging firms to underwrite a low-cost program to extend technical assistance to small and medium-sized entrepreneurs in the Third World, a realistic, if very partial, measure to deal with some of the dissatisfaction with the inequality generated by the current stage of globalization (Hurt 2003).

Creating resources

Nonetheless, the longer history of international cooperation suggests that something more may be possible. Many of the international institutions created over the last century *created* resources that that they then allocated by "politically efficient" means that often hid the redistributive element. For example, the original international intellectual property regime not only created a form of property in the monopoly rights given to inventors, authors, and trademark owners, it also created a real duty on the part of patent owners to work their patents in every international market, or else lose the right to maintain it. Until the recently created WTO system—the invention of a tiny coalition of American pharmaceutical, information technology, and entertainment firms—international technology regimes gave lower prices to industrializing nations (Sell 2003; Penrose 1973). The recent responses of pharmaceutical companies to international pressure over the costs of AIDS drugs suggest some possibility that the "global lawmakers" may relearn the older lesson. Similarly, the Biodiversity Treaty, with its sections on intellectual property, may eventually serve to create similar resources for industrializing nations.

Long after governments put the first global intellectual property regimes in place, international institutions also "created" resources through the drawn-out process of renegotiating Germany's war debts. By fiat, governments reduced the war debts, originally created by fiat. Of course, the negotiators accompanied their moves with much hand waving about "responsible international financial practices." It was, nonetheless, a politically efficient action that obscured the redistributive elements from the masses within Belgium, France, Italy, and the US, and from their elected representatives.

In 1991, the distinguished Mexican economist, Victor Urquidi (1991: 7) argued that powerful governments should do something similar in order to assure some level of redistribution to the less-industrialized world:

> The essence of the [current] problem, so clearly foreseen by Keynes at the time of the German reparations . . . is that for the debt to be repaid . . . the debtors must develop a sufficiently large export surplus.

The recession-induced collapse of world markets for Third World goods in the 1980s made that impossible. Therefore:

> many countries went into default, which made them ineligible for loans or other forms of financial assistance. Others kept on meeting their interest payments at the expense of growth and development. What came to be termed the "reverse transfer," that is the net out-transfer of financial resources from the developing to the industrialized countries, was the equivalent of reparations payments as if a war had been lost. In fact, the war on poverty, the great struggle for development, had to be given up.

Other cases where international institutions have created resources and then redistributed them exist. For example, the Bretton Woods institutions used the initial deposits of gold and hard currencies by the US (and the very few other original members whose money was convertible) to create a pool of loan fund that the Fund and Bank expanded both by fiat and by borrowing. As a result, the Keynesian proposal to use additions to Fund reserves as a pool of funds for development assistance remained a hardy perennial in discussions of international public finance until the floating exchange rate system appeared in the early 1970s. The new system made the "reserve-expansion/foreign assistance Link" idea less relevant. Nevertheless, it might be a better use of analysts' time to develop proposals of this sort rather than on finding new ways to importune reluctant donors and point out their inconsistency in endorsing multilateral programs without providing the necessary financing.

Programs analogous to the "Link" would establish regular (even if initially, small) sources of development finance linked to some growing aspect of the world economy. Ruben P. Mendez (1992) suggests some possible directions. The most interesting are those that could be connected back to the traditional, proven way in which benefactors have played a role in extending the activities of world organizations by allowing new programs to be demonstrated in practice before all states are required to bear their part of the burden.

The Norwegian initiative to impose a carbon tax on North Sea oil (Sandvold 1993) is a case that could be linked to such a process. States that might be willing to impose such a tax include the pro-development oil producers (Canada and Mexico as well as Norway), similar countries with significant roles in the oil trade (for example, the Netherlands and Finland). The oil companies who have signed on to the Global Compact or who have executives on the BCSD might join them. All might agree to impose a small unit fee on the oil they process and then give the funds to the Global Environmental Facility. The retail vendors of oil thus "taxed" would be able to advertise to Green consumers, explaining the major benefit to the environment that derives from a slight increase in price. If some firms' expectations about the significance of the Green segment of the market prove correct, then the forces of the market would generate significant development funds. Moreover, governments committed to a Green industrial development path would have an incentive to join in imposing the tax on all the oil sold in their countries.

Of course, one thing that should be noted about such a proposal— which is also true about all the ways in which international institutions have "created" resources—is the reliance on a particular power of some social group, a power that is amplified at the same time that it is some- what hidden by the international institution. In this example, it is the (hypothetical) power of Green consumers and governments committed to a Green industrial development path. In the case of the renegotiation of war debts and the original funding of the Bretton Woods institutions, it was the power of international finance. These interests failed to back the "reserve-expansion/aid link" or most attempts to forgive Third World debt. In the case of the original intellectual property regimes, inventors and industrializing countries both supported the compromise.

The powers that could help resolve the unresolved environmental, labor, and development issues of the current industrial order may change very rapidly. In 1992, the Japanese Ministry for International Trade (MITI) concluded that, "environmental concerns will drive the next generation of economic growth," and, therefore, more government money had to be spent in the, "strategic repositioning of Japanese industry," to take advan- tage of this development (Menon 1992: 5). This commitment to a Green industrial path, one shared by the contemporary German government, made new international environment regimes look much more likely a decade ago, when Japan was a global economic powerhouse. Now, after years of economic stasis, Japanese preferences seem less likely to shape the global order.

Therefore, it may be unclear whose powers one would wish to see ampli- fied in order to establish new international regulatory regimes. The history of international labor institutions should serve as a further caution. In the past, international regulatory efforts tended to privilege workers in the industrialized world. It is probably true that, a century ago, workers in the most "advanced" of the "newly industrializing countries" of the day (for example, in the Danish and Swedish empires) did benefit from the self-interested international labor legislation promoted by the German Kaiser to encourage social order within his nation where both industry and labor movements were more advanced. Equally, it may be true that workers today in South Korea or Malaysia will, in the end, benefit from international labor pacts pushed by an American government responding to domestic social forces with interests similar to those that motivated the Kaiser a century ago. Nevertheless, as Robert W. Cox (1996b: 47) reminds us, the first movement for international labor regulation was, "part and parcel of the nationalistic movement which was bringing European states into conflict both within Europe and more especially in the areas of imperial expansion beyond Europe."

Certainly, we should be attentive to each of the unresolved dimensions of global governance in the early twenty-first century to avoid the breakdown that took place at the beginning of the twentieth. Realistically, though, it may be impossible to find common ground among the First World and Third World groups marginalized in the transition to the Information Age. Christopher Candland (2002: 5) notes, "Labor activists in industrialized and industrializing countries who are normally allied in their belief that international capital should be made more socially accountable are sharply divided over linking labor standards to trade." That is, of course, the way that past international labor conventions have been enforced, and the only way that social active consumer groups in the North might contribute to higher labor standards in the South. Similarly, Candland points to "the multitude of social, political, material, ideological, and gender conflicts" that would need to be overcome in order to create effective transnational development coalitions. Yet, many Northern activists on the Left still see such coalitions as the only way to narrow the international income gaps that have grown during the liberal fundamentalist phase of the Information Age transition.

Prospects for cosmopolitan democracy

In fact, no matter how attractive progressive Northern programs for a more just form of global governance may be, they may be irrelevant to many activists in the South. As a major case in point, a realistic assessment of the political and cultural barriers to the movement for "cosmopolitan democracy" should make us skeptical about that goal.

As we have seen, the advocates of cosmopolitan democracy are a group of prominent political philosophers, activists, and policy-makers, including some of the most eminent living Western democratic theorists. They support the continued spread of liberal democratic political systems across the nations of the world along with the strengthening and democratization of international institutions. In a world in which the economy has outrun the boundaries of the state, argument goes, we need stronger international institutions to redress the social balance, and we need to democratize those institutions to assure that they serve the larger common good.

Advocates of cosmopolitan democracy see reason for optimism in the support for their program that recently has come from the leaders of international institutions. International agencies, from UNICEF to the IMF, have become material supporters of democratic movements throughout the world. Significant leaders, such as former UN Secretary General Boutros-Ghali (1995) as well as Kofi Annan (1998) have unexpectedly used their positions to advocate the entire cosmopolitan program, including the real democratization of strengthened international institutions through direct election of delegates or peoples' assemblies and one person, one vote forms of representation.

The typical argument that such optimism is misplaced comes from more conservative Western theorists who believe in the cultural particularity of liberal democratic norms that underlie the cosmopolitan program. Those norms, they claim, are rooted in the notions of equal dignity of all human beings and of individual rights and responsibilities that come from the Western tradition of Natural Law. It should not be surprising, therefore, that liberal democracy can thrive in the historically Catholic nations of Latin America, or that it has its firmest grip in Eastern Europe's Catholic and Protestant (not Orthodox) nations, and that the new African states with the most lively democratic politics—South Africa, Cape Verde—are those where Western Christianity has most successfully entrenched the Natural Law tradition. This is still a strange argument, one that ignores the experience of India and Japan as well as the quite similar claims about a moral community of mankind and about the equal obligations we owe to each other in Buddhist, Confucian, Hindu, and Muslim traditions.

The lack of realism does not come from the "democracy" in the cosmopolitan vision. It comes from its cosmopolitanism. For the next generation, at least, the focus of egalitarian movements in the Third World is likely to remain more on the local, national, and regional rather than the global level. It is logical for egalitarian social movements, even in poor regions with highly skewed economies, to place top priority on creating political democracy thus opening a safe political space in which to campaign for their significant economic priorities. The egalitarian politics of developing nations with undemocratic states or with marginally democratic states is likely to focus on democratization at home, whether the county's economy is relatively egalitarian (such as that of Indonesia) or relatively inegalitarian (such as that of Nigeria). In democratic and highly inegalitarian states (for instance, in Brazil and many of the other newer democracies and also in the wealthy states with growing economic inequality, such as the US) there may be two equal priorities: fighting for greater economic equality and protecting against attempts by the privileged to roll back the democratic victories. Only in those states that are democratic, egalitarian, and wealthy (that is, Japan and some in Western Europe) is the program of cosmopolitan democracy likely to be a priority, even though everywhere it deserves to be considered a plausible ideal, the sort of utopia that it is reasonable to mark our progress against.

In Chapter 4, I discussed the range of political options that energize the current generation of students in the industrialized world. There, "working for cosmopolitan democracy" may be a primary strategy. In much of the rest of the world, strengthening and reforming the state is more relevant.

What would be a reasonable agenda for those concerned with both strengthening and democratizing all of governance, globally? Beyond attention to democratic politics at home, in most parts of the world activists would do well to support the agencies, governments, and individuals willing to sponsor the international conferences where reform of the difficult labor, development, and environmental issues can take place. Because it will be hard to find benefactors wealthy enough to back the redistributive aspects of effective regimes that cross the North–South divide, backing new regimes that create resources will be essential. Therefore, the history of such innovations should become required reading. Creating resources means looking for institutional designs that husband and amplify the power of those willing to work for a more humane order—the power of progressive consumers, of firms that have become self-interested in a more benign world, and of the marginalized people themselves, those who will otherwise remain victims of the Information Age world order rather than its citizens.

12 To mingle, meet, and know

Marginalization and the privileged

Recall that the end of the most significant recent analyses of global patterns of income inequality, World Bank economist Branko Milanovic (1999: 51) asks how such levels of inequality can possibly continue. "Such a high inequality," he says, "is sustainable precisely because the world is not unified, and rich people do not mingle, meet, or even know about the existence of the poor other than in the most abstract way."

When she first read Milanovic, one of my students, a Francophone Caribbean woman who had grown up in the Philippines where her parents taught at an elite International Baccalaureate school, found that statement unconvincing. She wondered whether the economist had any experience with great urban centers like Manila or Port-au-Prince. Her parents' students, among the richest of the rich, easily ignored the impoverished men and women who served them and the thousands whose neighborhoods they crossed to get between the barred gates of their homes and the barred gates of the school. "Certainly, people can mingle without every really meeting, knowing, or caring about the poor. Nothing is going to convince privileged people to be concerned with those on the margins."

This final chapter makes that difficult case, the case that the conditions of the marginalized, and their own knowledge of those conditions, are of concern to the privileged. I initially frame the problem as one of searching for the benefactors of international institutions that might effectively manage the remaining problems of the Information Age world order. The chapter then turns to the "common sense" of the world's privileged, and, in particular, to the simple liberal arguments made for unregulated globalization, for a world without conscious concern for the marginalized. I outline a series of prudential and ethical concerns that arise for the world's privileged when uncritical versions of the liberal argument become a reality. One of those concerns points to the centrality of the knowledge of the marginalized to the resolution of the moral dilemmas faced by the privileged. In that context, I argue for an International Relations that learns from the world's poor. I close by shifting from merely prudential issues to argue that working to overcome the inequalities that divide humanity may

be one of the few ways to give greater meaning to the lives of those with
gross material advantage.

The unfinished business of building the next world order

Why, in a book about the international political economy of marginalization and development should the last chapter focus on the human needs,
the development, of the world's privileged?

In the first instance, my concern is practical. As Braithwaite and Drahos
conclude, no matter how creative the intellectual and political leadership
provided by egalitarian social movements, ultimately, the institutions that
regulate and tame capitalist globalization will be put into place by the
very privileged, "the global lawmakers . . . the men who run the largest
corporations, the US and the EC" (Braithwaite and Drahos 2000: 629).

As the last chapters have argued, the major unfinished business of the
Information Age world order involve creating institutions to overcome
labor and Third World conflicts and to deal effectively with global environmental problems. These are, of course, the issues that have driven
almost a decade of anti-globalization protests outside the meetings of
the IMF and World Bank, the WTO, and the World Economic Forum.
They are the issues at the center of the simultaneous, alternative, World
Social Forum that brings together critical liberal economists and social
activists opposing the imposition of a liberal fundamentalist world by an
increasingly unilateralist US government.

In 2004, the Indian writer and political activist, Arundhati Roy, opened
the Forum by bitterly condemning the US's new version of Britain's
nineteenth-century liberal imperialism (Roy 2004):

> New Imperialism is already upon us. It's a remodeled, streamlined
> version of what we once knew. For the first time in history, a single
> Empire with an arsenal of weapons that could obliterate the world in
> an afternoon has complete unipolar economic and military hegemony.
> It uses different weapons to break open different markets. There isn't
> a country on God's earth that is not caught in the crosshairs of the
> American cruise missile and the IMF chequebook. Argentina's the
> model if you want to be the poster-boy of neoliberal capitalism, Iraq
> if you're the black sheep.

Yet, history tells us that the last attempt to establish a liberal empire,
the British program before the First World War, proved relatively ineffective at creating the expanding market areas demanded by capitalist
industrialism. The functionalist, cooperative, Public International Unions
had to do that job. Moreover, in the subsequent industrial era, sponsors
and benefactors had to be found for an even more benign system that

responded to some of the concerns of the marginalized that the liberal imperialists had ignored, in particular, the concerns of industrial workers and of natives of the colonized world.

Not surprisingly, then, in today's world, where the imperialist United States blocks discussion of labor and environmental agreements that might secure the liberal world order without force, Secretary General Kofi Annan has launched his Global Compact, the program that circumvents governments and asks progressive business leaders to promote fundamental human rights, labor, and environmental norms directly (Ruggie 2001; Hughes and Wilkinson 2001). Within this context of unresolved issues of global regulation and extreme, possibly misplaced reliance on the positive motivations of private enterprise, it is worth remembering the entire range of reasons (not just the pecuniary ones) why all the "global lawmakers," (and not just progressive corporate leaders) have concern for those who have so far been left out of the planning for the Information Age world order. The place to start is with the central arguments that all the lawmakers salute, the liberal arguments in favor of largely unregulated globalization.

The Liberal fundamentalist case

Today's basic argument in favor of globalization remains Cobdenite. It is the argument that goes back to David Ricardo, and in a slightly different form, to Adam Smith, the argument that favors the widest possible geographic division of labor. In the form that Ricardo gave it to us, it is the argument of comparative advantage.

Under most conditions, the argument remains correct. Under most conditions, regions of the world will be better off—if the material abundance is their aim—when they trade with one another and specialize in the lines in which they have a comparative advantage. The so-called "New International Economics" (Krugman 1986) of the 1980s did point out that the old "import substitution-style" arguments about using trade policy to protect "infant industries" have a good deal of validity, even when the new industry is a fundamentally new sector located in an already industrialized nation. Moreover, it is certainly true that many of the global institutions with influence over Third World governments have ignored the lessons of the New International Economics. Nonetheless, as advocates of that kind of analysis are often at pains to point out: they still accept the basic case for comparative advantage. Under most conditions, if a country really wishes to get wealthier, it will open its borders to the products, investment, and workers of all other countries.

Globalization benefits some, but it harms others

If that is true, why does anyone oppose such policies? Some globalization advocates are apt to tell us that the opponents are either ignorant or they are "rent-seekers" attempting to preserve an unjust advantage gained by "protectionist" barriers to trade, investment, and migration. Yet, that reaction overlooks the fundamental argument made by the more learned advocates of comparative advantage. No one argues that *everyone* within a country will benefit when barriers come down. Certainly, in the North, there will be the industrial workers who will lose their jobs to equally skilled and less well paid workers in the South. In the South, capitalists and workers in uncompetitive sectors will lose when the goods and services from the North flood in. The argument for comparative advantage is only that the *total* income of the countries involved, the *Wealth of the Nations*, will be greater, not the wealth of every one (or even most) of their citizens. For the liberal magic to work, for *everyone* within a nation to benefit, the nation must have governors willing and able to tax the greater benefits coming to some individuals (the newly rich manufacturing capitalists of the South, the software magnates of the North) and redistribute the wealth to those immediately harmed.

Liberal internationalism arrives as part of an ideological package

Even relatively sophisticated economists who tout the benefits of open borders are apt to overlook the simple political facts that make such redistribution rare. States often adopt liberal international policies as part of an entire package brought in by a liberal party associated with traders, financiers, and highly competitive manufacturers. The package will not be based on the sophisticated, nuanced political economy of university professors willing to imagine careful policies to distribute both the benefits and pains of globalization. The package will, more likely, be based on the "common sense" of men interested in the gains they will achieve, as well as on the rules of thumb of "practical" analysts who have absorbed the basic liberal faith in markets. The liberal package is likely to recommend that those harmed by the new stage of globalization be given the discipline of the market rather than recommend that their welfare is served by the redistribution of globalization's benefits. Recall (from Chapter 6) how, at the time of the Irish famine, the abolition of the Corn Laws—the paradigmatic liberal internationalist victory—marked the end of the Tory redistributive policies that had curbed death and immigration in the first months of the disaster. The Great Famine also deserves to be recalled as the paradigmatic result of liberal common sense.

Of course, a century and a half later, the common sense of the privileged no longer sees famine as an appropriate discipline for a backward people. Nevertheless, the policy packages sometimes offered to the poorest states after they have faced external shocks (such as the rapid rise in oil prices in the 1970s) bear a family resemblance to the Whig policy in Ireland. In Africa, in particular, the first round of structural adjustment in the late 1970s and 1980s required governments not only to undermine their elite base by eliminating uncompetitive nationalized industries and protected bastions of local capitalists, governments also had to harm their popular base by cutting subsidies to consumers and eliminating an array of services. In a second phase, after the first round of structural adjustment had led to some combination of political instability (due to the weakening of the state's legitimacy), increased government corruption (due to attempts to circumvent external requirements), and continued economic malaise, international lenders began to demand more comprehensive programs for "good governance" whereby relatively ineffective, limited democratic states were required to constitutionalize neoliberal norms, in part, to tie the hands of future governments that might wish to reassert greater state control (Abrahamsen 2001; Bøås and McNeill 2003, 50–89). In Africa in the late twentieth century, as in Ireland in the middle of the nineteenth, liberal internationalism arrived with the revolutionary agenda of eliminating the forces that could tame the market.

Moreover, while Social Darwinism may no longer be part of the common sense of the world's lawmakers, in many parts of the world—certainly in my own country, the United States—the ideological layer of liberalism still lies atop a thick layer of denominational Protestantism that enjoins us to limit charity to the "deserving," hard-working, and grateful poor (Augelli and Murphy 1988, Chapter 3). Place this very particular Protestant ethic on top of that layer of the peculiar statism that underlies all liberal economics since Smith, and you have justification for ignoring any growing international inequality: The most important factor affecting *their* economy is the policy of *their* governments, and if their governments are so venal or stupid not to adopt liberal fundamentalist policies, then we have no responsibility to close the growing gap between our material conditions and theirs. We have no responsibility even if, in their society, material stagnation means more destitution.

Globalization fuels resentment: prudential reasons for concern

If we imagine the "global lawmakers" to be men of little compassion very much at ease with hypocrisy, then the readily overlooked aspects of the liberal package would hardly be a problem. "Yes," they might, in more honest moments, think, "globalization always harms some, but it benefits us, and, all the better that it comes in as part of political programs that absolve us of responsibility for those who are harmed, either here at home or abroad."

Few of the privileged are so vile. As Gertrude Stein said, the only thing different about the rich is, "They have money." Yet, even the heartless few have prudential reasons for considering the lot of those people that globalization continues to marginalize.

Amy Chua's (2003) *World on Fire: How Exporting Free Market Democracy Breeds Ethnic Hatred and Global Instability* outlines the prudential argument quite well. Chua, a Yale Law School professor, has no difficulty with the liberal fundamentalist concept of "market democracy," the concept that Erskine Childers (1997: 272) called "intellectual rubbish" and "insidiously undemocratic trickery." Chua's first worry is not that the contemporary world order creates meaninglessly weak democratic states, but that marketization always tends to rebound to the advantage of limited groups, identity groups that easily become sources of more widespread resentment. Chua lays out the problem this way:

> Market-dominant minorities can be found in every corner of the world. The Chinese are a market-dominant minority not just in the Philippines but throughout Southeast Asia. In 1998, Chinese Indonesians, only 3 percent of the population, controlled roughly 70 percent of Indonesia's private economy, including all of the country's largest conglomerates. More recently, in Burma, entrepreneurial Chinese have literally taken over the economies of Mandalay and Rangoon. Whites are a market-dominant minority in South Africa—and, in a more complicated sense, in Brazil, Ecuador, Guatemala, and much of Latin America. Lebanese are a market-dominant minority in Nigeria. Croats were a market-dominant minority in the former Yugoslavia. And Jews are almost certainly a market-dominant minority in post-Communist Russia.
>
> (p. 6)

The economic advance of these minorities fuels political organization by ethno-nationalists and may lead to violent ethnic conflict or even genocide.

There may be no simple lesson that all the global lawmakers will take from this finding. Some may have concluded that the relatively recent (post-1985) American presumption that limited democracy can always accompany marketization is invalid. William Robinson (1996) correctly points out how revolutionary this change in US foreign policy in the second Reagan administration was. Rather than working to undermine popular democratic forces throughout the Third World, Reagan, his immediate successor, and then Clinton actively supported democratization, with the proviso that economic liberalization and the "good governance" of a limited state accompany it. The second Bush administration appears to have gone back to the older pattern. In places large and small—Pakistan, Venezuela, Haiti, the Central African Republic—honoring "democracy" now seems less important than securing strong allies and assuring that the advice of the Bretton Woods institutions is followed.

Yet, the one consistent lesson from Chua's analysis would be to support strong democratic states, committed to liberal international economic relations, but able to transfer the benefits of globalization from the small minorities that first gain them to the less-well-off majorities whose resent-ment would otherwise be fueled. Radical Afrikaaner political economist, Janis van der Westhuizen (2002), explains that it is the realization of exactly the problem Chua identifies that has fueled post-apartheid South Africa's search for models of "Ethnic Redistribution with Growth." In South African analysts' minds, two models stand out: the Malaysian model of using redistribution in a growing economy to create a class of Malay capi-talists, and the Afrikaaner experience in seizing the state created by the anglophone elite and using it to raise Afrikaaners to their level. Both models required a strong, interventionist state, one supporting a capitalist economy, certainly, but not the radically downsized state suggested by "market democracy."

Chua closes her book by arguing that Americans, themselves, consti-tute a "global market-dominant minority" that experiences the resentment of the world's majority. The analogy is apt, as is the analogous pruden-tial consequence: just as elites concerned with avoiding ethnic conflict in the Third World should support states strong enough to engage in ethnic redistribution with growth, at a global level, it would be prudent for the privileged to support powerful institutions that would redistribute part of the world's wealth. In the terms used in Chapter 2, it would be prudent to have global institutions that really do what they have always promised to do. In the early years of US hegemony, the years immediately after the Second World War, this is precisely what the United States did for its European allies and for Japan. That is why we still hear so many calls for a new "Marshall Plan" for Africa, Latin America, South Asia, the Arab world, or the South in general.

Why are such calls ignored? There is a relevant, and extensive, literature on why the United States has become increasingly hostile to international institutions and to any fundamentally redistributive global policies (Agrawala and Andresen 1999; Holloway 2000; Patrick and Forman 2002). Yet, much of that literature misses the cyclical nature of elite interest in tam-ing markets and redistributing some of the wealth. These cycles are just as relevant to the behavior of the privileged in Europe or Japan as they are to the more-often bewailed actions of the US government.

These long cycles persist, in part, because a long sequence of innovations is needed before a period of benign hegemony can begin. Consider, for example, the problem for world leaders who have become convinced of Chua's argument and ready to support stronger states capable of ethnic redistribution. Where would they look for policy guidance? Probably not to contemporary economics and international political economy (IPE). Both mainstream economics and IPE treat states that have adopted liberal eco-nomic policies, especially "market democracies," as normative. Political economists want to understand the forces that take a state away from this ideal. They rarely consider the forces that give rise to the adoption of the normative policies (Nelson 2003), let alone consider what is needed to

establish and give legitimacy to the different ideal of a powerful state committed to ethnic redistribution. Similarly, political economists concerned
with international institutions and development are likely to spend their
time thinking only about the policies of *Third World* governments as the
dependent variable. The conditions under which effective redistributive
international institutions might be created have not been explored.

Beyond the prudential

The greatest moral dilemmas faced by the world's privileged stem from
unequal influence granted to them by their wealth. One of the main themes
of this book has been that inequality is the enemy of human development;
it harms those at the bottom of the hierarchy. In fact, there is even strong
evidence that inequality, by itself, contributes to the ill health of the marginalized. Neither human beings, nor, for that matter, other primates, cope
well with the levels of inequality that are typical in the contemporary world
(Marmot and Wilkinson 1999; Kawachi *et al.* 1999).

   The world's marginalized know the power of the world's privileged.
The disadvantaged know that there are a wide range of collective decisions, in which they have no part, that affect their material well-being,
their security, their sense of self-worth, and their prospects for self-
actualization. These fundamentally undemocratic decisions include those
made by "democratic" means when Northern citizens choose their *globally* powerful leaders. Similar decisions are not really hidden from the eyes
of the marginalized even when they are made in the market. Market
outcomes *are* predictable consequences of market power, of wealth.
Indonesians can expect 70 percent of the market's benefits to go to the 3
percent of the people who have 70 percent of the private wealth. The
same can be said at a global level about the expectations the world can
have about how the market will benefit the 4 percent of humanity that
make up the "global market-dominant minority" in the US, or the similarly sized, and similarly privileged, minority in the EU.

Responsibly wielding power: learning from those on the margins

For better or worse, the materially privileged have great influence over
the marginalized, but theirs is a power difficult to wield responsibly. Those
of us who are part of the world's privileged find it difficult to have anything
more than the most abstract kind of compassion for all the people we
influence when we vote for our leaders and when we make our market
choices. Peter Singer (1999, 2002) might want the average European
or American to try to conjure up the faces of the dozen or two dozen
children we leave in destitution by refusing to make marginal changes in
our consumption, sacrifices equivalent to a tax of 1, 2, or 3 percent of

our incomes. Yet, it is difficult to see these faces. We do not, in fact, mingle or know the world's destitute.

Mormon ethicist and business consultant Steven R. Covey (1990) tells us that "highly effective people" are able to keep a close match between their "circle of influence" and their "circle of concern." Those who, by luck or misfortune, can influence more people than they can fully understand and have compassion for the need to delegate their influence in order to achieve their own goals.

Using a commercially savvy self-help guru as an authority for global ethics is meant to be jarring. Covey's point, of course, is to get business leaders to lighten-up and let others sweat the small stuff. He is not asking the privileged to give up ultimate power. Yet, that, in fact, would be the logical conclusion of the argument he is making, certainly if the goal of the privileged, influential person is to foster real democracy and to give everyone the opportunity for self-realization. In fact, the self-realization of the privileged people, themselves—their greatest sense of competence, honesty, and responsibility—can only come by giving up the influence they have over all those outside their circle of concern.

Yet, it is difficult to imagine how even the "global lawmakers" could make a world of relatively equal market power and truly democratic and effective global institutions. Perhaps the best that can be expected is that the powerful would begin to delegate more. That would allow the knowledge and the interests of the marginalized to play a role. This is, in fact, the central characteristic of "hegemony" in Antonio Gramsci's sense of the word. It is also what distinguished the Marshall Plan from almost every subsequent program of international economic assistance. Europeans decided on the projects to be funded, how they were to be done, and how they would be evaluated. The Americans insisted only that the Europeans cooperate and work toward the kind of economic integration that might end the century and a half of Franco-German conflict (Hogan 1987, 26–53).

The Marshall Plan was more successful than most later development assistance projects. Self-help guru Covey could explain why: the Americans delegated almost all responsibility to the people who had the knowledge to make the Plan work. Now, more cases teach the same lesson. They include some of the work of development NGOs as well as some of the work of the human-development-oriented UNDP (Tooze and Murphy 1996).

The argument made in this section has implications for the social sciences, and not just for development studies. International Relations (IR) claims a place among the disciplines not only as the main site of research on war and peace, statecraft, and international inequality. IR scholars argue that we nurture distinctive and valuable qualities of mind including the habit of approaching issues with a global perspective, that is, from the standpoint of all of humanity at once. Our critics correctly notice that the "global perspective" we claim to adopt and teach is often just that of the most powerful people in the most powerful states, the only people arrogant enough to believe that they can speak for the world. In IR, therefore, more perhaps than in other social sciences, it is essential to try to learn from the world's marginalized. It is essential to a goal we have set for ourselves and that we have not achieved.

The primary aim of contemporary critical theory in IR has been to let a wide range of previously excluded voices be heard within the academic and public dialogues about international affairs (Wyn Jones 2001). It is unclear whether critical theorists have been successful, and, no doubt, the effectiveness of the different strands of critical theory has differed. A distinct feminist IR theory that learns from the lives of women certainly exists, but the ability of global political economy to express the range of voices of the world's racially and economically marginalized can be questioned. There is still no disciplinary norm that enjoins students and scholars of global political economy to do field work among the world's marginalized—to meet, to spend time with, and to know the people for whom critical scholars claim to speak. Until such a norm exists, until it is habitually followed, the field is likely to remain less than "highly effective" at one of the core things we claim to do.

The material matters less than we sometimes believe it does

One of the ironies about many popular business writers, including Covey, is that they undermine both the ethical and psychological foundations of liberal capitalism by reminding their readers that material things contribute to happiness much less than do physical and emotional security, friendship, and the ability to pursue a calling. The UNDP's Human Development Index also tries to remind us of this. It is an imperfect measure, but instructive. For example, in the 2003 report, the United States shares the status of "high human development" with 54 other countries. In 53 of those, GDP per capita (taking into account purchasing power) is less than in the US. That is to say, 53 other societies find a way to provide the material conditions needed for a decent life while taking less, per capita, of the world's material goods. In 22 of the 53 countries, "high human development" is achieved with less than half the income of the average American. Or, to put it another way, Americans might be able to give to others half of what they gain each year and still have access to all that really matters.

Honoring our ancestors, assuring that we have taken only what has been given, releasing ourselves from clinging

For many Americans, our ethical concerns for the plight of the world's marginalized may be even greater. Those of us whose families fled Ireland's

Great Famine (or the Swedish famine a generation later, or any of the myriad other immigrant tragedies) dishonor their memory by ignoring those who, today, suffer from the same policies that turned our great grandparents into economic exiles. Tom Hayden (2001: 269) writes:

> We may climb the corporate ladder—by some estimates one-third of American CEOs are Irish American—but these material gains are often achieved at the expense of deeper spiritual benefits. . . . We can become a permanent caste of Reagan Democrats, adopting the same superior pretensions and free-market nostrums that doomed our own ancestors to catastrophic suffering, or we can learn from our origins to identify with the landless, the hungry, the poor, and the immigrants . . . We can reap the privileges of being white or, remembering the shame of being classified as simians and asking what is whiteness but privilege?, we can transcend the superficiality of our skin color to join in solidarity with those who are darker than ourselves. We can dismiss . . . as inferior the two billion people living on wages of one US dollar per day, and in doing so live lives of perfect denial of our own origins. Or we can see ourselves mirrored in the roughened, unkempt, tearful faces of today's persecuted, and act to alleviate their suffering as we once hoped others might do for us.

Even those of the world's privileged who do not share the experience of the "successful" immigrants have reason to question whether their material advantage has been earned fairly. It is not necessary to be convinced that the Third World's "underdevelopment" was, in part, a consequence of "the drain of economic surplus from the satellite after its incorporation as such into the world capitalist system," (Frank 1967: 10). It is only necessary to suspect that some of the privilege we now have is unearned; that some of what we have was not given freely to us or to our ancestors.

Finally, there is the problem faced by all of us who have prestige, honor, wealth, and power. Our advantages are addictive, hard to give up. We cling to them, and that clinging itself, ultimately, is painful not only for others, but also for us. In 1998, Nadine Gordimer, the South African novelist who won the 1991 Nobel Prize for Literature wrote a post-apartheid, metaphorical tale, a horror story, about a white couple—decent, kind, humane—trying to protect all they have and what they care for. They wall their house and top it with loops of razor wire, as so many decent and kind South Africans have done since 1994, the common response to the robberies, break-ins, and violence that have marked the first decade when everyone can freely move throughout the country. The story closes with the couple's beloved only child, increasingly isolated and living in his own beautiful fantasy world of knights and dragons, pretending "to be the Prince who braves the terrible thicket of thorns to enter the palace and kiss the Sleeping Beauty back to life." Crawling into the coiled tunnel at the compounds' edge, he is caught, and killed, by the razor wire. It clutches him and drags his body in, exactly as the contractors, "The People for Total Security," promised it would.

Gordimer (1998) frames the tale with her own reflections about life in her new politically equal, but still economically divided country. The story is a metaphor for the clinging that is destroying the privilege, psychically and morally. Yet, even she—democrat, open admirer of Marx, life-long warrior for equality—has nothing but sad compassion for those who use walls and wire to try to save what they have.

Coda: a copper box for cars

For most of us in the privileged world, the tragedy and insanity of what we do to preserve our advantage is rarely as stark and clear as the things a critical observer can see in Johannesburg, or Port-au-Prince, or perhaps even in Manila. Yet, I am almost certain that, if we open our eyes, we can always find examples in our own backyards.

A case in point: a few years back, the Trustees, the governing board of the college where I teach, walked around the campus with some of our historians of art and architecture and noted that a horrible "sub-urbanization" had taken place even in the 30 or 40 years since most of the Trustees had been students. Little could be seen of the landscape imagined by Wellesley College's nineteenth-century founder, a visionary philanthropic capitalist who wanted to create a place where women could "revolt against the slavery" in which they were held "by the customs of society—the broken health, the aimless lives, the subordinate position," (Palmieri 1997: 10). The College was to be a laboratory for social trans-formation where even the landscape would work toward that end. Frederick Law Olmstead, the architect of New York's Central Park and the "Emerald Necklace" of green spaces surrounding the city of Boston, provided the blueprint. Yet, by 2000, Olmstead's bucolic landscape was filled with auto-mobiles. Tarmac covered what were once open meadows and Subarus and Volvos lined what were once empty carriage roads.

This "suburbanization" came about without anyone's intention. The existence of the College itself, and its beautiful public landscape, contributed to the value of property in the surrounding community. By the early 2000s, a house or condominium within walking distance cost eight times the annual salary of an average senior faculty member, 16 times the salary of an entering assistant professor, or 32 times the salary of the average member of the clerical staff. Almost everyone who works at the College now has to commute, and, after more than a decade of Republican governors convinced that users should bear the entire costs of public services, the network of trains and buses that once converged on the College was now very thin.

The bus that I used to take disappeared when the General Motors factory, ten miles to the West, moved to Latin America. (That factory had been important to me in another way. Its United Auto Workers' contract stipulated that the union could bring organizers from other countries there to learn about American practices. I used to take my International Organization students there to see a practical demonstration of the ways in which international labor solidarity could be built in this "global" age.)

In any event, my story, and a hundred others like it, left the campus, in the eyes of today's Trustees, looking too much like one of the local shopping malls. They resolved to restore Olmstead's, and the founder's, vision, not by intervening in the housing market, not by lobbying for a more rational system of public transportation, but by finding a place to hide all those cars.

The solution was a huge garage at the College's gate, partially sunken, partially (to treetop height) above ground. Of course, to restore the campus's beauty, the above ground part had to be hidden, as it eventually will be, by a forest of young, green-barked birch trees, trucked in from distant nurseries. To have the concrete building blend in with the forest, the builders attached a bamboo thicket of tree-high poles to exterior walls, a thicket that eventually will be verdigris. Right now, however, when we enter the College's gates, it is entirely too clear that here is a bunker, sheathed in precious metal, designed to lock up all the expensive little precious and metal worlds that we individually inhabit as we go to and from work. This seems far from the place that the College's philanthropic founder imagined, in 1875, would counterbalance the "male" world of "crass commercialism, social isolation, and death," (Palmieri 1997: 9).

Speaking at the UNDP, at the 1997 launching of the "Decade for Elimination of Poverty," Nadine Gordimer (1999: 183) asked:

> those who possess and control great wealth ... [to] look at the economic structures in their own countries which have made that wealth possible and yet have created conditions that make philanthropy necessary—political and economic regimes that have failed to establish the means ... by which people may provide for themselves in self-respect and dignity.

That critical reflection, that commitment to understanding the place of the privileged in the larger world of marginalization, may be an essential program for our own "development." Gordimer closes the book in which she placed her UNDP address by remembering the words Nehru wrote in a colonial prison about the shared human struggle to give meaning to our lives as we try to confront, consciously:

> the problems of individual and social life, of harmonious living, of a proper balancing of an individual's inner and outer life, of an adjustment

of the relation between individuals and groups, of a continuous becoming something better and higher, of social development, of *the ceaseless adventure of man.*

(Quoted in Gordimer 1999: 236)

For the world's privileged, to engage in that adventure requires moving out of our precious metal boxes, out from behind our walls and wires, to mingle, meet, and know.

Notes

1 Institutions, marginalization, development

1   The allusion is to Keynes (1936: 383):

> The ideas of economists and political philosophers . . . are more power-
> ful than is commonly understood. Indeed the world is ruled by little
> else. Practical men who believe themselves to be quite exempt from any
> intellectual influences, are usually the slaves of some defunct economist.

2   Cadbury's purchase of the soft-drink giant, Schweppes, solved that problem in
    1969, and it began the rapid evolution of the British chocolate giants into
    "normal," less philanthropic, companies (Swift 1998).

2 World organizations and human needs

1   Lederach (1998) introduces many of these techniques from different contexts,
    drawing heavily on Curle (1971). Lederach is a Mennonite mediator and devel-
    opment worker who has done significant work for the United Nations, although
    the limits of what has been possible in his own work illustrate the argument
    made in this chapter: the world organizations work for the short- or medium-
    term management of many fundamental conflicts and are ill-equipped to work
    for their long-term resolution.

2   However, consider Cheru (1990) who sees many Africans' disregard for govern-
    ment and the investment, emotional and material, into economies of affection
    as fundamentally revolutionary activities designed to transform an intolerable
    status quo.

3   This is confirmed by the generally improving trends in Human Development
    noted in the UNDP's *Human Development Reports*. A conviction that material trends
    were improving was important to Stephen D. Krasner's (1981) argument that
    the NIEO demands of the 1970s reflected the interests of governing elites rather
    than popular aspirations (see Chapter 7).

4 Social movements and liberal world orders

1   The last of the three phrases has the greatest surface validity. It comes from
    Henk Overbeek (1990, 1993), Kees van der Pijl (1998), and others of the
    Amsterdam School of international political economy.

2   See John S. Henley's contribution to Stopford and Strange (1992).

3   Jonathan A. Fox (2000) outlines the limitations of this democratic opening in
    the procedures of the Bank.

4   This perspective on the connection between large or "bulky" investments and the beginnings of new industrial eras is consistent with Systems Dynamics arguments about the long wave; see Sterman and Mosekilde (1994) as well as Modelski and Thompson (1995).

5   It is interesting to compare Wallach's own account of her work in Geneva in the early 1990s ("There was no openness, and the level of arrogance was amazing. As disheartening as it was, it was also a motivating factor for an enormous amount of political organizing" ("Lori's War" 2000: 32) with Braithwaite and Drahos's (2000: 31) empirical conclusion, based on hundreds of interviews in Geneva, that Wallach's (and Ralph Nader's) organization was the most effective of the international model mongers during those years.

5 The promise of democratic functionalism

1   Chandler (1962) outlines the process in the United States. Chandler with Hikino (1990: 240-295), comparing the US experience with the relatively similar experience in Germany and the different experience of the United Kingdom and other industrialized countries in which fewer companies developed within the leading industries of the Second Industrial Revolution. Yates (1985) provides an outstanding summary of the shift from direct control to functional structures to more complex divisional forms.

2   See Peter Drucker (1994) on the rediscovery of Follett by organization theorists. In 1994, the American Political Science Association inaugurated a Mary Parker Follett prize for the best article employing historical methods. In 1998, Pennsylvania State University Press published a new edition of *The New State*, with forewords by a leading American political theorist (Benjamin R. Barber) and a leading scholar of women and politics (Jane Mansbridge).

3   Not coincidentally, Schlafly worked closely with Republican leaders to produce an effective film promoting American unilateralism, "Global Governance: The Quiet War Against American Independence," (Eagle Forum 1998).

6 International institutions, decolonization, and "development"

1   I wrote the original version of this chapter with the late Enrico Augelli. I have revised this version extensively and it refers to a great deal that has gone on since his death.

2   Julius Nyerere's assessment in his introduction to Mason Sears's *The Years of High Purpose* (1980) is typical.

3   On the shifting arguments that have justified support for "development" within the United States, in particular, see Augelli and Murphy (1988: 75-96). For all donor countries, see Cassen *et al.* (1982).

4   Enrico Augelli and I analyzed the accuracy of the analysis with reference to Africa (Augelli and Murphy 1989). A commentator (Novati 1989) said that we still adopted "the World Bank position," and suggested a number of ways in which what we took to be internal factors impeding Africa's development were, in fact, external factors.

7 What the Third World wanted: the meaning of the NIEO

1   Critical liberal internationalists sympathetic to the South's proposals, including Gwin (1977) and Hart (1982) played minor roles in the Carter administration.

2   See the critical comments of US democratic socialist leader, Michael Harrington (1977: 220-251).

3   Rothschild (1944) gives a prescient Keynesian justification for the poorer states'
    position. Wilcox (1949) documents the postwar economic conferences where the
    Asian, Latin American, and the few free African states began to share views.
4   From the debates in the UN General Assembly's Second Committee (UNGA),
    references include the country whose representative is speaking, the year of the
    actual meeting, and the page number in the English translation and summary
    where the speech is reported.
5   Nwekwe (1980: 94-107) calls the Third World response to falling trade shares
    "The Nigerian Initiative of 1961" and notes (p.99) that Gosovic and Ruggie
    (1976) were unaware of the Nigerian action as a direct antecedent to calls for
    a NIEO in 1974.
6   Compare the resolutions of regional (Asian, African, and Latin American) meet-
    ings to Group of 77 meetings in Moss and Winton (1976: 20-34, 99-159, 208-309).
7   In the 1960s, debate between more and less radical states resulted in an agreement
    not to mention any region's principles in the Group's consensus if they conflicted
    with those advocated by another region (Moss and Winton 1976: 99-159).

10 Political consequences of the new inequality

1   At least, the cards in the back of many books I used in the early 1990s showed
    that they had checked them out. Keohane lived on the Wellesley campus while
    writing *After Hegemony*. Courses at MIT, where Kindleberger taught, and Wellesley
    are cross-listed and the facilities of both campuses are open to both faculties.

11 Leadership and global governance for the Information Age

1   On the situation in Indonesia, see Candland and Nurjanah (2001).

References

Abrahamsen, Rita (2001) *Disciplining Democracy: Development Discourse and Good Governance in Africa*. London: Zed Books.

Adelman, Carol C. (1988) *International Regulation: New Rules in a Changing World Order*. Washington, D.C.: Institute for Contemporary Studies.

Adorno, Theodor W., Else Frenkel-Brunswick, Daniel J. Levinson, and R. Nevitt Sanford (1950) *The Authoritarian Personality*. New York: Harper.

Agrawala, Shardul, and Steinar Andresen (1999) "Indispensability and Indefensibility? The United States and the Climate Treaty Negotiations." *Global Governance* 5(4): 457–482.

Ake, Claude (1995) *Democracy and Development in Africa*. Washington, D.C.: Brookings Institution Press.

Ali, Tariq (2003) *Bush in Babylon: the Recolonisation of Iraq*. London: Verso.

Al-Mashat, Abdel Monheim (1985) *National Security in the Third World*. Boulder, Colo.: Westview Press.

Amin, Samir (1987) "The Crisis: the Third World, North–South and East–West," in Emmanuel Hansen (ed.) *Africa: Perspectives on Peace and Development*. London: Zed Books.

Amsden, Alice H. (2001) *The Rise of "The Rest" Challenges to the West from Late-Industrializing Economies*. New York: Oxford University Press.

Annan, Kofi (1998) "The Quiet Revolution." *Global Governance* 4(2): 121–138.

Ansprenger, Franz (1989) *The Dissolution of Colonial Empires*, London: Routledge.

Ashley, Richard K. (1980) *The Political Economy of War and Peace: the Sino-Soviet-American Triangle and the Modern Security Problematique*. New York: Nichols Publishing Company.

Ashworth, Lucian M., and David Long (1995) "David Mitrany, the Functional Approach, and International Conflict Management." NPSIA Occasional Paper No. 9. Ottawa: Norman Paterson School of International Affairs, Carleton University.

Augelli, Enrico (1986) "Il 'dialogo politiche' secondo Washington." *Politica Internationale* 14(1): 108–211.

Augelli, Enrico and Craig N. Murphy (1988) *America's Quest for Supremacy and the Third World: a Gramscian Analysis*. London: Pinter Publishers.

—— (1989) "The International Economy and the Development of Sub-Saharan Africa," in Enzo Caputo (ed.) *Which Cooperation with Africa in the 90s?* Rome: Istituto Italo-Africano.

—— (1993) "Gramsci and International Relations: a General Perspective with Examples from Recent US Policy toward the Third World," in Stephen Gill (ed.) *Gramsci, Historical Materialism, and International Relations.* Cambridge: Cambridge University Press.

—— (1995) "La nuova teoria-della pace delle Nazioni unite," in Gian Giacomo Migone and Olga Re (eds) *A cinquant'anni dalla nascita delle Nazioni unite,* a special issue of *Europa/Europe* 4(4): 97–121.

Azar, Edward E., and Nadia Farah (1981) "The Structure of Inequalities and Protracted Social Conflict: a Theoretical Framework." *International Interactions* 7(4): 317–335.

Azar, Edward E., and Chung-in Moon (1986) "Managing Protracted Social Conflicts: Facilitation and Development Diplomacy." *Millennium* 15(3): 393–408.

Bairoch, Paul (1993) "Was there a Large Income Differential before Modern Development?," in his *Economic and World History: Myths and Paradoxes.* Chicago: University of Chicago Press.

Bakker, Isabella (ed.) (1994) *The Strategic Silence: Gender and Economic Policy.* London: Zed Books.

Barnett, Michael (1995) "The New United Nations Politics of Peace: From Juridical Sovereignty to Empirical Sovereignty." *Global Governance* 1(1): 79–97.

—— (2001) *Eyewitness to a Genocide: the United Nations and Rwanda.* Ithaca, N.Y.: Cornell University Press.

Bell, Daniel (1977) "The Future World Disorder." *Foreign Policy* 27: 109–135.

Bell, Phillip W. (1956) *The Sterling Area in the Post-War World: Internal Mechanisms and Cohesion, 1946–1952.* Oxford: Oxford University Press.

Benedetti, Fanny and John L. Washburn (1999) "Drafting the International Criminal Court Treaty." *Global Governance* 5(1): 1–38.

Berkovitch, Nitza (1999) *From Motherhood to Citizenship: Women's Rights and International Organizations.* Baltimore, Md.: Johns Hopkins University Press.

Berlinguer, Giovanni, Douglas Bettcher, Nick Drager, Tim Evans, Godfrey Gunatilleke, Wendy Harcourt, Craig N. Murphy, Derek Yach, and Meg Wirth (eds) (1999) Special issue on "Equity in Health in the Age of Globalization." *Development* 42(4): whole issue.

Block, Fred (1977) *The Origins of International Economic Disorder.* Berkeley, Calif.: University of California Press.

Bøås, Morten and Desmond McNeill (2003) "The Changing Priorities of Multilateral Institutions: from Technical Aid to Good Governance," in their *Multilateral Institutions: a Critical Introduction.* London: Pluto Press, pp. 50–89.

Boli, John, and George M. Thomas (1999) *Constructing World Culture: International Nongovernmental Organizations since 1875.* Stanford, Conn.: Stanford University Press.

Boutros-Ghall, Boutros (1995) "Democracy: a Newly-Recognized Imperative." *Global Governance* 1(1): 3–11.

Braithwaite, John, and Peter Drahos (2000) *Global Business Regulation.* Cambridge: Cambridge University Press.

Brandt Commission (1980) *North–South: a Programme for Survival.* Cambridge, Mass.: MIT Press.

—— (1983) *Common Crisis North–South: Cooperation for World Recovery.* Cambridge, Mass.: MIT Press.

Bronfenbrenner, Martin (1976) "Predatory Poverty on the Offensive: the UNCTAD Record." *Economic Development and Cultural Change* 24(4): 825–831.

Brown, William A. Jr (1950) *The United States and the Restoration of World Trade.* Washington, D.C.: The Brookings Institution.

Burton, John (1979) *Deviance, Terrorism, and War.* New York: St Martin's Press.

Butterworth, Robert L. (1978) *Moderation through Management.* Pittsburgh, Pa.: University of Pittsburgh Center for International Studies.

Calhoun, Craig (2000) "Report from the President." *Social Science Research Council Items and Issues* 2: 10–13.

Cammack, Paul (2002) "The Mother of All Governments: the World Bank's Matrix for Global Governance," in Rorden Wilkinson and Steve Hughes (eds) *Global Governance: Critical Perspectives.* London: Routledge.

Camps, Miriam, and Catherine Gwin (1981) *Collective Management: Reform of Global Economic Organization.* New York: McGraw-Hill.

Candland, Christopher (2002) "How Are International Labor Standards Established?" Prepared for the Annual Conference of the International Studies Association. New Orleans, La. March.

Candland, Christopher, and Siti Nurjanah (2001) "Indonesia after Wahid: the New Authoritarianism." *Royal Institute of International Affairs Briefing Paper.* New series no. 28, December.

Cardoso, Fernando H. (1977) "The Originality of a Copy: CEPAL and the Idea of Development." *CEPAL Review* second half: 7–40.

Carr, Edward Hallett (1939) *The Twenty Year's Crisis, 1919–1939.* London: Macmillan.

Cassen, Robert with Richard Jolly (eds) (1982) *Rich Country Interests and Third World Development.* London: Croom Helm for the Overseas Development Council.

Cavallari, Giovanni (1990) *Instituzione e individuo nel Neoidealismo Anglosassone: Bernard Bosanquent e Mary Parker Follett.* Milan: Angeli.

Chabal, Patrick (1983) *Amilcar Cabral: Revolutionary Leadership and People's War.* Cambridge: Cambridge University Press.

Chandler, Alfred D., Jr. (1962) *Strategy and Structure: Chapters in the History of American Industrial Enterprise.* Cambridge, Mass.: MIT Press.

Chandler, Alfred D., Jr., with Takashi Hikino (1990) *Scale and Scope: the Dynamics of Industrial Capitalism.* Cambridge, Mass.: Harvard University Press.

Charnovitz, Steve (1997) "Two Centuries of Participation: NGOs and International Governance." *Michigan Journal of International Law* 18(2): whole issue.

Chase-Dunn, Christopher K. (ed.) (1982) *Socialist States in the World System.* Beverly Hills, Calif.: Sage Publications.

Chen, Martha Alter (1995) "Engendering World Conferences: the International Women's Movement and the United Nations." *Third World Quarterly* 16(3): 477–494.

Chenery, Hollis, Montek S. Ahluwalla, C. L. G. Bell, John H. Duloy, and Richard Jolly (1974) *Redistribution with Growth.* New York: Oxford University Press.

Cheru, Fantu (1990) *The Silent Revolution in Africa: Debt, Development, and Democracy.* London: Zed Books.

Childers, Erskine (1997) "The United Nations and Global Institutions: Discourse and Reality." *Global Governance* 3(3): 269–276.

Chilton, Patricia (1995) "Mechanics of Change: Social movements, transnational coalitions, and the transformation processes in eastern Europe," in Thomas Risse-Kappen (ed.) *Bringing Transnational Relations Back In.* Cambridge: Cambridge University Press.

Choucri, Nazli, and Robert C. North (1975) *Nations in Conflict: National Growth and International Violence.* San Francisco, Calif.: W. H. Freeman.

Choucri, Nazli, Robert C. North, and Susumu Yamakage (1992) *The Challenge of Japan before World War II and After: a Study of National Growth and Expansion.* London: Routledge.

Chua, Amy (2003) *World on Fire: How Exporting Free Market Democracy Breeds Ethnic Hatred and Global Instability.* New York: Doubleday.

Clapp, Jennifer (1998) "The Privatization of Global Environmental Governance: ISO 14000 and the Developing World." *Global Governance* 4(3): 295–316.

Clark, John Maurice (1923) *Studies in the Economics of Overhead Costs.* Chicago: University of Chicago Press.

Commission on Global Governance (1995) *Our Global Neighborhood.* New York: Oxford University Press.

Commons, John R. (1924) *The Legal Foundations of Capitalism.* Madison, Wis.: University of Madison Press.

Cornia, Giovanni Andrea (1999) "Rising Inequality in an Era of Liberalization and Globalization." *Work in Progress: a Review of Research Activities of the UN University* 16(1): 12–13.

Council on Economic Priorities (2001) "Mission of the CEP Accreditation Agency." Found on the internet at www.cepaa.org/, January 16, 2004.

Covey, Stephen R. (1990) *The Seven Habits of Highly Successful People.* New York: Simon & Schuster.

Cox, Robert W. (1980) "The Crisis of World Order and the Problem of International Organization in the 1980s." *International Journal* 35(2): 370–395.

—— (1992) "The United Nations, Globalization, and Democracy." The John W. Holmes Memorial Lecture. Providence, R.I.: Academic Council on the United Nations System.

—— (1996a) "Structural Issues of Global Governance: Issues for Europe," in Robert W. Cox with Timothy J. Sinclair (eds) *Approaches to World Order.* Cambridge: Cambridge University Press.

—— (1996b) "The Idea of International Labor Regulation," in Robert W. Cox with Timothy J. Sinclair (eds) *Approaches to World Order.* Cambridge: Cambridge University Press.

Cox, Robert W., with Michael G. Schechter (2002) *The Political Economy of a Plural World: Critical Reflections on Power, Morals, and Civilization.* London: Routledge.

Cox, Robert W., Harold K. Jacobson, *et al.* (1973) *The Anatomy of Influence: Decision Making in International Organizations.* New Haven, Conn.: Yale University Press.

Curle, Adam (1971) *Making Peace.* London: Tavistock.

Cutler, A. Claire, Virginia Haufler, and Tony Porter (eds) (1999) *Private Authority and International Affairs.* Albany, N.Y.: SUNY Press.

Davidson, Basil (1989) *The Fortunate Isles: a Study in African Transformation.* Trenton, N.J.: Africa World Press.

Deudney, Daniel (1996) "Building Sovereigns. Authorities, Structures, and Geopolitics in Philadelphian Systems," in Thomas J. Biersteker and Cynthia Weber (eds) *State Sovereignty as a Social Construct.* Cambridge: Cambridge University Press.

Deutsch, Karl W. (1966) *Nationalism and Social Communication.* Cambridge, Mass.: MIT Press.

Deutsch, Karl W., S. A. Burrell, R. A. Kann, M. Lee, Jr *et al.* (1957) *Political Community in the North Atlantic Area: International Organization in Light of Historical Experience.* Princeton, N.J.: Princeton University Press.

Dodgson, Richard (1999) "The Women's Health Movement and the International Conference on Population and Development: Global Social Movements, Population, and the Changing Nature of International Relations." Doctoral dissertation in International Politics, University of Newcastle upon Tyne.

Douglas, Ian R. (1999) "Globalization as Governance: Toward an Archaeology of Contemporary Political Reason," in Aseem Prakash and Jeffrey A. Hart (eds) *Globalization and Governance*. London: Routledge.

Dowrick, Steve and Muhammad Akmal (2003) "Contradictory Trends in Global Income Inequality: a Tale of Two Biases." Prepared for the UNUU/WIDER Conference, "Inequality, Poverty, and Human Well-Being." Helsinki, May.

Drucker, Peter (1994) "Introduction," *Mary Parker Follett—Prophet of Management: a Celebration of Writings from the 1920s*. Boston, Mass.: Harvard Business School Press.

Eagle Forum (1998) "Global Governance: the Quiet War Against American Independence." Documentary film. Alton, Ill.: Eagle Forum.

Eckhardt, William (1987) "Rudolf Rummel—Apostle of Peace and Justice through Freedom." *International Interactions*, 13(3): 183–223.

Elsenhans, Harmut (1991) *Development and Underdevelopment: the History, Economics, and Politics of North–South Relations*. New Delhi: Sage Publications.

Erasov, Boris (1972) "Cultural Personality in the Ideologies of the Third World." *Diogenes* 78(2): 123–140.

Evans, Tim (1998) "Bangladesh Country Report." Global Health Equity Initiative, Social Determinants Project, Santa Fe, N.M., October.

Fanon, Frantz (1961) *The Wretched of the Earth*. San Francisco, Calif.: Grove Press.

Farmer, Paul (2003) *Pathologies of Power: Health, Human Rights, and the New War on the Poor*. Berkeley, Calif.: University of California Press.

Farrenkopf, John (1991) "The Challenge of Spenglerian Pessimism to Ranke and Political Realism." *Review of International Studies* 17(3): 267–284.

Fayol, Henri (1937) "The Administrative Theory in the State," in Luther H. Gulick (ed.) *Papers on the Science of Administration*. New York: Institute of Public Administration, Columbia University.

Finnemore, Martha (1996) *National Interests in International Society*. Ithaca, N.Y.: Cornell University Press.

Follett, Mary Parker (1918) *The New State: Group Organization, the Solution of Popular Government*. New York: Longmans, Green.

—— (1937) "The Process of Control," in Luther H. Gulick (ed.) *Papers on the Science of Administration*. New York: Institute of Public Administration, Columbia University.

—— (1942) *Dynamic Administration: The Collected Papers of Mary Parker Follett*, (Henry C. Metcalf and L. Urwick, eds). New York: Harper & Brothers.

—— (1954) *The Illusion of Final Authority: Authority Must Be Functional and Functional Authority Carries with It Functional Responsibility*. Washington, D.C.: US Bureau of Public Assistance.

Fomerand, Jacques (1996) "UN Conferences: Media Events or Genuine Diplomacy?" *Global Governance* 2(3): 361–377.

Forgacs, David (ed.) (1988) *An Antonio Gramsci Reader: Selected Writings, 1916–1935*. London: Lawrence & Wishart.

Fox, Jonathan A. (2000), "The World Bank Inspection Program: Lessons from the First Five Years." *Global Governance* 6(3): 279–318.

Frank, Andre Gunder (1967) *Capitalism and Underdevelopment in Latin America*. New York: Monthly Review Press.

——— (1981) *Crisis in the World Economy*. New York: Holmes & Meier.

Friedeberg, A. S. (1969) *UNCTAD 1964: the Theory of the Peripheral Economy at the Center of Global Discussion*. Rotterdam: University of Rotterdam Press.

Friedman, Thomas L. (1999) *The Lexus and the Olive Tree*. New York: Farrar, Straus, Giroux.

Fromm, Erich (1973) *The Anatomy of Human Destructiveness*. New York: Holt, Rinehart, and Winston.

Gaer, Felice D. (1995) "Reality Check: Human Rights Nongovernmental Organizations Confront Governments at the United Nations." *Third World Quarterly* 16(3): 389–404.

Galtung, Johan (1971) "A Structural Theory of Imperialism." *Journal of Peace Research* 8(2): 81–118.

——— (1988) "International Development in Human Perspective," in Roger A. Coate and Jerel A. Rosati (eds) *The Power of Human Needs in World Society*. Boulder, Colo.: Lynne Rienner Publishers.

Gardner, Lloyd C. (1964) *Economic Aspects of New Deal Diplomacy*. Madison, Wis.: University of Wisconsin Press.

Geertz, Clifford (1964) "Ideology as a Cultural System," in David Apter (ed.) *Ideology and Discontent*. New York: Free Press.

Gill, Stephen (2003) *Power and Resistance in the New World Order*. Houndsmills, Basingstoke: Palgrave Macmillan.

Gilpin, Robert (2000) *The Challenge of Global Capitalism: the World Economy in the 21st Century*. Princeton, N.J.: Princeton University Press.

Gledistsch, Karen S., and Michael Don Ward (2000) "War and Peace in Space and Time: the Role of Democratization." *International Studies Quarterly* 44(1): 1–29.

Golway, Terry (1997) *The Irish in America*. New York: Hyperion.

Goodman, Paul (1998) *Of One Blood: Abolitionism and the Origin of Racial Equality*. Berkeley, Calif.: University of California Press.

Gordimer, Nadine (1998) "Once Upon a Time," in Graeme Friedman and Roy Blumenthal (eds) *A Writer in Stone: South African Writers Celebrate the 70th Birthday of Lionel Abrahams*. Cape Town: David Philip Publishers.

——— (1999) *Living in Hope and History*. New York: Farrar, Strauss, Giroux.

Gordon, David M. (1980) "Stages of Accumulation and Long Economic Cycles," in Terence K. Hopkins and Immanuel Wallerstein (eds) *Processes of the World-System*. Beverly Hills, Calif.: Sage Publications.

Gordon, David M., Richard Edwards, and Michael Reich (1982) *Segmented Work, Divided Workers: the Historical Transformation of Labor in the United States*. New York: Cambridge University Press.

Gosovic, Branislav (1972) *UNCTAD: Conflict and Compromise*. Leiden: A. W. Sifthoff.

Gosovic, Branislav, and John Gerald Ruggie (1976) "On the Creation of the New International Economic Order: Issue Linkage and the Seventh Special Session of the United Nations General Assembly." *International Organization* 30(2): 309–345.

Gramsci, Antonio (1971) *Selections from the Prison Notebooks*. (Quintin Hoare and Geoffrey Nowell Smith, eds and trans.) New York: International Publishers.

——— (1991) *Prison Notebooks*. Vol. 1 (Joseph A. Buttigieg, ed. and trans.) New York: Columbia University Press.

Gray, Loren (2003) "Getting Ready for Recovery." *Harvard Business School Working Knowledge for Business Leaders*. November 3. Found on the internet at hbswk.hbs.edu/item.jhtml?id=3762&t=finance, January 16, 2004.

Greaves, H. R. G. (1931) *The League Committees and World Order*. London: Oxford University Press.

Groom, A. J. R. (1995) "From Revolution to Reform," in *Approaches to Conflict and Cooperation in International Relations: Lessons from Theory for Practice, a Lecture Series*. Found on the internet at www.kent.ac.uk/politics/research/kentpapers/groom1. html, January 16, 2004.

Grown, Caren, Diane Elson, and Nilufer Cagatay (eds) (2000) Special Issue on "Growth, Trade, Finance, and Gender Inequality." *World Development* 28(7).

Gruber, Lloyd (2000) *Ruling the World: Power Politics and the Rise of Supranational Institutions*. Princeton, N.J.: Princeton University Press.

Guillén, Mauro F. (1995) *Models of Management: Work, Authority, and Organization in a Comparative Perspective*. Chicago: Chicago University Press.

Gurr, Ted Robert (2000) *Peoples Versus States: Minorities at Risk in the New Century*. Washington, D.C.: US Institute of Peace.

Gwin, Catherine (1977) "The Seventh Special Session: Toward a New Phase in the Relations Between the Developed and Developing States," in Karl P. Sauvant and Hajo Hasenpflug (eds) *The NIEO: Confrontation or Cooperation between North and South*. Boulder, Colo.: Westview Press.

Haas, Ernst B. (1958) *The Uniting of Europe*. Stanford, Calif.: Stanford University Press.

—— (1964) *Beyond the Nation-State*. Stanford, Calif.: Stanford University Press.

—— (1983) "Regime Decay: Conflict Management and International Organization, 1945–1981." *International Organization* 37(2): 189–256.

Haas, Peter M. (1990) *Saving the Mediterranean: the Politics of International Environmental Cooperation*. New York: Columbia University Press.

—— (1992) "From Theory to Practice: Ecological Ideas and Development Policy." Harvard University, Center for International Affairs Working Paper 92–2.

—— (ed.) (1997) *Knowledge, Power, and International Policy Coordination*. Columbia, S.C.: University of South Carolina Press.

Habermas, Jürgen (1971) "Knowledge and Human Interests: a General Perspective," in Jeremy J. Shapiro (trans.) *Knowledge and Human Interests*. Boston, Mass.: Beacon Press.

Hall, Rodney Bruce, and Thomas J. Biersteker (2003) (eds) *The Emergence of Private Authority in Global Governance*. Cambridge: Cambridge University Press.

Harrington, Michael (1977) *The Vast Majority: A Journey to the World's Poor*. New York: Simon & Schuster.

Harris, Nigel (1987) *The End of the Third World: Newly Industrializing Countries and the Decline of an Ideology*. Harmondsworth: Penguin Books.

Hart, Jeffrey A. (1982) *Political Forces in the Global Economy: Explaining Negotiations for the New International Economic Order*. London: Macmillan.

Hasenclever, Andreas, Peter Mayer, and Volker Rittberger (1997) *Theories of International Regimes*. Cambridge: Cambridge University Press.

Hayden, Tom (2001) *Irish on the Inside: in Search of the Soul of Irish America*. London: Verso.

Held, David (1995) *Democracy and the Global Order: From the Modern state to Cosmopolitan Governance*. Cambridge: Polity Press.

—— (1997) "Democracy and Globalization." *Global Governance* 3(3): 251–267.

Helleiner, Gerald K. (ed.) (1987) *Africa and the International Monetary Fund*. Washington, D.C.: International Monetary Fund.

Hewson, Martin and Timothy J. Sinclair (1999) "The Emergence of Global Governance Theory," in Martin Hewson and Timothy J. Sinclair (eds) *Approaches to Global Governance Theory*. Albany, N.Y.: SUNY Press.

Higer, Amy (1997) Transnational Movements and World Politics: the International Women's Health Movement and Population Policy. Doctoral dissertation in the Department of Politics, Brandeis University, Waltham, Mass.

Hirschman, Albert O. (1977) *The Passions and the Interests: Political Arguments for Capitalism before Its Triumph*. Princeton, N.J.: Princeton University Press.

Hobson, John A. (1965[1902]) *Imperialism: a Study*. Ann Arbor, Mich.: University of Michigan Press.

—— (1912) *The Evolution of Modern Capitalism*. London: Walter Scott Publishing Company.

—— (1915) *Towards International Government*. London: George & Allen Unwin.

Hobson, John M. (2000) *The State and International Relations*. Cambridge: Cambridge University Press.

Hogan, Michael J. (1987) *The Marshall Plan: America, Britain, and the Reconstruction of Western Europe, 1947–1952*. Cambridge: Cambridge University Press.

Holborn, Louise (1975) *Refugees: a Problem of Our Time*. Metuchen, N.J.: Scarecrow Press.

Holloway, Stephen (2000) US Unilateralism at the UN: Why Great Powers Do Not Make Great Multilateralists." *Global Governance* 6(3): 361–381.

Holsti, Ole (1962) "The Belief System and National Images: a Case Study." *Journal of Conflict Resolution* 6(3): 244–252.

—— (1976) "Foreign Policy Viewed Cognitively," in Robert Axelrod (ed.) *Structure of Decision*. Princeton, N.J.: Princeton University Press.

Horsefield, J. Keith (1969) *The International Monetary Fund: 1945–1965*. Washington, D.C.: International Monetary Fund.

Hughes, Steve, and Rorden Wilkinson (2001) "The Global Compact: Promoting Corporate Responsibility?"*Environmental Politics* 10(1): 155–159.

Hurt, Harry, III (2003) "A Path to Helping the Poor, and His Investors." *The New York Times*. August 10.

Hyden, Goran (1980) *Beyond Ujamaa in Tanzania*. Berkeley, Calif.: University of California Press.

IFRC (International Federation of Red Cross and Red Crescent Societies) (1997) *World Disasters Report*. Oxford: Oxford University Press.

International Panel of Eminent Personalities to Investigate the 1994 Genocide in Rwanda and the Surrounding Events (2000) *Rwanda: the Preventable Genocide*. Addis Ababa: Organization of African Unity.

Jackson, Robert H. (1990) *Quasi-States: Sovereignty, International Relations, and the Third World*. Cambridge: Cambridge University Press.

Jacobson, Harold K. (1974) "WHO: Medicine, Regionalism, and Managed Politics," in Robert W. Cox and Harold K. Jacobson (eds) *The Anatomy of Influence: Decision Making in International Organizations*. New Haven, Conn.: Yale University Press.

—— (1984) *Networks of Interdependence: International Organizations and the Global Political System*, 2nd ed. New York: Alfred A. Knopf.

James, C. L. R (1977) *Nkrumah and the Ghana Revolution*. Westport, Conn.: Lawrence Hill.

Johnson, Harry (1977) contributions in Jagdish Bhagwati (ed.) *The New International Economic Order: the North–South Debate*. Cambridge, Mass.: MIT Press.

Jolly, Richard, Frances Stewart, and Giovanni A. Cornia (eds) (1992) *Adjustment with a Human Face: Protecting the Vulnerable and Promoting Growth*. Oxford: Oxford University Press.

Jones, Charles A. (1987) *International Business in the Nineteenth Century: the Rise and Fall of a Cosmopolitan Bourgeoisie*. New York: New York University Press.

Joyce, James Avery (1945) *World Organization: Federal or Functional?* London: C. A. Watts.

Joyner, Christopher (1999) "The United Nations and Democracy." *Global Governance* 5(3): 33–58.

Kant, Immanuel (1957[1795]) *Perpetual Peace*. (Lewis White Beck, ed. and trans.) Indianapolis: Bobbs Merrill.

Katzenstein, Mary Fainsod (1998) *Faithful and Fearless: Moving Feminist Protest Inside the Church and Military*. Princeton, N.J.: Princeton University Press.

Kaul, Inge, Isabelle Grunberg, and Marc A. Stern (eds) (1999) *Global Public Goods: International Cooperation in the 21st Century*. New York: Oxford University Press.

Kawachi, Ichiro, Bruce P. Kennedy, and Richard G. Wilkinson (1999) *The Society and Population Health Reader: Income Inequality and Health*. New York: The New Press.

Keck, Margaret E., and Kathryn Sikkink (1998) *Activists beyond Borders*. Ithaca, N.Y.: Cornell University Press.

Kelley, Casey D. (2000) "The Modern Global Man: the Moderation of the Masculine Model and International Relations." Wellesley College, Department of Political Science, NSF Aire Student-Faculty Research Collaboration.

Kelman, Herbert (1979) "An Interaction Approach to Conflict Resolution and Its Application to Israeli-Palestinian Relations." *International Interactions* 6(2): 99–122.

Keohane, Robert O. (1984) *After Hegemony: Cooperation and Discord in the World Political Economy*. Princeton, N.J.: Princeton University Press.

—— (1989) *International Institutions and State Power: Essays in International Relations Theory*. Boulder, Colo.: Westview Press.

—— (2002) *Power and Governance in a Partially Globalized World*. London: Routledge.

—— (1971 [1920]) *The Economic Consequences of the Peace*. New York: Harper.

Keynes, John Maynard (1936) *The General Theory of Employment, Interest, and Money*. New York: Harcourt, Brace.

Kidron, Michael (1968) *Western Capitalism Since the War*. London: Weidenfeld & Nicolson.

Kim, Jim Yong, Joyce V. Millen, Alec Irwin, and John Gresham (eds) (2000) *Dying for Growth: Global Inequality and the Health of the Poor*. Monroe, Me.: Common Courage Press.

Kindleberger, Charles P. (1973) *The World in Depression, 1929–1939*. Berkeley, Calif.: University of California Press.

Kopp, Karl (1941) "The League of Nations and Raw Materials." *Geneva Studies*. 11(3): whole issue.

Krasner, Stephen D. (1974) "Oil is the Exception." *Foreign Policy* 14: 68–83.

—— (1980) "The United Nations and the Struggle for Control of North–South Relations." Unpublished paper. Department of Political Science, University of California, Los Angeles.

—— (1981) "Transforming International Regimes: What the Third World Wants and Why," *International Studies Quarterly* 25(2): 119–148.

Krugman, Paul R. (ed.) (1986) *Strategic Trade Policy and the New International Economics*. Cambridge, Mass.: MIT Press.

—— (1990) *The Age of Diminished Expectations: US Economic Policy in the 1990s.* Cambridge, Mass.: MIT Press.

Larin, Kathryn, and Elizabeth McNichol (1997) *Pulling Apart: a State-by-State Analysis of Income Trends.* Washington, D.C.: Center on Budget and Policy Priorities.

Lasch, Christopher (1977) *Haven in a Heartless World.* New York: Basic Books.

Lederach, John Paul (1998) *Building Peace: Sustainable Reconciliation in Divided Societies.* Washington, D.C.: United States Institute of Peace.

Lee, John (1937) "The Pros and Cons of Functional Organization," in Luther H. Gulick (ed.) *Papers on the Science of Administration.* New York: Institute of Public Administration, Columbia University.

Lee, Kelly, and Richard Dodgson (2000) "Globalization and Cholera: Implications for Global Governance." *Global Governance* 6(2): 213–236.

Lee, Susan, and Christine Foster (1997) "The Global Hand." *Forbes Magazine.* April 21: 85–114.

Libby, Roland L. (1976). "External Co-optation of a Less Developed Country's Policy Making: the Case of Ghana, 1969–1972." *World Politics* 29(1): 67–89.

Lih, Lars (1990) *Bread and Authority in Russia, 1914–1921.* Berkeley, Calif.: University of California Press.

Lipietz, Alain (1987) *Mirages and Miracles: the Crises of Global Fordism.* London: Verso.

—— (1988) "Building an Alternative Movement in France." *Rethinking Marxism* 1(3): 80–99.

—— (1989) "The Debt Problem, European Integration, and the New Phase of World Crisis." *New Left Review* 178 (November/December): 37–50.

Long, David, and Lucian M. Ashworth (1999) "Working for Peace: the Functional Approach, Functionalism, and Beyond," in Lucian M. Ashworth and David Long (eds) *New Perspectives on International Functionalism.* Houndsmills, Basingstoke: Macmillan Press.

"Lori's War" (2000) *Foreign Policy* (Spring): 28–58.

Loxley, John (1987) "Alternative Approaches to Stabilization in Africa," in Gerald K. Helleiner (ed.) *Africa and the International Monetary Fund.* Washington, D.C.: International Monetary Fund.

Luo, Xiaowei (2000) "The Rise of the Social Development Model: Institutional Construction of International Technology Organizations, 1856–1993. *International Studies Quarterly* 44(1): 147–175.

Lynch, Cecelia (1999) "The Promise and Problems of Internationalism." *Global Governance* 5(1): 83–103.

MacFarlane, S. Neil (1985) *Superpower Rivalry and Third World Radicalism: the Idea of National Liberation.* Baltimore, Md.: Johns Hopkins University Press.

MacPhee, Craig R. (1979) "Martin Bronfenbrenner on UNCTAD and the GSP." *Economic Development and Cultural Change* 27(3): 357–363.

Manley, Robert H. (1978) "The World Policy System: an Analysis." *International and Comparative Public Policy* 2: 35–141.

Markovitz, Irving L. (1977) *Power and Class in Africa.* Englewood Cliffs, N.J.: Prentice-Hall.

—— (ed.) (1987) *Studies in Power and Class in Africa.* New York: Oxford University Press.

Marmot, Michael, and Richard G. Wilkinson (eds) (1999) *Social Determinants of Health.* Oxford: Oxford University Press.

Marx, Karl, and Fredrick Engels (1932[1848]) *Manifesto of the Communist Party*. New York: International Publishers.

Maslow, Abraham H. (1968) *Toward a Psychology of Being*. 2nd ed. Princeton, N.J.: Van Nostrand.

Matthaei, Julie (2001) "Healing Ourselves, Healing Our Economy: Paid Work, Unpaid Work and the Next Stage of Feminist Economic Transformation." *Review of Radical Political Economics* 33(4): 461–494.

Mayall, James (1975) "Functionalism and International Economic Relations," in A. J. R. Groom and Paul Taylor (eds) *Functionalism: Theory and Practice in International Relations*. New York: St Martin's Press.

—— (1990) *Nationalism and International Society*. Cambridge: Cambridge University Press.

Mayoux, Linda (1998) "From Vicious to Virtuous Circles? Gender and Micro-Enterprise Development." UNRISD UN Fourth World Conference on Women Occasional Paper No. 3, Geneva, May.

Melchior, Arne, Kjetil Telle, and Henrik Wiig (2000) "Globalization and Inequality: World Income Distribution and Living Standards, 1960–1998." Royal Norwegian Ministry of Foreign Affairs Studies on Foreign Policy Issues Report 6B.

Mendez, Ruben P. (1992) *International Public Finance*. New York: Oxford University Press.

Menon, Bhaskar (1992) *International Document Review: the Weekly Newsletter on the United Nations*. March 6.

Metcalf, Henry C., and L. Urwick (1942) "Introduction," in Henry C. Metcalf and L. Urwick (eds) *Dynamic Administration: the Collected Papers of Mary Parker Follett*. New York: Harper & Brothers.

Meyer, Mary K., and Elisabeth Prügl (eds) (1999) *Gender Politics in Global Governance*. Lanham, Md.: Rowman & Littlefield.

Milanovic, Branko (1999) "True World Income Distribution 1988 and 1993: First Calculation Based on Household Surveys Alone." World Bank Development Research Group Paper No. 2244, December. Washington, D.C.: World Bank.

Miller, Carol (1991) "Women in International Relations? the Debate in Interwar Britain," in Rebecca Grant and Kathleen Newland, (eds), *Gender in International Relations*. Bloomington, Ind.: University of Indiana Press.

Milner, Helen V. (1997) *Interests, Institutions, and Information*. Princeton, N.J.: Princeton University Press.

Mitrany, David (1933) *The Process of International Government*. New Haven, Conn.: Yale University Press.

—— (1934) "Political Consequences of Economic Planning." *Sociological Review* 26: 332–342.

—— (1936) *The Effect of War in Southeastern Europe*. New Haven, Conn.: Yale University Press.

—— (1943) *A Working Peace System: An Argument for the Functional Development of International Organization*. London: Royal Institute of International Affairs.

—— (1948) "The Functional Approach to World Organization." *International Affairs*. 24(4): 350–363.

—— (1975) *The Functional Theory of Politics*. London: London School of Economics/ Martin Robertson.

Modelski, George and William R. Thompson (1995) *Leading Sectors and World Powers: the Coevolution of Global Economics and Politics.* Columbia, S.C.: University of South Carolina Press.

Molina, Mario J. (1993) "Science and Policy Interface," in Nazli Choucri (ed.) *Global Environmental Accords: Implications for Technology, Industry, and International Relations.* Cambridge, Mass.: MIT, UNEP, UNDP, World Bank, and Business Council on Sustainable Development.

Moss, Alfred George, and Harry N. M. Winton (1976) *A New International Economic Order: Selected Documents, 1945–1975.* New York: UNIPUB.

Moynihan, Daniel Patrick (1975) "The United States in Opposition." *Commentary* March: 31–44.

—— (1978) *A Dangerous Place.* Boston, Mass.: Little Brown.

Murphy, Craig N. (1984) *The Emergence of the NIEO Ideology.* Boulder, Colo.: Westview Press.

—— (1987) "Learning the National Interest in Africa." *TransAfrica Forum* 4(1): 49–63.

—— (1992) "The UN's Capacity to Promote Sustainable Development: the Lessons of a Year that Eludes All Facile Judgment," in Albert Legault, Craig N. Murphy, and W. Ofuatey-Kodjoe (eds) *The Capacity of the UN System in 1992.* Providence, R.I.: Academic Council on the UN System.

—— (1994) *International Organization and Industrial Change: Global Governance since 1850.* Cambridge: Polity Press.

—— (1995) "Globalization and Governance: 'Passive Revolution' and the Earlier Transitions to Larger Scale Industrial Economies in the United Kingdom, Germany, the Northeastern United States, and Northeastern Japan." Prepared for the Annual Meeting of the American Political Science Association, Chicago, September.

—— (1996) "Seeing Women, Recognizing Gender, Recasting International Relations." *International Organization* 5093: 513–538.

—— (1998a) "Globalisation and Governance: A Historical Perspective," in Roland Axtmann (ed.) *Globalisation in Europe.* London: Pinter Publishers.

—— (1998b) "Understanding IR: Understanding Gramsci." *Review of International Studies* 24(3): 417–425.

—— (1999) "Inequality, Turmoil, and Democracy: Global Political-Economic Visions at the End of the Century." *New Political Economy* 4(2): 289–304.

—— (2001a) "Critical Theory and the Democratic Impulse: Understanding a Century-Old Tradition," in Richard Wyn Jones (ed.) *Critical Theory and World Politics.* Boulder, Colo.: Lynne Rienner Publishers.

—— (2001b) "Egalitarian Social Movements and New World Orders," in William Thompson, (ed.) *Evolutionary World Politics.* London: Routledge.

—— (2002) "Pinpointing the Significance of Women's Empowerment, Recognizing Political Opportunities, Anticipating Transnational Coalitions," in Craig N. Murphy (ed.) *Egalitarian Politics in an Age of Globalization.* London: Palgrave.

Murphy, Craig N., and Douglas R. Nelson (2001) "International Political Economy: a Tale of Two Heterodoxies." *British Journal of Politics and International Relations* 3(3): 393–421.

Næss, Arne (1989) *Ecology, Community, and Lifestyle: Outline of an Ecosophy.* (David Rothenberg, trans.) New York: Cambridge University Press.

Nandy, Ashis (1983) *The Intimate Enemy: Loss and Recovery of Self Under Colonialism.* Delhi: Oxford University Press.

—— (2002) "The Beautiful, Expanding Future of Poverty: Popular Economics as a Psychological Defense." *International Studies Review* 4(2): 107–121.

National Advisory Council on International Monetary and Financial Policies (1983) "Special Report to the President and Congress on the Proposed Increases in the Resources of the International Monetary Fund." Washington, D.C.: US Department of the Treasury, March.

Nelson, Douglas R. (2003) "Political Economy Problems in the Analysis of Trade Policy." Research Professorship Inaugural Lecture. School of Economics. University of Nottingham. November.

Novati, Giapaolo Calchi (1989) "Comment on 'The International Economy and the Development of Sub-Saharan Africa,'" in Enzo Caputo (ed.) *Which Cooperation with Africa in the 90s?* Rome: Istituto Italo-Africano.

Nussbaum, Martha (2000) *Women and Human Development: the Capabilities Approach.* Cambridge: Cambridge University Press.

—— (2002) "Capabilities and Social Justice." *International Studies Review* 4(2) 123–135.

Nwekwe, G. A. (1980) *Harmonization of African Foreign Policies 1955–1975: the Political Economy of African Diplomacy.* African Research Studies No. 14. Boston, Mass.: Boston University African Studies Center.

Nyerere, Julius (1980) "Introduction," in Mason Sears, *Years of High Purpose, from Trusteeship to Nationhood.* Washington, D.C.: University Press of America.

O'Brien, Robert, Anne Marie Goetz, Jan Aart Scholte, and Marc Williams (2000) *Contesting Global Governance: Multilateral Economic Institutions and Global Social Movements.* Cambridge: Cambridge University Press.

Oestreich, Joel E. (1998) "UNICEF and the Implementation of the Convention on the Rights of the Child." *Global Governance* 4(2): 183–198.

O'Loughlin, John, Michael Don Ward, Corey L. Lofdahl, Jordin S. Cohen, David S. Brown, David Reilly, Kristin S. Gleditsch, and Michael Shin (1998) "The Diffusion of Democracy, 1946–1994." *Annals of the Association of American Geographers* 88(4): 545–574.

Overbeek, Henk (1990) *Global Capitalism and National Decline: The Thatcher Decade in Perspective.* London: Unwin, Hyman.

—— (ed.) (1993) *Restructuring Hegemony in the Global Political Economy: the Rise of Transnational Neoliberalism in the 1980s.* London: Routledge.

Palmieri, Patricia Ann (1997) *In Adamless Eden: the Community of Women Faculty at Wellesley.* New Haven, Conn.: Yale University Press.

Parkinson, Fred (1977) *The Philosophy of International Relations: a Study in the History of Thought.* Beverly Hills, Calif.: Sage Publications.

Patrick, Stewart and Shepard Forman (eds) (2002) *Multilateralism and US Foreign Policy: Ambivalent Engagement.* Boulder, Colo.: Lynne Rienner Publishers.

Penrose, Edith (1973) "International Patenting and the Less-Developed Countries." *Economic Journal* 83(3): 768–786.

Perigord, Paul R. (1926) *The International Labor Organization.* New York: D. Appleton.

Pertot, Vladimir (1972) "The Influence of Changes in Concepts of Foreign Trade," in *The International Economics of Control.* Edinburgh: Oliver and Boyd.

Pijl, Kees van der (1984) *The Making of an Atlantic Ruling Class.* London: Verso.

—— (1990) "Socialization and Social Democracy in the State System," in Wibo Koole, *et al.* (eds) *After the Crisis: Political Regulation and the Capitalist Crisis.* Amsterdam: University of Amsterdam Department of International Relations.

—— (1998) *Transnational Classes and International Relations.* London: Routledge.

Pincus, Jonathan (1967) *Trade, Aid, and Development.* New York: Council on Foreign Relations.

Polanyi, Karl (1957) The Great Transformation: the Political and Economic Origins of Our Time. Boston, Mass.: Beacon Press.

Prebisch, Raul (1950) *The Economic Development of Latin America and Its Principal Problems.* Lake Success, N.Y.: United Nations.

—— (1984) "Five Stages in My Thinking on Development," in Gerald M. Meier and Dudley Seers (eds) *Pioneers In Development.* New York: Oxford University Press.

Pynchon, Thomas (1984) "Is it OK to be a Luddite?" *The New York Times Book Review.* October 28.

Rapoport, Anatol (1960) *Fights, Games, and Debates.* Ann Arbor, Mich: University of Michigan Press.

—— (1979) *Conflict in Man-Made Environment.* Harmondsworth: Penguin Books.

Reich, Wilhelm (1970) *The Mass Psychology of Fascism.* (Vincent R. Carfagno, trans.) New York: Farrar, Straus & Giroux.

Reinalda, Bob, and Bertjan Verbeek (1998) *Autonomous Policy Making by International Organizations.* London: Routledge.

Reinicke, Wolfgang H. (1998) *Global Public Policy: Governing without Government?* Washington D.C.: The Brookings Institution.

Reinsch, Paul S. (1911) *Public International Unions, their Work and Organization: a Study in International Administrative Law.* Boston, Mass.: Ginn.

Robertson, A. F. (1984) *People and the State: an Anthropology of Planned Development.* Cambridge: Cambridge University Press.

Robinson, William I. (1996) *Promoting Polyarchy: Globalization, U.S. Intervention, and Hegemony.* Cambridge: Cambridge University Press.

Robinson, William I., and Jerry Harris (2000) "Towards a Global Ruling Class? Globalization and the Transnational Capitalist Class." *Science & Society* 64(1): 11–54.

Rockefeller Brothers Fund (2000) Global Interdependence Initiative. Found on the internet at www.rbf.org/initiatives.html, March 16, 2001.

Rosenau, James N. (1981) "The Elusiveness of Third World Demands: Conceptual and Empirical Issues," in W. Ladd Hollist and James N. Rosenau (eds) *World System Structure: Continuity and Change.* Beverly Hills, Calif.: Sage Publications.

—— (1992) *The United Nations in a Turbulent World.* Boulder, Colo.: Lynne Rienner Publishers.

—— (1995) "Governance in the Twenty-First Century." *Global Governance* 1(1): 13–44.

—— (1997) *Along the Domestic-Foreign Frontier: Exploring Governance in a Turbulent World.* Cambridge: Cambridge University Press.

Rosenau, James N. and Ernst-Otto Czempiel (1992) *Governance without Government: Order and Change in World Politics.* Cambridge: Cambridge University Press.

Ross, Dorothy (1991) *The Origins of American Social Science.* New York: Cambridge University Press.

Rostow, W. W. (1948) *The British Economy of the Nineteenth Century.* Oxford: Oxford University Press.

—— (1953) *The Process of Economic Growth.* Oxford: Oxford University Press.

Rothschild, K. W. (1944) "The Small Nation in World Trade." *Economic Journal* 54(1): 26–37.

Roy, Arundhati (2004) "Do Turkeys Enjoy Thanksgiving?" Address given at the opening of the World Social Forum, Bombay, January 18.

Roy, Ramashray (1988) "Three Visions of Needs and the Future: Liberalism, Marxism, and Gandhism," in Roger A. Coate and Jerel A. Rosati (eds) *The Power of Human Needs in World Society.* Boulder, Colo.: Lynne Rienner Publishers.

Ruggie, John Gerald (1998) *Constructing the World Polity: Essays on International Institutionalism.* London: Routledge.

—— (1999) Covering letter to Mark W. Zacher. *The United Nations and Global Commerce.* New York: United Nations Department of Public Information.

—— (2001) "global_governance.net: the Global Compact as Learning Network." *Global Governance* 7(4): 371–378.

Sandvold, Haakon (1993) "Industry-Environment-Sustainability," in Nazli Choucri (ed.) *Global Environmental Accords: Implications for Technology, Industry, and International Relations.* Cambridge, Mass.: MIT, UNEP, UNDP, World Bank, and Business Council on Sustainable Development.

Sassen, Saskia (2003) *Denationalization: Economy and Polity in a Global Digital Age.* Princeton, N.J.: Princeton University Press.

Schattschneider, E. E. (1975) *The Semisovereign People.* Hinsdale, Ill.: The Dryden Press.

Schechter, Michael G. (2002) "Critiques of Coxian Theory: Background to a Conversation," in Cox with Schechter.

Schlafly, Phyllis (2002) "Feminism Meets Terrorism." Found on the internet at www.eagleforum.org/column/2002/jan02/02-01-23.shtml, January 16, 2004.

Schmidheiny, Stephan (1992) Changing Course: a Global Perspective on Business and the Environment. Cambridge, Mass.: MIT Press.

Schnabel, Albrecht and Ramesh Thakur (eds) (2001) *Kosovo and the Challenge of Humanitarian Intervention: Selective Indignation, Collective Action, and International Citizenship.* Tokyo: UN University Press.

Scott, Andrew M. (1977) "The Logic of International Interaction." *International Studies Quarterly* 23(4): 429–460.

Sears, Mason (1980) *Years of High Purpose.* Lanham, Md.: University Press of America.

Sell, Susan (1996) "North–South Environmental Bargaining: Ozone, Change, and Biodiversity." *Global Governance* 2(1): 97–118.

—— (2003) *Private Power, Public Law: the Globalization of Intellectual Property Rights.* Cambridge: Cambridge University Press.

Sen, Amartya (1999) *Development as Freedom.* New York: Alfred A. Knopf.

Sherr, Lynn (2001) *America the Beautiful: the Stirring True Story Behind Our Nation's Favorite Song.* New York: Public Affairs.

Shipman, Gordon (1931) "Science and Social Science." *Social Forces* 10(1): 38–48.

Shotwell, James T. (ed.) (1934) *The Origin of the International Labor Organization.* New York: Macmillan.

Shoup, Laurence H., and William Minter (1977) *Imperial Brain Trust.* New York: Monthly Review Press.

Sinclair, Timothy J. (1994) "Passing Judgement: the Credit Rating Processes as Regulatory Mechanisms of Governance in the Emerging World Order." *Review of International Political Economy* 1(1): 133–159.

Singer, Peter (1999) "The Singer Solution to World Poverty." *The New York Times Magazine,* September 5.

—— (2002) *One World: The Ethics of Globalization.* New Haven, Conn.: Yale University Press.

Singh, Jyoti Shankar (1977) *A New International Economic Order: Toward a Fair Redistribution of the World's Resources.* New York: Praeger Publishers.

Smith, Adam (1982[1776]) *An Inquiry into the Nature and Causes of the Wealth of Nations.* Indianapolis: Liberty Fund, Inc.

Smith, Emily T. (1993) "Growth vs. Environment." *Business Week* 3265 (May 11): 66–75.

Smith, Jackie, Charles Chatfield, and Ron Pagnucco (eds) (1997) *Transnational Social Movements and Global Politics: Solidarity beyond the State.* Albany, N.Y.: SUNY Press.

Smyth, Douglas C. (1977) "The Global Economy and the Third World: Coalition or Cleavage?" *World Politics* 29(4): 584–609.

Sondermann, Fred (1977) "The Concept of the National Interest." *Orbis* 21(2): 121–138.

Sorokin, Pitrim A. (1937) *Fluctuations of Social Relationships: War and Revolution*, vol. 3 of *Social and Cultural Dynamics.* (T. E. Hulme, trans.) Cincinnati: American Book Company.

Stead, William T. (1899) *The United States of Europe.* New York: Doubleday and McClure.

Sterman, John D., and Erik Mosekilde (1994) "Business Cycles and Long Waves: a Behavioral Disequilibrium Perspective," in Willi Semmler (ed.) *Business Cycles: Theory and Empirical Methods.* Boston, Mass.: Kluwer Academic Publishers.

Stiglitz, Joseph E. (2002) *Globalization and Its Discontents.* New York: W. W. Norton.

Stopford, John M., and Susan S. Strange (1992) *Rival States, Rival Firms: Competition for World Market Shares.* Cambridge: Cambridge University Press.

Strange, Susan S. (1986) *Casino Capitalism.* Oxford: Blackwell Publishers.

—— (1996) *The Retreat of the State: The Diffusion of Power in the World Economy.* Cambridge: Cambridge University Press.

Streeten, Paul (1981) "Constructive Responses to the North–South Dialogue," in Edwin Reuben (ed.) *The Challenge of the New International Economic Order.* Boulder, Colo.: Westview Press.

Streeten, Paul, Shahid Javed Burki, Mahbub ul Haq, Norman Hicks, and Frances Stewart (1981) *First Things First.* New York: Oxford University Press.

Swift, Richard (1998) "Chocolate Capitalism: How the Avuncular Image of the Chocolate Business has Melted into the Giant Corporations that Dominate the Trade Today." *New Internationalist* 304 (August). Found on the internet at www.newint.org/issue304/farmer.htm, January 12, 2004.

Tarrow, Sidney (1998) *Power in Movement: Social Movements and Contentious Politics*, 2nd ed. Cambridge: Cambridge University Press.

Teske, Robin L., and Mary Ann Tétreault (eds) (2000) *Conscious Acts and the Politics of Social Change.* Columbia, S.C.: University of South Carolina Press.

Thakur, Ramesh, and William Maley (1999) "The Ottawa Convention on Landmines: a Landmark Humanitarian Treaty in Arms Control." *Global Governance* 5(3): 273–302.

Therborn, Göran (1980) *The Ideology of Power and the Power of Ideology.* London: Verso.

Thérien, Jean-Philippe (1999) "Beyond the North–South Divide: the Two Tales of World Poverty." *Third World Quarterly* 20(4): 723–742.

—— and Carolyn Lloyd (2000) "Development Assistance on the Brink." *Third World Quarterly* 21(1): 21–38.

Tickner, J. Ann (1987) *Self-Reliance versus Power Politics: the American and Indian Experiences in Building Nation States.* New York: Columbia University Press.

—— (1990) "Reaganomics and the Third World: Lessons from the Founding Fathers." *Polity* 23(1): 53–76.

—— (1992) *Gender in International Relations: Feminist Perspectives on Achieving Global Security.* New York: Columbia University Press.

—— (2002) "Feminist Perspectives on 9/11." *International Studies Perspectives* 3(4): 333–350.

Tilly, Charles (1978) *From Mobilization to Revolution.* New York: McGraw-Hill.

—— (1998) *Durable Inequality.* Berkeley and Los Angeles, Calif.: University of California Press.

Tinbergen, Jan (coordinator) (1976) *Reshaping International Order: a Report to the Club of Rome.* New York: E. P. Dutton.

Tooze, Roger, and Craig N. Murphy (1996) "The Epistemology of Poverty and the Poverty of Epistemology in IPE: Mystery, Blindness, and Invisibility," *Millennium: Journal of International Studies* 25(3): 681–707.

Tucker, Robert W. (1977) *The Inequality of Nations.* New York: Basic Books.

Tzannatos, Zafiris (1999) "Women and Labor Market Change in the Global Economy: Growth Helps, Inequalities Hurt and Public Policy Matters." *World Development* 27(3): 551–569.

ul Haq, Mahbub (1976) *The Poverty Curtain.* New York: Columbia University Press.

UNDP (United Nations Development Programme) (1998) *Human Development Report 1998: Consumption for Human Development.* New York: Oxford University Press.

—— (2003) *Human Development Report 2003—Millennium Development Goals: A Compact among Nations to End Human Poverty.* New York: Oxford University Press.

UNEP (United Nations Environmental Programme) (1994) "A Successful Start to Informal Trade-Environment Talks." Geneva: UNEP Press Release, February 18.

UNGA (United Nations General Assembly) (Second Committee) (1946–1974) *Summary Records of the Meetings the (United Nations General Assembly) Second (Economic) Committee.* New York: United Nations. (References in the text include the country whose representative is speaking, the year of the meeting, and the page number in the English translation and summary where the speech is reported.)

Urquidi, Victor L. (1991) "Can the United Nations System Meet the Challenges of the World Economy." The John W. Holmes Memorial Lecture. Providence, R.I.: Academic Council on the United Nations System.

Urwick, L. (1937) "The Function of Administration: with Special Reference to the Work of Henri Fayol," in Luther H. Gulick (ed.) *Papers on the Science of Administration.* New York: Institute of Public Administration, Columbia University.

US Department of Treasury (1982) "United States Participation in the Multilateral Development Banks in the 1980s." Washington, D.C.: US Department of the Treasury, February.

Uvin, Peter (1998) *Aiding Violence: the Development Enterprise in Rwanda.* West Hartford, Conn.: Kumarian Press.

Vale, Peter (1995) "Engaging the World's Marginalized and Promoting Global Change: Challenges for the United Nations at Fifty." *Harvard International Law Journal* 36(2): 283–294.

Van der Westhuizen, Janis (2002) *Adapting to Globalization: Malaysia, South Africa, and the Challenges of Ethnic Redistribution with Growth.* Westport, Conn.: Praeger.

Veblen, Thorstein (1966) *Imperial Germany and the Industrial Revolution.* Ann Arbor, Mich.: University of Michigan Press.

Wallace, Michael D., and J. David Singer (1970) "Intergovernmental Organization in the Global System 1815–1964." *International Organization* 24(2): 239–271.

Wallerstein, Immanuel (1980) "Friends as Foes." *Foreign Policy*, 40 (Fall): 119–131.

—— (1999) *The End of the World as We Know It: Social Science for the Twenty-First Century*. Minneapolis, Minn.: University of Minnesota Press.

Washburn, John L. (1996) "United Nations Relations with the United States: The UN Must Look after Itself." *Global Governance* 2(1): 81–96.

Waterman, Peter (1998) *Globalization, Social Movements, and the New Internationalisms*. London: Mansell.

Weber, Thomas (1999) "Gandhi, Deep Ecology, Peace Research and Buddhist Economics." *Journal of Peace Research* 36(3): 289–307.

Weiss, Thomas G. (ed.) (1998) *Beyond UN Subcontracting: Task Sharing with Regional Security Arrangements and Service Providing NGOs*. Houndsmills, Basingstoke: Macmillan Press.

Weiss, Thomas G., and Leon Gordenker (eds) (1996) *NGOs, the UN, and Global Governance*. Boulder, Colo.: Lynne Rienner Publishers.

WHO (2001) *The Framework Convention on Tobacco Control: a Primer*. Geneva: World Health Organization.

Wilcox, Clair (1949) *A Charter for World Trade*. New York: Macmillan.

Wilkinson, Rorden (2000) *Multilateralism and the World Trade Organisation: the Architecture and Extension of International Trade Regulation*. London: Routledge.

Williamson, John (1990) *Latin American Adjustment: How much has Happened?* Washington DC: Institute for International Economics.

Wilson, Woodrow (1898) *Division and Reunion: 1829–1889*. New York: Longmans, Green.

Woolf, Leonard S. (1916) *International Government*. London: George & Allen Unwin.

Wright, John (1851) *Christianity and Commerce, the Natural Results of the Geographic Progression of Railways: A Treatise on the Advantage of Universal Extension of the Railways in Our Colonies and Other Countries and the Probability of Increased National Intercommunication Leading to the Early Restoration of the Land of Promise to the Jews*. London: Dolman.

Wright, Quincy (1930) *Mandates under the League*. Chicago: University of Chicago Press.

—— (1942) *A Study of War*. Chicago: University of Chicago Press.

Wyn Jones, Richard (ed.) (2001) *Critical Theory and World Politics*. Boulder, Colo.: Lynne Rienner Publishers.

Yates, JoAnne (1985) "Internal Communication Systems in American Business Structures: A Framework to Aid Appraisals." *American Archivist* 48(2): 141–158.

Yoshiro, M. Y. (1968) *Japan's Managerial System: Tradition and Innovation*. Cambridge, Mass.: MIT Press.

Young, Oran R. (1994) *International Governance: Protecting the Environment in a Stateless Society*. Ithaca, N.Y.: Cornell University Press.

—— (1999) *Governance in World Affairs*. Ithaca, N.Y.: Cornell University Press.

Zacher, Mark W. (1979) *International Conflict and Collective Security 1946–1977*. New York: Praeger Publishers.

—— (1999) *The United Nations and Global Commerce*. New York: United Nations Department of Public Information.

Index

eBooks

eBooks – at www.eBookstore.tandf.co.uk

A library at your fingertips!

eBooks are electronic versions of printed books. You can store them on your PC/laptop or browse them online.

They have advantages for anyone needing rapid access to a wide variety of published, copyright information.

eBooks can help your research by enabling you to bookmark chapters, annotate text and use instant searches to find specific words or phrases. Several eBook files would fit on even a small laptop or PDA.

NEW: Save money by eSubscribing: cheap, online access to any eBook for as long as you need it.

Annual subscription packages

We now offer special low-cost bulk subscriptions to packages of eBooks in certain subject areas. These are available to libraries or to individuals.

For more information please contact webmaster.ebooks@tandf.co.uk

We're continually developing the eBook concept, so keep up to date by visiting the website.

www.eBookstore.tandf.co.uk